CONTENTS

LIST OF ILLUSTRATIONS

LIST OF MAPS

LIST OF TABLES

PREFACE

At the beginning of the 21st century, peace had been established for only a few years throughout Central America. Seven years later, that peace has endured. Fledgling democratic institutions have survived as well. Electoral politics have replaced military coups; democratic presidents govern where dictators once ruled. After centuries of repression, these achievements are remarkable.

The events of these past seven years also demonstrate just how difficult it has been to maintain that peace and develop more transparent and trusted democracies. The transition to democracy has not ended death threats as a political tool nor has it been attended by any reduction in social inequalities, poverty, or unemployment. Lack of economic opportunity has resulted in increased emigration to wealthier nations to the extent that more Belizeans live outside that country than within it and the total remittances sent back to Central American countries almost match some national budgets.

Illegal drug transshipment from South America to the United States and money laundering have brought violence to the isthmus and now provide other economic alternatives to Central Americans, ones that have corrupted the military and other officials, particularly in Guatemala, El Salvador, and Nicaragua. In the hope of stimulating the regional economy by more legitimate means, governments have adopted capitalist reforms and signed new trade agreements, such as CAFTA–DR, but many Central Americans, their expectations raised by the promise of democracy, are becoming disillusioned by the lack of improvement in their lives. As in other parts of Latin America, they are demanding an end to globalization, and their votes may lead to more populist governments, such as those already found in Brazil and Venezuela. This book includes coverage of these challenges to Central America's peace and democracy.

ACKNOWLEDGMENTS

I have been fortunate to have generous friends and diligent advisers to assist me in the preparation of this book, especially with the illustrations in it. Without Peter Selverstone, the book would have lost most of its photographic insight into life in Central America; without Naomi Smith, many individuals in this history would have names but not faces. Cherra Wyllie happily created her beautiful drawings, and Geri Anderson, Roger Cooper, and Mary Alice Raymond dug through their albums to find just the right shots for this book.

Many individuals and institutions are mentioned in the text and captions for their contributions, but two scholars deserve special mention. Jack Spence of the University of Massachusetts in Boston and Efraín Barradas of the University of Florida both spent valuable time in order to share their expertise with me–Jack on the civil wars of the 1980s and the implementation of the peace accords as well as their aftermath and Efraín on Central American literature and poetry.

Lawrence Foster provided critical research assistance with unflagging patience. I also want to thank others for their kindhearted efforts on my behalf. Oswaldo Chinchilla gave me assistance at the Museo Popol Vuh in Guatemala City and George Colman provided me with helpful materials on recent Central American history. Patricia Maza-Pittsford, former Consul General of El Salvador in New York; Roberto Rosenberg, former Trade Commissioner of Guatemala in New York; and Roberto Morgan, publisher of *Presencia Panamena e Hispana News* were all very helpful with photographs for the book.

NOTE ON PHOTOS

Many of the illustrations and photographs used in this book are old, historical images. The quality of the prints is not always up to modern standards, as in many cases the originals are from glass negatives or the originals are damaged. The content of the illustrations, however, made their inclusion important despite problems in reproduction.

INTRODUCTION

Central America is a tiny region, broken into seven even smaller nations. Yet over 5 million North Americans visit these countries on their annual vacations, visiting Mayan ruins in Guatemala and Belize, exploring the rain forests of Nicaragua and Costa Rica, snorkeling in Honduras, and cruising through the Panama Canal. An increasing number retire to the region each year, taking advantage of the tax incentives in Panama and the low cost of living in Nicaragua. And each year, impoverished Central Americans make their way to the United States as both documented and undocumented immigrants. Over the past decades, the number residing in the United States has accumulated to almost three million, one-third of them from the smallest nation of them all, El Salvador. Yet Central America is poorly understood and its history is known by too few.

The isthmus has been strategically important to the United States since the Monroe Doctrine was formulated in 1823. It became critical to U.S. interests with the construction of the Panama Canal, the path between the Caribbean Sea and the Pacific Ocean. With immigration issues gaining importance in the political debate in the United States and the so-called Chávez-Castro alignment in Latin America increasingly demanding the U.S. government's attention, there are more reasons than ever to learn about the region's history.

Central America is not much larger than Spain. Yet Central America is home to 45 distinct indigenous groups, among them the Mayan and Kuna Indians, that continue to follow their separate traditions and speak their own languages. In Guatemala, a nation about the size of Tennessee, there are 24 indigenous languages spoken. Central America is a land where peoples have mingled, creating groups such as the African-Indian Garífunas and Miskitos, but above all, creating an overwhelmingly *mestizo*, or mixed Indian and European, population, with definite traces of African. With the exception of Belize, Central American nations are predominantly Catholic and Spanish speaking; their colonial heritage results from three centuries of Spanish domination and feudalism in contrast to the more democratic and industrialized British institutions brought to North America.

Tragic misunderstandings have resulted from the cultural contrasts between the "colossus of the North" and the slender isthmus. The United States has interfered with, invaded, and even occupied Central American nations, and U.S. mercenaries, such as William Walker, have felt free to take over entire nations. And not all interventions are confined to the past, as demonstrated by the United States threatening remarks during the 2006 Nicaragua's presidential election regarding the leftist candidate. Not too surprisingly, slogans like "Yankee go home!" often best summarize the resulting Central American attitude. Yet there is a mutual dependency, and a need for a more sophisticated understanding.

For 3 million years, the Central American isthmus has been both barrier and bridge, separating two vast oceans and linking two immense continents. The result has been a fabulous mosaic of landscapes, flora and fauna, and peoples, but also a history that has often been as explosive as its volcanoes. This history will be brief, but comprehensive, beginning with the geological formation of the isthmus and the peopling of the Americas, and spanning 3,000 years of civilization, from early pre-Columbian civilizations to the most recent political and economic challenges confronting Central America.

This history, to be brief, will focus on the seminal events and broad cultural patterns that have shaped Central America. It will probe deeply enough, however, to expose the regional differences that contribute to the individuality of the seven modern nations that share the isthmus: Belize, Costa Rica, El Salvador, Guatemala, Honduras, Nicaragua, and Panama. Yet this history of Central America does not, and cannot, attempt to provide a thorough history, complete with lists of presidents, of each nation.

Despite the limits imposed by its length, this history will nonetheless aim to be intellectually engaging. Special themes, such as the causes of political unity and disunity in Central America, and the environmental pressures on the land from volcanic eruptions and earthquakes to banana plantations and ecotourism, will be developed throughout the book. Other themes, such as the fate of the indigenous peoples and their cultures since the Spanish conquest, will reveal the variety of human experience on the isthmus and the great contrasts that exist among the nations dividing it.

Accounts of political and cultural events too often give a monolithic and dehumanized impression of society. In addition to the special themes that will be examined in this history, close-ups of individuals, ethnic groups, such as the Quiché (also spelled K'iché) Mayans, and regional movements will be used to enrich or contrast with the main events of that history. The book will examine, for example, the Spanish founding of the 16th-century utopian village of Verapaz to contrast with the brutalities of the Spanish conquest; it will compare the different impact of the British and Spanish empires on the isthmus, as well as spotlight such groups as the Garífuna (Black Caribs) and the semi-autonomous Kuna Indians of Panama. Illustrations will reveal the ethnic and geographic complexity of the region as well as its architecture. Quotations will add the intimacy of eyewitness reports and the texture of sacred texts; poems will give voice to aspirations not found in official documents.

There is, of course, no nation of Central America. Five nations—Guatemala, El Salvador, Honduras, Nicaragua, and Costa Rica—share a long history together. Under Spain, they were administered for several centuries as the Kingdom of Guatemala. After independence, they formed their own federation. And although circumstances caused them to divide the land into five autonomous states, they have repeatedly attempted to unite into a single sovereign state. From 1821 to 1960, there were 25 efforts at unification, and another serious effort was initiated as recently as 1997. These five nations provide the focus of this history. Panama and Belize, one a part of a South American country until the 20th century and the other a British colony until two decades ago, are now usually considered Central American nations. They, too, will be discussed insofar as they influenced events in Central America or shared in its history.

It is hoped that this book, however brief, will shed light on Central America and illuminate the indomitable spirit of its people to create a better society for themselves, often against tremendous odds.

1

THE LAND AND ITS FIRST PEOPLES

Whatever might be is simply not there; only the pooled water, only the calm sea . . . only murmurs, ripples, in the dark, in the night. Only the Maker, Modeler alone, Sovereign Plumed Serpent, the Bearers, Begetters are in the water, a glittering light. And then the earth rose because of them, it was simply their word that brought it forth. . . . For the forming of the earth they said "Earth." It arose suddenly, just like a cloud, like a mist, now forming, unfolding. Then the mountains were separated from the water; all at once the great mountains came forth. . . . And the earth was formed first, the mountain-plain. The channels of water were separated; their branches wound their ways around the mountains. The waters were divided when the great mountains appeared.

■

Popol Vuh, *Book of the Quiché Mayans (Tedlock 1985, 72–75)*

Three million years ago the isthmus of Central America was formed, dividing the sea into the Atlantic and Pacific Oceans and joining the two massive continents, of North and South America. The violent clashing of the earth's tectonic plates forced mountains to surface and pushed together lands from unknown locations in the sea; the thrusting and heaving of the earth's crust melded together these separate biosystems until, finally, in what scientists consider one of the most important geological events in the past 60 million years, the land bridge between the North and South American continents was complete.

The land bridge spanned 1,500 miles of sea and permitted the mingling of the diverse flora and fauna that had evolved during the many millions of years of continental separation. Profound changes occurred in both Americas in this massive exchange of species that included

I

South American monkeys and ceiba trees spreading north and North American jaguars and oaks adapting to more southern environments. More than half of the current land mammals of South America originally came from the north and then adapted and diversified in their new environment in what biologists call "the Great American Biotic Interchange." Central America was richly endowed in this process with temperate flora and fauna from the north as well as tropical species from the Amazon basin. As a result, the isthmus has more species of birds than exist in the United States and Canada combined.

Modern nations and their capitals and the major topographic features of Central America. Central America is a land of coastline: it stretches 1,500 miles along the Pacific coast and almost as far along the Caribbean. Yet the isthmus is only 127 miles at its widest, near the Nicaraguan-Honduran border, and a mere 29 miles wide at the Isthmus of Panama. (After map in CIA World Factbook, 1999)

Although only three-fourths the size of Texas, Central America encompasses an array of landscapes worthy of a continent. A wedge between two oceans, Central America has more coastline than land mass, yet it boasts everything from savannas and rain forests to highland pine and moss-laden cloud forests, from semi-arid, cactus-dominated plateaus and dry deciduous forests on the Pacific coast to Amazonian lushness and verdure along the Caribbean. The Nicaraguan Depression and the swamps of Panama's Darién barely rise above sea level while semi-alpine peaks soar to the 13,926-foot height of Volcán Tajumulco in western Guatemala. The dry and rainy seasons, not a change in temperature, divide the year everywhere except along the southern Caribbean, where the seasons are rainy and rainier. Temperatures vary greatly with altitude, if not with the seasons, from the hot, tropical lowland homes of spider monkeys and parrots to the temperate, springlike climate of oak- and fir-covered mountains and the frosty air of glaciated peaks. In Central America, even the oceans contrast: the vast and rough Pacific versus the shallow Caribbean, where the shores are protected by the second largest barrier coral reef in the world. All manner of wildlife and plants thrive in these diverse environments: 7 percent of the world's species are on this isthmus that constitutes only a small fraction (about .5 percent) of the earth's land mass.

The Ring of Fire

> ... there is a volcano that is the most terrifying thing ever seen,
> that throws from its mouth stones as large as a house, burning
> in living flames, and when they fall, they break in pieces and
> cover all the mountain with fire.
>
> ■
>
> Pedro de Alvarado, 1524 (Mackie 1972, 88)

The geological violence that created the isthmus still wreaks havoc upon it. Shifts and thrusts and fault lines in the earth's crust have created a spine of more than 350 volcanoes that parallel the Pacific coast from Guatemala into western Panama. Central America is one of the most turbulent regions in the Ring of Fire, a volcanic rim around the Pacific Ocean from South America into Asia that contains 75 percent of the world's active volcanoes. In Guatemala the volcanoes are the highest on the isthmus and the most active, with the dreaded Fuego, near Antigua, producing a glowing display against the night sky. The

3

CERÉN: THE POMPEII OF THE NEW WORLD

As for me, I bring down the sky, I make an avalanche of all the earth.

■

Popol Vuh, *Book of the Quiché Mayans (Tedlock 1985, 89)*

Volcanic eruptions have devastated pre-Columbian cities as well as historic ones. In 1976, a bulldozer at a construction site in central El Salvador accidentally uncovered part of Cerén, a pre-Columbian Mayan settlement buried under 17 feet of volcanic ash. Although the bulldozer destroyed some of the ancient structures, it also enabled archaeologists to discover complete households, their contents just where they were left at the end of the sixth century A.D. when the owners fled from the lava bombs and ash surges of the erupting Loma Caldera. Archaeologists can surmise the early evening hour of the eruption by the pots on hearths, the tools scattered about, and the rolled-up sleeping mats, items that together indicate a family gathering at the end of the workday. Plaster casts of ash-entombed gardens and fields have revealed the maturity of the fruit and maize on that fateful day, pinpointing August as the month of the disaster. Perishable items were so

---

volcanoes thrust their way along the Pacific side of Honduras, nearly edging El Salvador into the sea. They form memorable peaks on the islands of Lake Nicaragua and cluster into a smoking and gas-puffing cordillera in central Costa Rica. The volcanic spine is interrupted by the impressive granite range of the Talamanca Massif, but resumes its course in western Panama, where Volcán Barú appears like an explosive punctuation mark. From Guatemala into Panama, these threatening mountains dominate the Central American landscape.

At least 20 volcanoes are active, and another 20 may yet prove themselves to be so: Irazú in Costa Rica was declared extinct until it spewed ash over the heavily populated Meseta Central in 1963, killing 73 people and polluting the region for much of the decade. Young and unstable geologically, the Central American isthmus has been repeatedly devastated by both volcanic eruptions and earthquakes. In 1835, Cosiguina in northwestern Nicaragua exploded with a violence that

well preserved that archaeologists have been able to reconstruct a string of chiles that hung from a kitchen rafter and a cord that tied up a cornstalk almost 1,500 years ago. Cerén was uniquely preserved, but it was not the only pre-Columbian settlement devastated by a volcanic eruption. In El Salvador, Chalchuapa, part of the emerging Mayan civilization along the Pacific slope, was buried in about 250 C.E. by the Ilopongo volcano; the devastation was so great that the region was not resettled for two centuries. Farther south, the Chiriquí chiefdoms under the Volcán Barú in western Panama were forced to relocate in 600

Izalco last erupted in 1966; it is one of the more than 100 volcanoes in El Salvador. (Photo National Geographic Magazine, February 1922)

C.E. Even when these volcanoes were not erupting, they were an imposing presence in the pre-Columbian world: creation myths incorporated them into the sacred landscape and designated them the homes of the ancestral gods.

reduced the mountain to less than half its original height, from 6,600 to 2,660 feet. Fuego in Guatemala, Central America's most active volcano, has erupted over 60 times since the Spanish conquest; in 1971, it filled the ravines at its base with 66 feet of glowing lava and embers. Poás in Costa Rica spewed ash more than half a mile into the air in 1989; Arenal in Costa Rica approached the millennium with nightly fireworks; and Ilamatepec in El Salvador erupted for the first time in a century in 2005, forcing the evacuation of thousands from their homes. All are reminders of the explosive potential of Central America's volcanoes.

Earthquakes have damaged many Central American cities, and left them bereft of their architectural history—San Salvador has been rebuilt nine times since 1528. Antigua, Guatemala, the once magnificent regional capital of the Spanish empire, never was rebuilt after its destruction by earthquake in 1773; instead the capital relocated to Guatemala City, and Antigua was left to survive as a quiet town, its ruined churches eloquent testaments of the colonial past. The Nicaraguan city of León, abandoned in 1610, was first destroyed by earthquake and subsequently buried under layers of ash from repeated eruptions of Momotombo Volcano; León Viejo ("old León"), as the former capital is called, has been reduced to an archaeological site. Underlying such monumental devastation is the reality of human suffering: In 1976, an earthquake killed 25,000 Guatemalans and left 25 percent of the population homeless, and in 2001 an earthquake in El Salvador destroyed more than 100,000 homes.

Volcanism does have its benefits, however. Obsidian, or volcanic glass, provided cutting tools for the pre-Columbians, and volcanic ash the temper for making ceramics. Important lakes, such as Lago Atitlán in Guatemala, have formed 5,000 feet above the sea in collapsed volcanic cones. Fertile valleys below the isthmian volcanoes, repeatedly enriched by new deposits of ash and lava, have been among the most populous and prosperous regions throughout the millennia of human occupation. In recent decades, minor volcanic eruptions probably saved Costa Rica's central valley from economic collapse by renewing soils depleted from too many decades of coffee production and overpopulation.

The First Americans

I shall write the stories of our first fathers and grandfathers, one of whom was called Gagavitz ["Volcano"], the other Zactecauh ["Snow Mountain"], the stories they told to us; that from the other side of the sea we came to the place called Tulán, where we were begotten and given birth by our mothers and our fathers, oh, our sons!

■

The Annals of the Cakchiquels, Book of the Cakchiquel Mayans
(Recinos and Goetz 1967, 43)

The first humans in the New World were immigrants. The question of their origin has titillated the human imagination since Christopher Columbus's voyage in 1492 brought him to what he thought were the East Indies and the Indian people. Once the Europeans realized that entirely new continents had been encountered, they wondered who these descendants of Adam and Eve could possibly be. Speculation over the course of the centuries has identified the "Indians" as descendants of everything from the Lost Tribes of Israel to extraterrestrials. Scientists, using evidence from archaeology, tooth morphology, linguistics, and, most recently, DNA analysis, have been able to narrow the field considerably: They believe the first Americans were Asians. The exact reconstruction of how and when these Asians migrated to the New World is still a matter of lively discussion, but there is basic agreement that they first arrived in the Americas during the late Ice Age (40,000 to 10,000 B.C.E.), and that they crossed into the North American continent by way of Siberia.

The formation of the Central American isthmus was itself critical to the peopling of the Americas. This newly formed barrier between the seas created trade winds that eventually ushered in the Pleistocene, or late Ice Age, around 40,000 B.C.E. Pleistocene glaciers reduced the sea level in the Bering Strait, creating another land bridge, this one only 55 miles long but as wide as 1,000 miles in places, between North America and northern Asia. The landscape was therefore set for humans to cross into North America on foot and, perhaps, in coast-hugging boats, and to make their way south into the Americas. In Central America an ancient lava flow near Lake Nicaragua preserves the footprints of these early humans along with their prey, the bison. Fluted stone projectile points, similar to 11 500-year-old Clovis points found in New Mexico, date the arrival of these hunters in Central America.

Until 1997 it was accepted scientific opinion that humans did not arrive in the Americas before Clovis, and that bison, mastodons, and other big game enticed these hunters, most likely Mongolians, into the New World. The ice-free corridors and sustaining vegetation necessary for human migrations, or that of their prey, into the interior of North America simply weren't available before then. Although some paleontologists have long argued for much earlier dates for the peopling of the Americas, convincing evidence for their claims has been difficult to obtain given the erosion of the fossil record and the fact that the most obvious places to look for the hunting camps and human remains were submerged under the sea after the Pleistocene. A few archaeologists had discovered sites that they thought dated to several thousand years earlier than the Clovis culture—fingerprints in a cave in New Mexico, stone tools in a cave along the Amazon Basin—but their findings, which went against the grain of accepted theory, were hotly disputed.

In 1997 a scientific upheaval occurred, forcing the most conservative scientists to agree that the arrival of the first humans predated Clovis by at least 1,000 years. Incontrovertible evidence from the site of Monte Verde in Chile, more than 10,000 miles south of the Bering Strait, proved that humans had settled into a routine existence in the Americas at least 12,500 years ago. In order to have traveled so far south and to have adapted to new environments along the way, the humans must have arrived in the Americas even earlier, and probably before any ice-free interior corridor existed. Some believe these Americans must have traveled by shore-hugging boats along a now submerged portion of the west coast of North America, and they probably supported their families by fishing as well as hunting; the presence of massive glaciers and harsh climatic conditions would have made such journeys perilous. When an ice-free corridor opened the interior around 12,000 years ago, it is argued, the early Americans and their prey could make their way by land along the edge of the Rocky Mountains as well.

The new theory explaining an earlier arrival of humans will certainly be further elaborated, and debated, as evidence from new techniques, such as DNA analysis and the comparative analyses of Asian and Native American languages, challenge the traditional dating. Some scientists have already argued for an arrival of humans some 20,000 years ago— and a few have proposed an even more controversial 40,000 years ago.

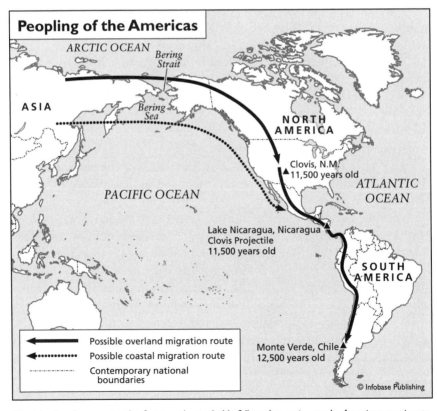

The inland and sea routes the first peoples probably followed to arrive on the American continents.

THE EARLIEST KNOWN AMERICANS

Distinguished as the oldest known human site in the Americas, Monte Verde, Chile, preserves an unusually revealing amount of information from 12,500 years ago; a ground cover of damp peat moss prevented the oxidation process that normally would have destroyed the Paleolithic remains. These remains are so old that the Monte Verdians may predate the development of racial characteristics in humans, although no such genetic evidence is available yet from the site. DNA tests have identified material preserved in a bog as mastodon meat, but Monte Verde proved that these big-game hunters also gathered berries, seeds, potatoes, and mushrooms, and they harvested shellfish from the Pacific Ocean, 30 miles away. Twenty or so people lived next to a creek at Monte Verde and shared a tentlike shelter roofed with animal hides; they had grinding stones and digging sticks, stone tools and ivory ones. Although no human bones were recovered from Monte Verde, a child's fossilized footprint was found beside a hearth.

Some also believe their analyses prove different waves of migration during the Pleistocene from various parts of Asia, not just Mongolia.

Scientists are confident, however, that millennia before Atlantis disappeared or before the Lost Tribes of Israel were lost, human beings arrived on the American continents through Siberia. They may have arrived in different waves of migrations from various parts of Asia, and they may have first reached South America more quickly than once thought by traveling along a coastal route. But around 10,000 B.C.E., they were cut off from the rest of the world when climatic changes caused the polar ice caps to melt and submerged the Bering land bridge and its coastal harbors. The Americans were left to evolve their own cultures and civilization.

The First Settlements

> . . . at that time the people had no corn or crops. They and the animals lived on fruits, also roots that they found in the forest. However, there was corn in the world. It was hidden . . .

■

Mopan Mayan myth (Bierhorst 1990, 86)

Millennia would pass before the Americans settled into permanent villages. With the end of the Ice Age, the hairy mammoths, the mastodons, and giant bisons that had originally sustained many of the first Americans became extinct due to a combination of drastically changed climate and overhunting through mass kills. As the grasslands changed to forests, the seminomadic Americans hunted small game, such as deer and peccary, and gathered seasonal seeds and fruits that, in Central America, included pineapples and pejibaye palm on the Caribbean coast and coconuts along parts of the Pacific. Those living in coastal regions added shrimp and other mollusks to their diet; and small bands of Central Americans—much like the contemporary and only partially sedentary Miskito Indians of eastern Honduras and northeastern Nicaragua—found the Caribbean an especially good provider, with its spiny lobsters and conch, green turtles and fish thriving in the shallow reefs and mangroves.

Not until domesticated crops supplemented the varied fare of the early bands of hunters and gatherers did permanent villages and more complex societies evolve in Central America. The isthmus, bridging the American continents, benefited from its neighbors: cultivated foodstuffs arrived from both the south and the north—and peoples, too. Most languages spoken in lower Central America, from the famous Kunas of Panama's San Blas region to the Miskitos of Honduras, derive from Chibchan, a language also found in northern South America. By 5000 B.C.E., tubers from the south, such as sweet potatoes, yams, and sweet manioc, were cultivated in Central America, where they would remain an important part of the diet throughout history, especially in the lower part of the isthmus. These root crops supplemented wild foods, but could not fully replace them.

Maize, or corn, a much more adequate food than tubers, arrived in northern Central America from Mexico around 2000 B.C.E. Archaeologists once thought that maize was first domesticated in the Pacific littoral and highlands of Guatemala and Chiapas, Mexico, because this small region has more varieties of maize than the entire United States. Although maize now is believed to have been first domesticated in central Mexico, its cultivation took root in such a way that it sustained the most sophisticated pre-Columbian civilization of Central America, that of the Mayans.

Maize, ground with limestone or shell, prevents rickets; eaten with its nutritional complements of chile, beans, and squash, it provides an unusually healthy but simple diet. Maize production permitted the proliferation of settlements in areas formerly uninhabited, from the Petén lowlands in Guatemala and Belize to the Pacific slope of Panama. Some regions, such as the cloud forests and rainiest sections of the Caribbean coast, were too wet year-round for productive maize farming; other areas, such as the savannas in the Petén rain forest, were too difficult to clear with Stone Age tools. In southern Central America, maize agriculture found a niche around 1000 B.C.E., eventually producing small sedentary villages along the most fertile Pacific slopes and valleys. Despite the prolonged dry season from November to May, much of Central America could produce enough crops in the rainy season to sustain permanent villages.

Corn basically defined the cultural areas of Central America. The north, where the land was intensively cultivated with irrigation canals, raised fields, and various other water collecting techniques, participated in the great Mesoamerican civilization of the Mayan region and Mexico; there, sophisticated agricultural techniques sustained city-states and, occasionally, empires. The south, where simple slash-and-burn agriculture prevailed, evolved into small, dispersed chiefdoms along the Pacific slope. The Mosquitía, on the Caribbean coast, where rains prevented farming from replacing foraging and fishing, supported seminomadic tribes. Although other factors, such as trade and cultural interaction, certainly contributed to these political and social variations, adaptability to maize agriculture brought with it the nucleated settlements and denser populations required for the development of complex societies and civilization.

The Rise of Pre-Columbian Civilization

In the Mayan region, which was to advance most precociously compared to the rest of Central America, the Pacific plain of Guatemala and Chiapas, Mexico developed first. This unusually fertile corridor from Soconusco down into El Salvador would, centuries later, provide the Aztecs and Spaniards with the cacao beans used for New World currency as well as frothy chocolate drinks fit for emperors. Not only had millennia of volcanic ash and lava enriched the coastal soils, but seasonal lakes permitted an extra crop of maize annually. The food surpluses increased wealth and leisure time, and helped to sustain larger populations. Out of this environment evolved the Ocós culture, a complex culture that evolved centuries before the southern isthmus even began settling down into scattered hamlets of fewer than 200 people. By 1700 B.C.E., the Ocós culture produced some of the earliest pottery in Central America and Mexico; by 1500 B.C.E. it had also developed a political hierarchy with a capital of 1,000 inhabitants ruling over small villages. Judging from elite

THE PEOPLE OF MAIZE

The young maize god was the Mayan symbol of world creation and renewal. In ancient myths, the fearsome gods of the Mesoamerican underworld decapitate the maize god, who is subsequently reborn at the dawning of this world. This theme of sacrifice and resurrection is integral to the pre-Columbian world view.

This stone *metate* from the Talamanca Massif is a monumental version of Mesoamerican grinding stones for maize. Some of these *metates,* clearly ceremonial in function, are almost 7 feet long and weigh more than 200 pounds. Although some archaeologists have thought these stone sculptures, found in Costa Rica and parts of Panama, might have functioned as thrones, they were associated at the site of Barriles with monumental stone pestles, one of which depicted a decapitated figure

An eighth-century C.E. Mayan stucco sculpture of the young maize god from the pre-Columbian city of Copán in Honduras. (Photo Alfred P. Maudslay, 1889)

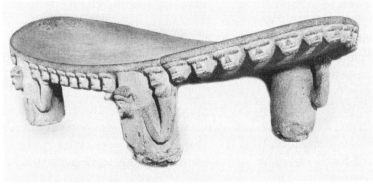

A monumental stone metate from Barriles (400–600 C.E.) and now in the Museo del Hombre de Panama. (Photo Thomas A. Joyce, 1916)

at each end. Archaeologists and art historians, among them Mark Miller Graham (1996, 247), now believe the skulls and other motifs that adorn the grinding stones indicate that their ancient function was human sacrifice: a kind of reenactment of the creation of humans from the sacrifice of the maize god.

> *When they made man, they fashioned him of earth, and they fed him with wood, they fed him with leaves ... But he did not talk, he did not walk, he had neither blood nor flesh, so our early fathers and grandfathers told us, oh, my sons! But at length they found whereof to make it ... corn was discovered [and] brought from out of the sea the blood of the tapir and the serpent, and with it maize was kneaded. With this dough the flesh of man was made by the Creator and Maker.*
>
> ■
>
> The Annals of the Cakchiquels, Book of the Cakchiquel Mayans
> (Recinos and Goetz: 1953, 46)

What rice is to Asians and what wheat is to Europeans, maize is to Mexico and Central America—and has been since pre-Columbian times. Corn not only sustained the first villagers and first empires, but it nourished the earliest beliefs about the creation of the world and the origins of humans. According to the *Popol Vuh,* the bible of the Quiché Mayans, the young maize god was central to the birth of the sun and world creation. After the maize god's sacrifice by decapitation (harvesting) and subsequent rebirth (sprouting), his mother, the "grandmother of day, grandmother of light," ground corn and mixed it with water to make the first humans. From the ancient hieroglyphic writings of the Mayans to the 20th-century oral traditions of the Bribri in the remote Talamanca Massif in Costa Rica, it is known that pre-Columbians believed the first humans were shaped from sacred cornmeal. In more recent times, Indians fought wars only to abandon them when the time came to prepare their *milpas,* or cornfields. In most indigenous regions today, maize tortillas and tamales continue to be the staff of life, and the cultivation of maize follows ancient rituals. Mayans cooked maize on three hearthstones in pre-Columbian times, and they continue to do so today, recalling the three-cornered stone where the maize god was reborn. Cornfields are laid out with great ceremony as cosmograms of the sacred world of maize. Since the beginning of civilization in the Americas, corn has been both holy and essential.

Northern Central America was an integral part of what archaeologists call Mesoamerican civilization. Mesoamerica did not coincide with any modern nation or single people, but rather encompassed most of Mexico, all of Guatemala, Belize, El Salvador and parts of Honduras, Nicaragua, and Costa Rica.

burials discovered in the capital village, sophisticated religious practices and social stratification developed in the Soconusco as well: archaeologists have found skeletons rubbed with red cinnabar and accompanied by polished stone mirrors that are known to be symbols of shamans and, in later Mayan civilization, rulers.

The Ocós culture was not unique in 1500 B.C.E. Throughout Mexico, densely populated and socially complex villages laid the foundation for the rise of civilization. And many of these villages were trading with each other in ideas as well as goods, just as they would until the Spanish conquest. Given the ruggedness of the Central American terrain—the near impenetrability of some areas of the Caribbean coast and the Darién in Panama, the ravines and high sierra that would isolate most regions of Central America throughout history—it comes as something of a surprise to learn about the connections the early village societies had with their far-flung counterparts. In the case of the Ocós culture, some archaeologists suspect that their pottery-making techniques may have diffused from farther south, from Ecuador, where pottery is known to date from before 3000 B.C.E., or from Panama, where cruder ceramics appear at one site as early as 2100 B.C.E. But what is most important for the Mayans is the similarity between Ocós pottery and that excavated under San Lorenzo, an Olmec village near the Gulf coast of Veracruz, Mexico. San Lorenzo grew in complexity and laid the foundation for Mesoamerican culture. The exchange between the Olmecs and the cultures of the Pacific corridor would lead to the rise of Mayan civilization in both Central America and Mexico.

The Olmecs and Mesoamerican Civilization

In the fertile, riverine environment of the Olmec heartland, the first monumental cities were constructed without metal tools, pack animals, or even wheeled vehicles. San Lorenzo sat on a natural salt dome modified by humans into a huge platform that was 2,000 by 3,000 feet in area. A few centuries later, the first American pyramid, 100 feet high, rose at La Venta, another Olmec city. Colossal sculptures, 20-ton portrait heads of shaman rulers, were carved from basalt transported from the volcanic Tuxtla Mountains, 30 miles from San Lorenzo and 80 miles from La Venta. Olmec rulers accumulated great wealth, and some found its way into elaborate offerings buried beneath the plazas and buildings: one offering contained 50 tons of polished green serpentine blocks.

The cost of such enormous human endeavor was subsidized by trade. The Olmecs probably exported surplus maize, but they also exported cacao, or chocolate beans, and exotic items such as jaguar hides and caiman skins for the elite. The trade was not solely in one direction. The Olmecs imported obsidian as well as precious and exotic materials, such as serpentine and jade. They polished the jade and carved it into works of art—portable items of prestige that, based on their wide distribution, other regions were eager to obtain. Never before had Mexico and Central America witnessed such wealth and concentrated power.

The Olmec civilization, dating from 1200 B.C.E., and perhaps earlier, and continuing until 400 B.C.E. is often said to be the mother culture of Mesoamerica. Mesoamerica traditionally has been defined as the pre-Columbian region that encompasses most of Mexico and reaches south through the Mayan area along the Pacific coast of Central America and, on occasion, dips into Costa Rica. It would almost be accurate to say

THE FIRST BALL GAME

. . . the Indians' games were extremely subtle, clever, cunning, and highly refined. [It is a pity] that so much heathenism and idolatry was mixed up with them!

■

Fray Diego Durán, 16th century
(Horacasitas and Heyden 1975, 313)

The world's first bouncing balls were made from rubber tapped from the tropical *Castilla elastica* tree found in the Olmec region, and the Olmecs exported these balls and, probably, a religious ceremony that was performed with them in a specially constructed court. This pre-Columbian ball game later figured prominently in Mayan creation mythology, in which ball-playing hero twins outwit and defeat the evil gods of the underworld in preparation for the dawning of the world and the rebirth of the maize god. The ball game endured as a Mesoamerican ritual for thousands of years. In the creation myth of the 16th-century Aztecs, the sun god slew the forces of night in a ball court. The Olmecs not only exported rubber balls, they also certainly performed a version of this ball game and may have invented the game itself. At San Lorenzo, archaeologists have excavated an earthen ball court as well as pottery painted with representations of ballplayers; and they retrieved waterlogged latex balls from an Olmec swamp. The ball game spread quickly into Central America: An early ball court has been found as far south as El Salvador, and another early site, this one located in the Soconusco region, had a 260-foot-long playing field flanked by mounds and benches. Unlike contemporary sporting events, the pre-Columbian "game" was a ceremony of state and played in the sacred precincts of cities. A match was a reenactment of creation and ended in the decapitation of the loser, just as the maize god was decapitated in the underworld. At the time of the Spanish conquest, the Aztecs demanded thousands of rubber balls each year as tribute from the Gulf Coast region. The Spaniards, fascinated by the athleticism of the ballplayers, who were permitted to hit the ball only with their hips and knees, took a team of players to Europe with them, and introduced the first bouncing, rubber ball to the Old World.

that Mesoamerica is the geographical region involved in the exchange of goods and ideas with the Olmecs, although the borders contracted and expanded slightly over time. From central Mexico, where the Aztecs would later base their empire, and from the Guatemala highlands, the Olmecs obtained obsidian, or the volcanic glass that was used by Mesoamericans to make the finest cutting tools. From Chiapas and Oaxaca, the Olmecs obtained magnetite for shamans' mirrors, and from various parts of the Mayan world, they traded for quetzal feathers and jade—the most precious items desired by Mesoamerican nobles. Throughout Mesoamerica, Olmec jades were placed in the graves of the privileged; Olmec boulder sculptures were carved from central Mexico to El Salvador. Olmec symbols of fire serpents and half human "were-jaguars" evolved into the gods of Mesoamerica; jade celts were hoarded as heirlooms by the Mayans and found as far south as Costa Rica.

This long-distance exchange stimulated the growth of cities and stratified societies beyond the Olmec region. Monumental architecture developed in a number of Mayan cities in Belize and the Guatemalan jungle of the Petén; by 750 B.C.E. 60-foot-high buildings covered what had formerly been a simple village at Nakbé. Olmec jades trace the influence of the mother culture to what would become the great Mayan city of Copán in Honduras and Seibal in the Petén. The Pacific region, in contact with the Olmecs since at least Ocós times, boasted numerous sophisticated cities, some from as early as 600 B.C.E., from Izapa in Mexico, La Blanca in Guatemala and Chalchuapa in El Salvador to Kaminaljuyú in the highlands, near what is now Guatemala City. By 400 B.C.E. hieroglyphic writing evolved and appeared in the art of the Oaxaca region of southern Mexico and in the former Olmec areas of Veracruz and Chiapas as well as in Mayan Guatemala. In central Mexico, Cuicuilco, which would be destroyed by a volcanic eruption, had a 75-foot-high stone pyramid. Well before 250 B.C.E., civilization was well established throughout Mesoamerica.

Mesoamerican Civilization

Their works were all good, all perfect, all wonderful, all marvelous; their houses beautiful, tiled in mosaics, smoothed, stuccoed, very marvelous . . . [They] were very wise, they were thinkers, for they originated the year count, the day count; they established the way in which the night, the day, would work . . .

■

Fray Bernardino de Sahagún (1950–82, Book 10), 16th century

Olmec civilization disappeared for reasons still not understood. But Mesoamerican civilization flourished for 2,000 more years, evolving and transforming itself until the Spanish conquest in 1519. Mesoamericans prided themselves on their great cities, their arts in mosaic and stone, their understanding of the stars and the seasons, and their priestly prophecies based on a sacred calendar, or day count. Through the millennia, Mesoamerican cities traded and exchanged ideas. Some-

SHAMANISM AND RULERSHIP

... thou [an Aztec emperor] speakest in a strange tongue to the god, the lord of the near, of the high ... he is within thee; he speaketh forth from thy mouth. Thou art his lips ...

■

Fray Bernandino de Sahagún (1950–82, Book 10), 16th century

The captain flew like an eagle, he was a great nobleman and a great sorcerer ...

■

Quiché Mayan document, 16th century
(Burkhart and Gasco 1996, 151)

Based on studies of Olmec art, archaeologists believe the earliest Mesoamerican rulers achieved their authority not just by controlling trade and rich agricultural lands, but also by claiming supernatural powers. Like shamans throughout the world, these individuals were thought to be able to magically call up invisible forces in mirrors and induce trances that would enable them to communicate with ancestral spirits and deities. Through self-sacrificial bloodletting rituals, dancing, and hallucinogens— pure tobacco is just one of many such plants that could have been used in the New World—shamans were believed to transform into their animal alter egos and travel to the supernatural world in order to mediate for the good of the community. Mesoamericans elevated the shaman to a sacred ruler who not only spoke with the gods, but also descended from them. Mesoamerican shaman-rulers can be found depicted in Olmec art with a combination of human characteristics and jaguar features, an animal

times they warred with each other, other times they formed alliances and intermarried. Throughout the shifting relationships, some regions rose into prominence while others declined. The Aztecs, the best known of all Mesoamericans, probably because they were flourishing at the time of the Spanish conquest, would be the final manifestation of this civilization (SEE chronology, appendix 8). They, like the Mesoamericans who preceded them, traded far and wide. They demanded, and

attribute that all Mesoamerican rulers would later take as their insignia. Later rulers can be seen communicating with ancestral deities in Classic-period Mayan carvings, and they are described as oracles in Aztec times, when the emperor, or *tlatoani* ("spokesman"), was said to be the lips of the gods. Shamanistic authority seems to have been prevalent during pre-Columbian times in lower Central America, too, where large ceramic vessels of women, many with jaguar traits, were found in elaborate Nicoyan burials worthy of chiefs. These ceramic figures may very well represent the earliest known women rulers in the Americas—and they would not be the last: female rulers can also be identified 500 years later, in the Mayan region. The same items found in these Preclassic tombs from Costa Rica and Nicaragua—shaman stools, sucking tubes, smoothed stones, and incense burners—are used today by the shamans of the few surviving Bribri and Cabecares of Costa Rica, whose clans are matrilineal.

The earliest woman chief? Nicoya-style ceramic (300 B.C.E.–300 C.E.) from Ometepe Island, Lake Nicaragua, of a seated and tattooed woman in a trance. A number of these ceramic effigies of female shamans have been excavated from unusually wealthy tombs in the Nicoya region; archaeologists speculate whether these prehistoric women, accompanied in death with precious carved jades, were the rulers of their tribes. (Drawing published by Thomas A. Joyce, 1916)

received, tribute from most regions outside their own capital of Tenochtitlán, located where Mexico City is today, yet they never dominated the region of the Mayans. They, like earlier cultures, received trade items from beyond Mesoamerica, including turquoise from what is now the southwestern United States and gold and copper, cacao and cotton, from Central America.

Many Cultures

Evolving for centuries and adapting to many different environments, Mesoamerican cities varied enormously. In Mexico alone, some 10,000 ruined Mesoamerican cities have been identified; in Guatemala, an additional 1,400. They did not all exist simultaneously, some endured for just a few hundred years, such as the Aztec capital, and others for almost a millennium, such as the Mayan city of Tikal in Guatemala and the Mexican highland city of Teotihuacán. Large, semi-arid highland basins encouraged massive states, such as the Aztec empire that dominated most of Mesoamerica; forested, lowland territories, where mahogany trees soared 150 feet high and rivers formed natural boundaries, encouraged many city-states instead of single empires, such as those created by the Mayans—although even Mayan cities ruled over smaller, subsidiary ones. Some cities were walled or protected by hilltop locations; others seem to have been easily accessible. Major cities, depending on their location, varied in population from 10,000 to 250,000, and they varied in social complexity, with the largest ones accommodating a royal family and many other noble dynasties as well as enclaves of artisans, merchants, farmers, and, probably, slaves. At the time of the Spanish conquest, with a population surpassing 30 million, Mesoamerica was the most densely occupied region of the New World.

Cultural differences also marked these American cities, whose modern descendants speak 80 distinct languages. The artistic diversity is just as remarkable: highland Mexican cities preferred geometric and powerfully expressive representations of gods in contrast to the delicate realism and human scale of most Mayan art. (SEE maize god photo on page 12.) Long texts in hieroglyphic writing were the hallmark of Mayan civilization, but such texts were surprisingly rare in the monumental art of central Mexico. Early Mayan buildings were covered with immense stucco images of deities, while the Mixtecs in Oaxaca covered their buildings in abstract mosaics made from thousands of small cut stones.

One Worldview

Although they varied greatly, Mesoamerican cultures also shared many characteristics. They were the only indigenous American cultures to compose books—books of folded bark paper, most often written in pictographs rather than the truer writing system of the Mayans. They had divine rulers chosen from noble dynasties; they practiced ancestor worship, a tradition that continues in a modified form today in Day of the Dead ceremonies. The cities, so impressive that the conquering Spaniards said they were grander than those in Europe—in fact, the Aztec capital was five times more populous than London—had temples built atop stepped pyramidal platforms and reached by steep stairways. Rooms, whether in residences or temples, were usually small, but the temples and palace structures were arranged around vast public plazas where rituals of state and religion were performed. Building facades were finished in stone or stucco. Sculptures of rulers and murals of battle scenes and religious rituals proclaimed the power and importance of each city-state. All these enormous human undertakings were accomplished with only Stone Age tools and human carriers for overland transport. Mesoamericans also shared a worldview expressed in their creation myths, their sacred calendar and astronomical tables for eclipses and the movements of Venus, and in their belief that human sacrifice was necessary to appease the gods.

Human Sacrifice

The practice of human sacrifice received considerable attention from the conquering Spaniards and in subsequent assessments of Mesoamerican civilization. The Spaniards reported that 20,000 war captives were sacrificed to dedicate a single temple to the Aztec's patron deity; time-motion computer simulations have cast serious doubt on the number of sacrifices reported. And 16th-century ethnohistoric documents, compiled by Spanish missionaries, indicate that fewer human sacrifices were associated with religious festivals than originally reported. Such considerations put the numbers into a more realistic perspective, yet they cannot dispel the simple truth that Mesoamericans practiced ritual human sacrifice and they did so with considerable invention: child sacrifice, decapitation, heart extraction, and disembowelment are only a few of the methods used.

Human sacrifice has been known throughout civilization from ancient China to ancient Roman gladiators. Even in Renaissance Florence, by

STONE AGE TECHNOLOGY

Mesoamericans built stone cities large enough for 250,000 inhabitants and constructed hulking pyramids, a few of which match or exceed the Great Pyramid of Giza in volume, if not in height. They had elaborate drainage systems and canals; aqueducts brought fresh water to the island capital of the Aztecs, and landfill projects, called *chinampas,* converted swamps into rich agricultural lands in the Petén. They built elevated, stucco-paved causeways—one was 62 miles long. They felled trees, hollowed logs for canoes, and carved and polished hard stones, such as jade, into exquisite figures. All this they did with Stone Age technology. Obsidian is sharp—sharp enough to be used for surgical tools in the 20th century—but its use is so limited that some have argued that the absence of bronze or steel in the Americas is alone proof that civilization developed without Old World contact. The principle of the wheel was known, as toys such as the one pictured demonstrate. In a mountainous land without draft animals, however, wheeled vehicles may have been more cumbersome than useful. The Mesoamericans overcame these shortcomings by relying on river and sea traffic when they could, and managing overland communication with relay runners and human carriers. The Spaniards themselves relied on the Mesoamerican system of *tlalmenes,* or human carriers, for well over a century, and complained that their horses were useless in the more rugged regions. In 1524, the conquistador Hernán Cortés, after losing his horse in the middle of the Petén jungle, was told by the Mayans that he should have used a canoe instead.

some accounts the epitome of Western civilization, feuding parties were known to play soccer occasionally with the severed head of an enemy. In Mesoamerica, human sacrifice was cloaked in religious fatalism. The creator gods, according to this pre-Columbian worldview, had destroyed previous creations when the people failed to honor them properly. To avoid the destruction of this world order, the world of maize, the creator gods required sacrifice. From death and sacrifice, the sun would be reborn each day and the world rejuvenated. Only the most valuable sacrifice, that of human beings, would properly honor the gods. The Mesoamerican belief in such a grim reality led to human sacrifices, particularly of war captives, as well as to painful acts of self-sacrifice—some Aztec priests could barely speak because their tongues were so swollen from piercing them with thorns.

In contrast to such brutal practices, the poetry and songs of the Mesoamericans express another side of their humanity:

> *My heart finally understands;*
> *for I now hear a song,*
> *I wonder at a flower*
> *which will not wilt.*

> ■

> *Nezahualcóyotl, King of Texcoco, 15th century*
> *(after León-Portilla 1969, 88)*

> *All is joyful at dawn.*
> *Let only happiness, only songs,*
> *enter our thoughts!*

> ■

> *Book of the Mayan Songs of Dzibalché*
> *(after León-Portilla 1969, 92)*

23

2

THE MAYANS AND
THEIR NEIGHBORS

*There had been five changes and five generations of people
since the origin of light, the origin of continuity, the origin of life
and humankind. And they built many houses. . . . And they also
built houses for the gods, putting these in the center of the
highest part of the citadel. They came and they stayed.*

■

Popol Vuh, *Book of the Quiché Mayans (Tedlock 1985, 208)*

Mayan civilization is the single most important culture of ancient
Central America. Mayan city-states ruled northern Central
America in what is now Belize, Guatemala, western Honduras, and much
of El Salvador while countless small chiefdoms fragmented the southern
part of the isthmus into a kaleidoscope of cultures. Mayan civilization not
only dominated the region in pre-Columbian times, but also it has capti-
vated world attention more than a thousand years after its collapse.

The soaring white temples of ruined Mayan cities, rising amid the
tropical verdure of the rain forest, create unforgettable images for
today's travelers. The naturalism and soft, curving lines of ruler portraits and palace scenes make Mayan art readily accessible and easily
admired; and the Mayan painting and calligraphic traditions have been
judged among the finest in the world by art historians. The decipherment of Mayan hieroglyphs in recent decades has also generated considerable attention by revealing the first written histories of the
Americas and giving voice to long forgotten rulers. The Mayans constructed hundreds of stone cities from the seventh century B.C.E. until
the Spanish conquest. Ravaged by time, eroded by rain and sun,
shrouded by vines and trees, these ruined cities have nonetheless survived as an extraordinary legacy from the pre-Columbian world.

An Enduring Culture (1000 B.C.E. to present)

The defining, or "Classic," period of Mayan civilization occurred between 250 C.E. and 900 C.E., when Mayan accomplishments in writing, astronomy, architecture, and art proliferated from one city-state to the next throughout the lowlands of the Petén and Yucatán. Yet Mayan civilization endured much longer than its Classic period. It first evolved along the Pacific coast and in the Guatemalan highlands during the period of Olmec civilization (SEE chapter 1), and by the seventh century B.C.E. monumental buildings were constructed in the Petén heartland and in Belize. The Mayans flourished after the Classic period, too, a fact often overlooked when considering the "mysterious" collapse of the Classic period Mayan world. But the collapse resulted in the abandonment of some Mayan cities, not the disappearance of the Mayans themselves. The Mayans never disappeared. Although most of the lowland cities in the Petén ceased to be occupied during the ninth century, other cities flourished during the Postclassic period (900 C.E. to the Spanish conquest) in northern Yucatán and the highlands of Guatemala.

Not only did Mayan civilization continue until the Spanish conquest, but more than 10 million Mayans live in the same regions today that their ancestors occupied centuries ago—a significant number considering there are only 2.5 million self-identified Native Americans in the entire United States. In Guatemala, Honduras, Belize, and in the Mexican regions of Chiapas and the Yucatán, many Mayans share traditions established more than 2,000 years ago, even though they now speak 24 distinct Mayan languages among them, such as Yucatec and Quiché. Some communities are still governed by ancient ritual calendars; others practice an oral tradition that previously was inspired by hieroglyphic books; a surprising number engage in festivals that reenact pre-Hispanic creation myths under a contemporary veneer of Catholicism. With the recent decoding of the ancient glyphic texts, Mayans are learning the writing system of their ancestors for the first time since the Spanish conquest.

The Mayans have endured. And the ancient Mayan civilization has survived in crumbling and once-buried cities, in eroded texts carved into plaster walls and stone sculptures as well as painted onto bark paper in the few surviving screen-fold books. From these scraps of evidence, archaeologists have reconstructed their cities and social institutions; art historians and ethnohistorians have identified the rulers and gods; and epigraphers, specialists in writing, have decoded their hieroglyphs and revealed the official histories of the city-states—the oldest written histories in the New World.

MAYAN CITIES

Classic period Mayan buildings, such as Tikal, were most often constructed of limestone, which was plentiful in the lowlands, and plastered. Time has eroded the paint that may have covered the buildings, although traces left at the ruins of Palenque in Chiapas, Mexico, indicate red—the Mayan color symbolizing the east, the rising sun, and rebirth—was often the color of choice. The Mayans invented the corbeled arch, a technique that gave height to rooms, a mansard shape to the roofs and an unusual gracefulness to their architecture. At cities like Uxmal, a kind of concrete was used, too, enabling the architects to create even more ample interior spaces, and at Chichén Itzá covered colonnades provided another form of interior space. The Mayans also distinguished themselves by planning their cities to conform to the natural setting rather than the more typical Mexican grid. Standing stone relief sculptures, called *stelae,* were erected in the main plazas and carved with ruler portraits accompanied by hieroglyphic texts boasting of their achievements. Stucco sculptures decorated building facades and murals frequently covered interior walls. Most Mayan cities had at least one ball court integrated into the ceremonial center of the city as well as architectural features for astronomical observations. Ritual complexes and ancestral shrines, plazas, and sweat baths could be found throughout every city, from the central plaza and lineage compounds for scribes and other members of the nobility, to the thatch-and-adobe or thatch-and-stick complexes of commoners. Private household orchards and gardens included avocado, papaya, and guava trees, medicinal and dye plants, agaves for rope making, and chiles for condiments. Many of the neighborhoods were connected to the center by paved causeways. More humble family compounds were found on the outskirts of the city, near the farmlands, which often were irrigated and fed by artificial reservoirs. Canals and reservoirs could also provide the cities with freshwater fish and mollusks. Beyond the city itself were provincial towns and hamlets under its dominion, all separated by forests where the residents might hunt.

The central plazas most often were devoted to dynastic authority; some probably functioned as markets. The city centers were the religious heart of the city, too, and constructed as sacred cosmograms; pyramids recreated sacred mountains, temples symbolized cave entrances to the underworld, and ball courts permitted the reenactment of the creation of the Mayan universe. Many royal tombs, filled with precious offerings of jade, painted pottery, obsidian, and shell, have been excavated from inside the base of "ancestor mountains"—actually steep pyramids, usually of nine stepped levels to represent the layers of the Mayan underworld.

Top: Temple I and the ceremonial plaza at the pre-Columbian city of Tikal, Guatemala (200 B.C.E.–900 C.E.). Located in the Petén jungle, Tikal had more than 3,000 buildings in a six-square-mile area. The heart of the city was this ceremonial plaza surrounded by two acropolises (one included residences for the royal family) and two of the city's five soaring temples—one 145 feet in height. On the plaza are stone monuments carved with rulers' portraits. Temple I (727 C.E.) is a nine-tiered funerary monument dedicated to Jasaw-Chan-K'awil, the 27th ruler of the city. Jasaw-Chan-K'awil's tomb has been excavated from inside the pyramid base. Below: A model of downtown Copán, an ancient city in Honduras. (Photo by Alfred P. Maudslay, 1889)

Classic Period Mayan Achievements

Although the Mayans created unique culture, they were an integral part of Mesoamerica and also actively traded goods and ideas with their neighbors to the south in Central America. An examination of their calendrical calculations, astronomy, and writing demonstrates the Mayans' distinctive genius and their essentially Mesoamerican character. The Mayans, more than the cultures in the central highland regions of Mexico, continued the tradition of Olmec naturalistic art and portrait sculptures and Olmec jade carving. Through their trade, the Mayans, like the Olmecs before them, exchanged these symbols of prestige with their isthmian neighbors to the south; in return, they received the art of metallurgy and, perhaps, the art of polychrome and pictorial ceramics, a tradition that is often considered a hallmark of Mayan civilization.

Astronomy

Then the face of the sun was eaten; then the face of the sun was darkened; then its face was extinguished. They were terrified on high, when it burned at the word of their priest . . .

■

The Chilam Balam of Chumayel, *a Yucatec Mayan book*
(Roys 1967, 76)

The Mayans were superb astronomers. They could calculate the 500-year cycle of Venus with only a two-hour margin of error. They predicted eclipses, such as the one described above by the priest of Chumayel, and they predicted equinoxes and solstices, the rise and set of Pleiades, and much more. Their solar calendar—indeed the calendar used by all Mesoamericans—was more accurate than that of the Spanish conquistadores. Without telescopes, but with carefully positioned window slats and specially aligned buildings, the Mayans exploited naked-eye astronomy to its limits. They recorded their impressive knowledge in carefully codified books, a few of which survive today.

The most fundamental use of such intense stargazing must have been to create a kind of farmer's almanac, or seasonal calendar for farming; in fact, some of the painted books predicted which periods would be propitious for planting maize, which would be periods of drought, and the like, and often just such knowledge, entered in an attempt to control the uncontrollable, is found in the few surviving Mayan books. Mesoamerican astronomers were astrologers who also read the sky to predict the fate of entire empires. For them, the myths of creation, called the "dawning" of this world, were interwoven with the sun and other celestial bodies that represented gods. Trained priests could see not just the movement of the stars, but also the activities of the gods themselves. Assisted by their books, the most learned priests interpreted the meaning of celestial events, advising rulers of the outcome. Most priestly advice and interpretation has been lost with the passage of time, but it is known that as the ships of the Spanish conquistadores approached Mexico, the Aztec ruler Moctezuma sent his court astronomers to read the omens in the sky, and they were not good. Even more routine royal decisions—the appropriate day to designate an heir apparent or to perform self-sacrificial bloodletting in honor of the gods—were determined only after consultation with the court astrologers.

Calendars and Computations

They measured to find the good hours; they measured to find the good days ... They measured to observe the rulership of the good stars, all the good years.

■

Book of Chilam Balam of Chumayel (Restall 1998, 137)

Mayan astronomy went hand-in-hand with Mayan mathematics. In addition to recording their observations, the astronomers developed cyclical tables on the movements of planets and stars, and with their mathematics they could predict celestial events far into the future as well as describe mythic events thousands of years into the past. The Mayans were among the first in the world to develop the concept of zero; at a time when the ancient Romans were struggling with their awkward numerical system, the Mayans used a positional-based mathematics much like ours, only theirs was a vigesimal, based on 20, not a decimal, based on 10.

Just as their astronomy was motivated by supernatural concerns, so Mayan numbers were far from mere abstractions. Numbers had patron gods, and certain combinations, such as 13 and 20, were infused with sacred meaning. The ritual 260-day calendar, shared by all Mesoamericans, was a combination of 20 named days rotating with the numbers 1 through 13. Some of the very first known examples of American writing are these sacred calendar dates recorded around 400 B.C.E. The approximately nine-month measure may have originated from such

29

elemental cycles as the duration of human gestation and the tropical agricultural season. Both rulers and farmers governed their lives by the prognostications of the sacred calendar. The sacred calendar, so essential to the pre-Columbian world order, has not yet lost its authority: in Quiché Mayan towns, such as Momostenango in Guatemala, venerated "daykeepers" divine the future and determine religious festivities based on the 260-day count.

Studying the movements of the heavens, the Mayans were fascinated by cycles, and especially overlapping cycles. For example, they delighted in noting that the eclipse tables equaled 46 rounds of the 260-day calendar. The most important overlapping cycle, however, was the Calendar Round that occurred every 52 years when the ritual 260-day calendar and the 365-day solar calendar ended on the same day. This 52-year cycle was the Mesoamerican equivalent of the century. Much like modern apocalyptic visions of the 2000 millennium, Mesoamericans feared the end of the world upon the completion of the Calendar Round. They believed the gods had destroyed previous worlds in the mythic past, and feared they would do so again if rituals honoring them were not properly performed. To keep the world on its course, Mesoamericans offered the sacrificial blood they believed the gods demanded. The sincerity of their belief is revealed in the self-inflicted wounds of rulers, who pierced their genitals with stingray spines and pulled thorns through their tongues in order to make blood offerings. Humans, usually war captives from enemy states, were sacrificed in a variety of gruesome ways, including heart excision and decapitation.

The 52-year cycle was a limited measure of time that made no distinction between one "century" and the next, in much the same way that the date '55 does not distinguish between 1855 and 1955. The Mayans, and a few other lowland cultures, supplemented the Mesoamerican "century" with the more sophisticated calendrical system of the Long Count. The Long Count began counting days at 13.0.0.0.0 4 Ahau 8 Cumku, a zero point in the past that happens to correlate with August 12, 3114 B.C.E. in our calendar and, according to Mayan creation myths, the dawning of the world of the maize people. From this starting point, the counting method could continue for 5,000 years without repetition. In contrast to the 52-year limit of the Calendar Round, the Long Count was an extraordinary advance. Not only did it enable the ancient Mayans to date events without confusion, but the Long Count also has enabled archaeologists to reconstruct the history of ancient Mayan civilization with unusual exactitude for the Classic Mayan civilization when such dates were routinely recorded from 292 C.E. until 909 C.E.

Hieroglyphic Writing

These [Mayan] people also made use of certain characters or letters, with which they wrote in their books their ancient matters and their sciences, and by these . . . drawings, they understood their affairs and made others understand them and taught them. We found a large number of these books in these characters and, as they contained nothing in which there were not to be seen superstition and the lies of the devil, we burned them all, which they regretted to an amazing degree, and which caused them much affliction.

◼

Bishop Diego de Landa, 16th century
(Tozzer 1941, 169)

The Mayans embraced the written word like no other culture before them, even the Olmecs or the Zapotecs, who may have invented writing. The Mayans painted books on bark paper, works that deteriorated and disappeared, but fortunately for modern historians they also wrote on their pottery and carved texts into stone monuments, small jades, and other precious items. Artisans at Copán, Honduras, patiently carved 2,200 glyph blocks into stone to create a dynastic history on a pyramidal staircase. Mayan hieroglyphs represented "true writing," a primarily phonetic symbol system unlike the pictographs found in most of Mesoamerica. And the Mayan scribes clearly took pleasure in writing, choosing between various styles in the way a calligrapher might choose capitals over small letters, or Gothic script versus Roman.

Although the calendrical hieroglyphs were decoded by the early 20th century, the content of other texts was a mystery until recent decades. Understanding only the numbers, early Mayanists developed a distorted, and very idealized, interpretation of the ancient culture, believing it to have been a peaceful society ruled by mathematical wizards and priests. The decipherment of the hieroglyphs, however, has revealed the ancient Mayans to be only too human. Far from peaceful, the Petén city-states literally fought one another continuously in the closing century of the Classic period. And far from contemplating matters removed from earthly concerns, Mayan rulers built great palaces, accumulated considerable wealth for themselves, and not only claimed their divine right to rule, but also their personal divinity.

The ongoing decipherments have opened an unexpected window onto the ancient Mayan world. Writings on public monuments declare the names of rulers, such as K´inch-Janab-Pakal (or "Great-Sun-Shield"), and

Sak K'uk ("White-Quetzal"), his mother who ruled before him at Palenque and one of several female rulers now identified in Mayan politics. Rulers described their royal lineage in great length, and often claimed to be descendants of the creator gods, dating their lineages back to 13.0.0.0.0 4 Ahau 8 Cumku. We now know from their own statements that these divine rulers ordered court architects to construct temples, married into the nobility of other city-states in order to forge political alliances, feasted and visited rulers from other cities, and appointed administrators in subordinate towns. They conducted wars, usually after checking that Venus was propitiously aligned, and captured enemy noblemen and if they could, enemy kings. They led their polities in religious rituals—in ball playing, dancing, burning incense, commemorating the cycles of time by erecting monuments, and sacrificing their own blood to nourish the gods, a painful procedure, but one believed to induce shamanistic visions and communication with the spirit world.

There is much these royal proclamations fail to mention—such as royal failures and natural disasters like hurricanes and drought. Devoted to the main dynastic events in the lives of kings and queens, these texts say little about the social fabric of the community, although they do mention scribes and sculptors, wives and princes. Otherwise, the nature of the lives of the people they ruled is omitted. The official histories have left such matters to archaeologists to reconstruct from fragments of pottery and bone.

The four surviving pre-Columbian Mayan books record not dynastic histories, but rather astronomical tables and their accompanying astrological prognostications. A few of them also describe mythic events and ceremonies that reenact the creation of time. Whether they represent the only kinds of books the Mayans wrote or are actually a distorted sample is hard to say. Many books have been lost—many burned by zealous Catholic friars, others disintegrated from age. Some manuscripts have been discovered in tombs, reduced to pulp by humidity and time. A few books continued to be used after the conquest, eventually becoming part of an oral tradition or rewritten in Latin script, an easier form of writing than the hieroglyphs with their hundreds of symbols. These books, among them the Quiché Mayan *Popol Vuh,* survive, corrupted by the centuries of cultural change, but nonetheless consistent with the myths of creation and political founding, with the sacred cycles of time and divinations that are found in Classic period hieroglyphs and art. Despite the cultural disruption that followed the Spanish conquest, Mayan respect for the word has survived here and there, among people who for centuries were kept basically illiterate. It

Lintel 24 from Yaxchilán, Chiapas, Mexico. The hieroglyphic text relates that the Mayan ruler of Yaxchilán, Lord Shield Jaguar, and his wife, Lady Xoc, engaged in autosacrifice on October 28, 709 C.E. In this scene, only Lady Xoc is seen providing blood for the gods by pulling a rope with thorns through her tongue. (Drawing by H. Chapuis, 1883)

33

Mayan vase with mythological bird (700–800 c.e.) from the Popol Vuh Museum, University of Francisco Marroquín, Guatemala City. Mayan cylindrical vases were painted in a variety of styles and some depicted palace scenes or mythological ones. The artists/scribes who painted the pottery sometimes signed their works in a glyph band at the top. These realistically painted vases were so valued that they were buried with their owners. Recent chemical analyses (as well as decipherments of some of the glyph bands around the rim) indicate that the owners used them as drinking vessels, often as chocolate mugs. Sometimes the chocolate was fermented, sweetened with honey, or mixed with corn gruel. Given that cacao beans were used as Mesoamerican currency, drinking chocolate was the height of conspicuous consumption. The Aztecs are known to have restricted consumption of the beverage to rulers—Moctezuma liked his laced with vanilla—and other members of the nobility. In 16th-century Nicaragua, Fray Fernández de Oviedo y Valdés noted (Reents-Budet 1994, 77) "... only the great and those who can afford it consumed it." (Photo courtesy Lawrence Foster)

survives today in Yucatán, where a village elder records his inherited wisdom in a tatty spiral notebook; it survives in the sacred calendar still interpreted by diviners in the highlands of Guatemala.

This is the beginning of the Ancient Word,
here in this place called Quiché. Here we shall inscribe,
we shall implant the Ancient Word, the potential and
source for everything done in the citadel of Quiché,
in the nation of Quiché people.

■

Popol Vuh, *Book of the Quiché Mayans*
(Tedlock 1985, 71)

Classic Period Collapse

Beginning in 810 C.E., one Mayan city after another was abandoned. Stone monuments with Long Count dates were no longer carved after 909 C.E., when the last known royal pronouncement was recorded. This collapse of the Petén cities, which happened incrementally over a period of at least 100 years, has baffled archaeologists for most of the 20th century. War, natural catastrophes, and overpopulation have been suggested as causes, and recent studies indicate that all three may have been factors in the collapse. Tropical forests are fragile environments when shorn of trees, and the Mayan city-states, many with populations of 50,000 or more, certainly must have strained the agricultural resources of the thin soil. Deforestation was a terrible reality of the ancient Mayan world: trees were felled to clear fields for farming, to make charcoal for cooking, to hollow out canoes, to fire pottery kilns, and to burn limestone for thousands of stucco-covered buildings—approximately 20 trees produced only a small pile of stucco. Add to this environmental degradation, the severe drought that is known to have occurred around this time, and it is not surprising that skeletal remains at some sites indicate malnutrition among commoners.

Not much more is needed as an explanation of the abandonment of the region than soil erosion, overpopulation, and drought. Yet archaeologists have also uncovered evidence of moated and fortified cities, and recent glyphic decipherments tell the tragic story of nearly continuous warfare as the greatest cities attempted to create empires at the expense of one another. The Petén was driven into decline, its majestic cities abandoned, and the region depopulated. When the conquistador Hernán Cortés crossed the Petén in 1524, he called it a wilderness.

The Postclassic Mayans (900–1524 C.E.)

After the Petén collapse, power and trade shifted to other regions. Mayans flourished in cities in northern Yucatán and highland Guatemala; they dotted the coasts of Belize and Honduras. These Mayans were literate, too, but they carved fewer texts into stone for later archaeologists to discover. Although the early Postclassic period boasts some very impressive cities, such as Chichén Itzá, the cities became less monumental and less finely constructed. In this period, politics seems less devoted to the cult of dynastic rulership and, as a result, the art is less focused on portraiture than that of the Classic period. Although Mayan style persists, it incorporates characteristics found elsewhere in Mesoamerica. In fact, this period throughout Mesoamerica shows an increasing intermingling of art styles, perhaps as a statement of new trade alliances brought about after the collapse of the Classic period Petén. Archaeologists argue that these trade and political alliances ushered in a new, more commercial era for the Mayans.

The later pre-Columbian Mayans did write books; however, only four survive in their original hieroglyphic form. Each book is proof of their continued devotion to astronomy and the calendar. Other books did survive, but they were gradually transformed by the conquest; the remaining copies are written in Mayan languages, but in Latin script rather than hieroglyphs, and they are infused with Christian symbolism and other post-Conquest events. These works, such as the *Popol Vuh, The Annals of the Cakchiquels,* and the various Books of the Chilam Balam, provide archaeologists and ethnohistorians with a wealth of material for understanding the ancient Mayan world.

When the Spaniards arrived, they found many Mayan cities in both Yucatán and highland Guatemala, cities built of stone and more densely populated than those they knew in Europe. These Mayans, like their Classic period cousins, were great traders and dominated much of Central American trade, especially its sea trade.

Long-Distance Trade in Central America

The Mayans engaged in long-distance trade from the time of the Olmecs until the Spanish conquest. Waterborne trade certainly contributed to their success as merchants. Archaeologists have identified an artificial river harbor at Lamanai in Belize from the seventh century B.C.E., as well as a massive masonry port in Yucatán, constructed 2,000 years later, that belonged to the inland Mayan city of Chichén

Itzá. A Mayan trading canoe off the coast of Honduras so impressed Christopher Columbus in 1502 that he talked about the wealth it promised for a voyage to the "unknown" land of Yucatán. The Mayans traded among and with the rest of Mesoamerica as well as with their neighbors in southern Central America. After the conquest, trade continued along the old routes until the Spanish economy developed enough in the 17th century to replace the last vestiges of the pre-Columbian system.

For several thousand years, the Mayans sold quetzal feathers from the cloud forests in Mexico and elsewhere, jade from western Guatemala, and jaguar pelts from the lowland rain forests. They produced honey and the finest quality of salt on the Yucatán Peninsula, they grew cotton and wove it into valued textiles throughout the lowlands, and they nurtured cacao in the fertile coastal plains along the Gulf of Mexico, the Pacific, and the Caribbean. They had access to obsidian from the Guatemalan highlands and chert (similar to flint), both essential for tools and weapons. At the time of the conquest, the Mayans also traded in slaves from other parts of Central America.

The Mayans produced some of the most valued goods in Mesoamerica for trade with the great cities of Mexico. In addition, they also exploited their strategic middle position to control trade between southern Central America and the rest of Mexico. The southern periphery of the Mayan world in Honduras and El Salvador produced cacao and cotton to supplement that grown in the Mayan heartland. These local elites participated in Mesoamerican culture by building cities of stone, carving stone portraits of rulers (but often with non-Mayan motifs and no accompanying text), and performing the ritual ball game.

The Nicoya Peninsula, at the crossroads to regions farther to the south, was also important to the Mesoamerican world. Nicaraguan and Costa Rican chiefdoms probably served as intermediaries in trade with the south—a considerable amount of imported gold has been found at Nicaraguan sites in the lakes region and imported carved jade has been excavated in Costa Rica. Pearls from the Gulf of Nicoya and cacao from the fertile coast added to the region's attraction as a trade center. The lower isthmus, more aloof from Mesoamerica than its northern counterparts, had many highly valued commodities: gold, pendants of semiprecious stones, such as agate and opal, and spondylus shells harvested from the bottom of the Caribbean Sea by divers.

Trade Routes

As a result of the isthmus's valuable resources, many separate trade routes developed there. One of the most important routes, first exploited by the Olmec, was along the Pacific coast. Another, most important during the Classic period of the Mayans in the Petén, cut across the center of the lowland jungle to the eastern edge of the Mayan realm where the cities of Copán and Quiriguá were established. And a sea route united the Gulf of Mexico with the Caribbean coast of Central America at trading ports on the Bay of Honduras. Various other routes linked the Caribbean, particularly at the Bay of Honduras, with the highlands and the Pacific.

Competition for isthmian goods must have been intense. Archaeological evidence indicates that during various periods central Mexican merchants gained a foothold in the region along some of these routes, especially along the Pacific coast, and the great Mexican city of Teotihuacán left its imprint on the Mayan city of Kaminaljuyú in highland Guatemala. Also, enclaves of peoples speaking central Mexican languages apparently occupied the Pacific region of both Nicaragua and Costa Rica, according to the earliest Spanish reports; some archaeologists believe these peoples may have been in the region as early as the ninth century C.E. The southern Central Americans were merchants, too, and may have tried to bypass northern intermediaries in Costa Rica and Nicaragua: at the time of the Spanish conquest, the Coclé in Panama sailed rigged canoes along the Pacific, perhaps as far as Mexico, exporting salt, hammocks, cotton, gold dust, and slaves.

Southern Isthmus

> From these Indians . . . we learned that up country there were many caciques [chiefs] who had heaps of gold, and people armed like ourselves.
>
> ■
>
> Ferdinand Colón, 1503 (Morison 1963, 344)

Although Mayan civilization was an integral part of Mesoamerica, the lower isthmus had no such close relationship with its northern neighbors. The Mesoamerican border is difficult to define with any exactitude, but it most definitely incorporated the western parts of El Salvador and Honduras within the Mayan realm. Mesoamerica's reach

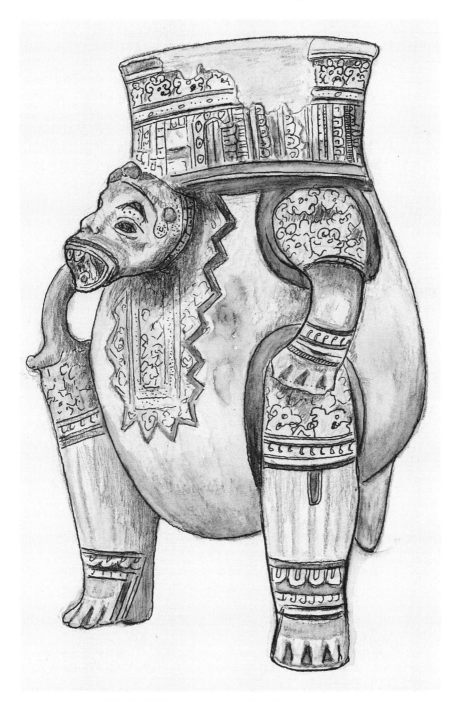

Nicoya Jaguar Vessel (1000–1500 C.E.) from Costa Rica. This polychrome vessel demonstrates the sophistication of ancient isthmian ceramics. (Drawing by Cherra Wyllie)

also fluctuated over time, extending south to touch Costa Rica and Nicaragua in Olmec times and again in the centuries before the conquest when peoples from central Mexico may have moved into the Nicoya region. However ill-defined the borders, many archaeologists refer to the lower isthmian cultures, along with what are now Colombia and Ecuador, as the Intermediate Area, after their location between the more complex civilizations of Andean South America and Mesoamerica. Stone cities were not constructed in the Intermediate Area, but peoples in the Nicoya region of Nicaragua and Costa Rica built earthen mound platforms to support temples and houses of the elite, arranging them around a central plaza in a manner reminiscent of Mesoamerican cities. Also, the first Spaniards to encounter them observed that they had books as well as stone sculptures of rulers, two other traits typical of Mesoamerica.

In Panama and the Talamanca region of Costa Rica, dispersed villages, some of them defensively palisaded and all smaller than 1,500 in population, showed none of the monumentality of the more northern regions of the isthmus. Self-sustaining chiefdoms, not complex states, ruled the Pacific slopes of the southern isthmus. These autonomous societies remained small and scattered, perhaps because the rugged terrain allowed little room for expansion. The chiefdoms never required complex administrative structures or architecture, although slab-lined tombs filled with well-crafted items were quite common.

Lacking impressive monumental cities or any surviving written records of their accomplishments, these chiefdoms have not always attracted the attention they deserve. Some areas, such as the Atlantic watershed of Nicaragua and Honduras, are practically unexplored; others, on the Pacific side of Costa Rica and Panama, have been heavily looted for gold. Even those sites that have been excavated have often failed to provide enough information to date them with any precision, or to clearly define their interrelationships with other regions. What is certain is that there were many distinctive and independent cultures.

Chiefdoms

However great the variety of cultures in Central America, trade united the isthmus. From 500 to 1100 C.E., the height of Mayan civilization, the southern chiefdoms increased in size and wealth under the stimulus of trade in luxury items of jade and gold as well as magnificent polychrome pottery. The chiefs who controlled this trade, which certainly included trade with Colombia—where some of the metallurgical techniques originated—became rich and powerful. The chiefs, according to the first Spanish explorers, also led their people in war (archaeologists have found weapons accompanying them in burials) and were the supreme religious authorities, much like the shaman rulers in Mesoamerica. After 800 C.E., and at the time of the collapse of many lowland Mayan city-states, some of these chiefdoms reached their highest level of complexity and wealth. During this period, southern Central American gold was traded to Mesoamerica in quantity for the first time.

Prestige befitting a chief required rituals and social stratification that often echoed the practices of the civilizations to the north and south. Chiefs commonly ordered their portraits carved into stone. In Nicaragua, the rulers were depicted wearing animal-spirit headdresses; in the Chiriquí region of Panama and Costa Rica, they were portrayed riding on the shoulders of a naked commoner or slave. At numerous Costa Rican sites, great granite spheres, the largest 7 feet in diameter and weighing 15,000 tons, were carefully worked and lined up in what may have been a cosmological or astronomical arrangement, just as buildings in Mesoamerica were aligned to measure and commemorate such events. Monumental grinding stones decorated with trophy heads were apparently used in maize rituals of human sacrifice (*see* Maize close-up, Chapter 1). The richest Coclé and Veraguas graves in Panama included sacrificed retainers as well as ornaments of semiprecious stones and hammered and cast gold jewelry. Linea Vieja graves in northern Costa Rica demonstrate not only wealth, but also an amazing diversity of foreign contacts, not just from Central America but also from Peru and the West Indies, from Mesoamerica and northern South America. Even in areas where gold was not mined, such as the Talamanca Massif of the Chiriquí culture, sculptures depict rulers wearing gold ornaments.

Cultural Exchange

Some archaeologists argue that the southern chiefdoms should be studied independently of the civilizations to the north and south. The isthmian cultures achieved self-sufficient societies of great stability and duration, and they produced exquisitely skilled work in both gold, semiprecious stones, and ceramics. Yet there seems little doubt that, as scattered and independent as the southern chiefdoms were, they were not isolated from the civilizations to the north and south. They gave the gift of metallurgy to Mesoamerica, where isthmian gold is found north of Mexico City and south to the Yucatán Peninsula. Most of the extraordinary gold work dredged from the famous sacred well of the Mayan

AMERICAN GOLD

Metallurgy in the New World was practiced for 2,000 years before the voyage of Christopher Columbus. The technology traveled slowly from Andean South America into southern Central America and, eventually, into Mesoamerica. Despite pre-Columbian expertise in metallurgy, few practical objects were made from any metal. Chert and obsidian were the primary materials for tools, although tweezers, fish hooks, and axes were sometimes made of copper during the late Postclassic period (1250–1519 C.E.). Gold was reserved for ornaments and ritual objects—animal pendants, hammered burial helmets, settings for emeralds and other jewelry, and bells for dance rattles and adornments as well as masks and offerings for religious ceremonies. Although copper and tin were mined as was silver, gold was the preeminent pre-Columbian metal. Its brilliance and color associated it with the sun god cult: in fact, a 36-pound gold Aztec sun disk was taken by the conquistadores to the Spanish court and marveled upon by European artists, among them Albrecht Dürer.

Diquis cast gold frog pendant (800–1500 C.E.) from Costa Rica, with a bifurcated tongue ending in mythological serpent heads. In the Collection of the Banco Central de Costa Rica. (Drawing by Cherra Wyllie)

Gold objects, usually strengthened with copper, were produced with a great variety of metallurgical techniques, including lost-wax castings, hammering, anneal-

city of Chichén Itzá (800–1000 C.E.) was made in the lower isthmus. And metallurgical techniques were copied in various parts of Mexico and resulted in that country's finest gold work: the lost-wax pendants of Oaxaca.

The lower Central American chiefdoms participated in and shared much of the culture of their neighbors in both northern South America and Mesoamerica. Bark cloth, hammocks, the Talamancan sculptural

ing, soldering, and welding. The technology appeared around 400 B.C.E., and perhaps much earlier, in Peru and Colombia. It took a millennium for metallurgy to reach Panama and Costa Rica, a surprisingly long time given that Colombia and Panama share a border. Once adopted, gold swept the isthmus. By 600 C.E., it had replaced jade in elite Costa Rican burials, and substituted for spondylus shell jewelry in Panama. At Sitio Conte (700–900 C.E.), a Coclé site in central Panama with one of the richest tombs yet discovered, gold distinguished a chief from his retainers in a mass burial: a hammered gold helmet covered his head, an elaborate pectoral his chest, and other ornaments adorned his wrists, ears, and nose. Traditions associated with gold endured well beyond the Spanish conquest, and as late as the 18th century, Franciscan friars observed gold figurines being buried with the dead in the Talamanca region.

Mesoamerica, despite its accomplishments in many areas, was a true latecomer in metallurgy. Not until the eighth century C.E. did the Mayans begin importing significant amounts of gold from the lower isthmus. Soon thereafter, extraordinary repoussé gold disks and copper and gold bells were thrown as offerings into the sacred well of Chichén Itzá. Many of the gold items retrieved by archaeologists from the well were from Costa Rica; quite a number were clearly made in Mesoamerican designs for export, rather than for local isthmian use. Other items employed isthmian gold and technology, but in a Mayan style so fluid as to suggest that they may have been made in the Yucatán, perhaps by a traveling isthmian goldsmith or by a Mayan apprentice to such a goldsmith. Apparently Mesoamerica quickly learned to value gold, creating its own goldsmiths and commerce in the precious metal. Although Nicaragua and Costa Rica continued to trade gold to Mesoamerica until the 16th century, Mexican metallurgists, especially those from Oaxaca, produced exceptional gold jewelry. By the time of the Spanish conquest, the Aztec emperor Moctezuma was receiving two tons of gold in tribute each year.

style, and exquisite gold objects speak to this region's affinities with Andean cultures. Ruler-shamans attired in quetzal-feathered headdresses and depicted with jaguar features indicate the acceptance of Mesoamerica's most potent political symbols; sacrificial grinding stones and contemporary oral traditions tell of a shared Mesoamerican worldview that included ancestor worship and creation myths centered on maize and human sacrifice.

Pre-Columbian Legacy

The Central American isthmus during the millennia of pre-Columbian civilization witnessed a diversity of cultural responses, from the literate and complex Mayan civilization and the exquisite artistry of the simpler Pacific coast chiefdoms to the more isolated tribal societies along parts of the Caribbean. These people, despite their different languages, varied art styles, and contrasts in social complexity, traversed rugged mountains, sailed through rough waters, and penetrated tropical jungles to trade with one another and exchange exotic rituals of ruler prestige as well as stories of world creation.

The legacy of ancient civilization in Central America did not end with the Spanish conquest. More than 20 percent of Central Americans live within the cultural framework and oral traditions of their native American ancestors. Their heritage includes the monumental ruined cities of Mayan civilization that have been reclaimed by archaeologists from the jungles and highland basins of northern Central America, and the Panamanian and Costa Rican gold pendants seen in museums throughout the world. Their ancestors participated in the most dramatic moments of Central American history: they battled the conquering Spaniards and suffered defeat and enslavement; some, such as the Miskito and rebel Mayans, allied themselves with English pirates and profiteers against Spain. The indigenous peoples have survived, sometimes at the forefront of history and sometimes in closed or remote societies that preserved ancient traditions. They have also survived through intermarriage, creating the *mestizo* population, part Indian and part European, which accounts for 62 percent of Central Americans. Today every isthmian nation's character is influenced by its indigenous culture, or its absence, from Costa Rica, where the native peoples have been practically extinct since the Spanish conquest, to Guatemala, where Mayans constitute approximately half the population. Central American history, and the diverse profiles of its various modern states, cannot be separated from the story of these Americans.

3

THE SPANISH CONQUEST
(1492–1541)

I I Ahau was the katun ... at the arrival of the foreigners.
Red were the beards of the sons of the sun,
The bearded ones who came from the east
When they arrived here near this land
As foreigners to the land ...
Thus we were made to weep for their coming, their
* arrival ...*

■

Book of Chilam Balam of Chumayel (Edmonson 1986, 115–17)

Everything that has happened since the marvellous discovery of
the Americas ... [seems] to overshadow all the deeds of famous
men past, no matter how heroic, and to silence all talk of other
wonders of the world. Prominent amid the aspects of this story
which have caught the imagination are the massacres of
innocent peoples ...

■

Friar Bartolomé de Las Casas, 1542 (1992, 3)

The Spanish conquest is a compelling story about the clash of two worlds, each previously unknown to the other. It encompasses the destruction of the Aztec and Incan Empires by conquistadores who numbered only in the hundreds, and it includes the prolonged struggle to subjugate the diverse peoples of Central America. Within decades of their arrival in the Caribbean in 1492, the Spaniards had destroyed the urban civilizations of the Americas and proclaimed themselves sovereign over a territory 40 times the size of Spain.

Central America was invaded from both the north and south, just as it had been since the isthmus was first formed. The isthmus, on the way to everywhere, was the gateway to both Mesoamerica and the Andes. The Spaniards arrived from Mexico and Panama as well as by sea—especially the Caribbean Sea, where they had established themselves on nearby islands. Crossing Panama, the Spanish found the Pacific Ocean and, subsequently, the Incan civilization; entering the Bay of Honduras, they encountered sophisticated Mayan traders from whom they learned about the land of Yucatán. The isthmus promised gold, access to new lands and, perhaps, a passage to India. Barraged from every angle, Central America was nonetheless not easily subdued. It would take more than four decades before the Spanish Crown could institute effective governmental controls, and even then, half the isthmus remained unexplored and unconquered.

Spain and the Conquistadores

> ... kingdoms granted and entrusted by God and His church to the Spanish Crown ...
>
> ■
>
> Friar Bartolomé de Las Casas (1992, 6)

In 1502 Christopher Columbus sailed into the Bay of Honduras and claimed the surrounding land for Spain. A decade had passed since he first stumbled upon the New World while looking for a route to Asia, the land of silk and ivory, cinnamon and cloves, porcelain and jade. Thinking that only a vast ocean separated Europe from the Orient, Columbus believed he had found the coast of Asia. On his fourth and final expedition, he explored the Caribbean coast of Central America, still seeking a passage to India. He found neither a strait to India nor the Pacific Ocean. In making the fateful decision to travel eastward from Honduras, he encountered dispersed thatch-and-cane houses along the undeveloped Mosquitía coast and peoples attired in little more than tattoos; had he moved in the opposite direction, he would have found Mesoamerican stone cities and the cotton-clad Mayans of Yucatán. Columbus returned to Spain a failed and forgotten man, leaving America to bestow its gifts of fame and fortune on others, such as Vasco Núñez de Balboa, explorer of Panama and the Pacific Ocean, and Pedro de Alvarado, the most influential conquistador of Central America. Even greater glory was left for Hernán Cortés, conquistador of Mexico, and Francisco Pizarro, conquistador of Peru.

These men, and the conquest and exploration of the New World, were the product of the Spanish war machine, at the time the greatest in Europe. Spain had fought the Crusades for 200 years. Just before Columbus's voyage, the Muslims had finally been expelled from Spain with the battle of Granada in 1491. The Catholic monarchs, Ferdinand and Isabella, were ready for new undertakings. Columbus's plan to find a sea route to the Orient appealed to them on two grounds: as an opportunity to save new souls for the good of the church and as a chance to secure trade routes for the good of its treasury.

Spain's treasury certainly needed a boost. Centuries of war and plundering had devastated the economy. A war machine was no substitute for commerce and adequate agriculture; soldiers, who thrived on plunder and adventure, disdained the patience and investment required for farming and industry. While the rest of Europe experimented with capitalism and industrialization, Spain remained basically feudal. The country seethed with unemployed soldiers, restless sons of soldiers, and penniless members of the nobility, impoverished by an inheritance system that favored the eldest son.

When Columbus returned from his first voyage laden with gold, parrots, and Indian slaves, Spain recognized a solution to its problems. Needing to legitimize the imperial undertaking of sending Columbus back to the New World, the Catholic monarchs appealed to Pope Alexander VI. With the stroke of his pen, he granted Spain sovereignty over the New World in exchange for its spiritual conversion of the heathens who inhabited it. Spain thus was entrusted with a new holy war. Under this divine mandate, Spaniards shipped out from Seville in the hope of making their fortunes, confident that God was on their side.

Spain in the Caribbean

The Spaniards who came to America were a mixed lot. Many, like Francisco Pizarro, were illiterate. Others were common criminals. Some, such as Cortés, Montejo, and Alvarado, were from the lesser nobility. A few were well-connected sons of the nobility, such as Pedrarias Dávila (Pedro Arias de Ávila), who was the younger brother of the count of Medelín. For decades, the war machine had employed their families and accustomed them to expect the spoils of conquest: Pedrarias, for example, had distinguished himself in the battle for Granada before trying his skills in Central America. Most conquistadores were Spaniards, but there were some from other European countries as well as a few African slaves. Whatever their class and background, they shared one thing: poverty.

They arrived in the Caribbean in the name of God and the Crown, but they were, in reality, determined fortune hunters. War booty, gold, and pearls—not manual labor—would make them rich. The hard work would be left for native slaves. Many planned to return to Spain, bringing with them the riches that would improve their standing in society. The dream was so tantalizing that some families contributed many of their members to the dangerous sea voyage and unknown territory. Pedro de Alvarado traveled with his four brothers, with whom he would entrust the conquest and governance of various parts of Guatemala; Francisco de Montejo traveled and fought with his son and nephew in Yucatán. Some regions of Spain were particularly swept by the dream—Cortés, Pizarro, the Alvarado brothers, and Pedrarias all came from the Extremadura area there.

As it turned out, the island colonies were not to everyone's liking. The mines were few, and the large estates, which required investment of time and money, could not satisfy any soldier's get-rich-quick scheme. Within a few years, there weren't any slaves either: European diseases and inhumane treatment had exterminated the Indian populations on Hispaniola (the island now shared by Haiti and the Dominican Republic) and Cuba. Spaniards raided other islands, kidnapping Indians and forcing them to work in the mines in the Spanish colonies; desperate for laborers, they even paid for African slaves.

The mines soon were depleted, and many Spaniards had to fall back on their estates for an income. If not wealthy, they at least lived like the gentry. Cortés spent all his money on clothing and gambling. Balboa became so encumbered by debts he was forced to escape Hispaniola as a stowaway on a ship heading for Panama. As the settlers became pressed for slaves and gold, they explored the Caribbean once again and quickly found their way to Panama, where Columbus earlier had reported large quantities of gold.

Panama: The First Settlement

I take and seize ... actual possession of these seas and lands, and coasts and ports and islands of the South ...

∎

Vasco Núñez de Balboa, 1513 (Anderson 1941, 176)

Major Conquest Routes

ATLANTIC OCEAN

Gulf of Mexico

Havana

CUBA

Santo Domingo

Mexico City 1521

Santiago HISPANIOLA

Puerto Caballos 1524

Caribbean Sea

Comayagua 1537

Trujillo 1525

Guatemala 1524

San Salvador 1525

León 1523

Portobelo 1510

Granada 1523

San José 1540

Panama 1519

Santa María de la Antigua 1510

N

Christopher Columbus (fourth voyage), 1502–03

Vincente Yañez de Pinzón & Juan Díaz de Solís, 1506

Vasco Núñez de Balboa, 1511–13

Gil González Davila, 1522

Pedro de Alvarado, 1523–26

Cristóbal de Olid, 1523

Hernán Cortés, 1524–25

PACIFIC OCEAN

0   300 miles

0   300 km

© Infobase Publishing

Central America was conquered from almost all directions: from Mexico and from both the Pacific Ocean and the Caribbean.

The fabulous conquests in Mexico and Peru have obscured the fact that the earliest European settlements on the American mainland were in Panama. Under the leadership of Vasco Núñez de Balboa, the first successful colony, Santa María la Antigua, was established in the unlikely location of the Darién in 1510. The Darién, a low-lying spit of the isthmus that joins South America to the rest of the Americas, is today a region of dense rain forest and one of the most pristine tropical wildernesses in the world. Its remoteness has preserved the traditions of semi-nomadic Indians, such as the Kuna and Emberá. In settling in the Darién, the Spaniards had only a confused idea of where they were and absolutely no idea that the wealthy civilizations of Mexico and Peru existed. Yet the region, though quickly abandoned for more temperate climes, led to some of Spain's greatest discoveries.

As early as 1498, Christopher Columbus, sailing along the northern coast of South America, suspected the massive mountains and major rivers there indicated a mainland, unlike the islands that already were being settled by Spaniards. The presence of monkeys and pearls convinced Ferdinand of Spain that the coast of Asia had finally been reached. The king quickly dispatched ships to explore the area, and although they returned with pearls, gold, and slaves, India was not found.

Eventually the search for a strait to India attracted Rodrigo de Bastidas (1501), Columbus (1502–3), and others to Panama; they found a great bounty in gold as well as news of a southern sea nearby— Columbus optimistically thought it would be the Ganges River. The gold tempted Columbus to establish a trading post in Veraguas, but he was soon expelled by angry Indians, and the enterprise ended in disaster. Not until the Spaniards became disgruntled with the situation on the islands was the search for Panamanian gold and the southern sea revived. In 1513, after he had befriended the Indians of Darién and established the settlement of Santa María, Balboa was taken to the Pacific Ocean by native guides.

The Darién, officially designated Castilla del Oro ("Golden Castile") by the Crown, had access to gold from both Colombia and Panama and provided a relatively short, overland route between the Atlantic and Pacific oceans, a fact that would become even more critical with the conquest of Peru in 1532. Santa María was abandoned for the more temperate climate of Panama City in 1519, and the overland shipment of goods and people from the Pacific to Spanish ships in the Atlantic shifted to a route closer to that of today's Panama Canal. By 1519 Panama's strategic location had led to a permanent settlement and exploration of the Pacific Ocean, but in that same year attention would shift to Mexico and Hernán Cortés's march on the highland capital of the Aztecs.

Mayans on the Eve of the Conquest

Moctezuma, ruler of the Aztec Empire, sent messengers to his allies and his enemies, warning them of the impending invasion by the conquistadores. He suggested the time had come to unite against this common foe. On the eve of the conquest, the Aztecs dominated most of Mesoamerica; their island capital of Tenochtitlán was the largest city in the land, indeed one of the largest in the world, with a population approaching 250,000. Less than 100 years after becoming an independent state, the upstart Aztec nation had forced alliances on formerly powerful states and subjugated many others into paying tribute. Aztec troops marched to wherever there was resistance; permanent military garrisons were established where rebellions simmered. Aztec merchants, who also functioned as military spies, controlled many of the ancient trade routes. Yet even the powerful Aztecs viewed the white, bearded Spaniards with fear.

The Mayans traded with the Aztecs and even emulated Aztec culture. Nobles in both Yucatán and Guatemala adorned themselves with luxury items imported from the Aztecs and painted their palace walls with frescoes in the style of central Mexico. Pleased to bask in the reflected glory of Mesoamerica's most powerful empire, the Mayans were nonetheless vigilant at maintaining their independence; the Quiché Mayans even prohibited Aztec merchants from entering their kingdom in the Guatemalan highlands. Just before the Spanish conquest, however, the Aztecs seemed poised to expand into the various Mayan regions. Their merchants were encountered by Spanish expeditions at trading outposts on both the Pacific and Caribbean coasts of Central America; and their language, Nahuatl, was the lingua franca of trade. While consolidating their power along the periphery of the Mayan world, the Aztecs also took direct control in the southeast and by 1500, they had incorporated parts of Chiapas, including the cacao lands of the Soconusco, into the empire.

Aztec expansion in the Soconusco region met with resistance from the Mayan kingdom of the Quiché. Since the 14th century, the Quichés had ruled over most of highland Guatemala and the rich lands of the Pacific coast from their fortified capital of K'umarcaaj or, as it eventually was called in Nahuatl, Utatlán. The Quiché confederacy was the largest kingdom in all of Central America. It was a state created by the military prowess of the legendary founder K'ucumatz (1375–1425) and his son, Quik'ab (1425–75), men whom the Quichés believed had shamanistic powers. A hieroglyphic codex from Utatlán, lost after the Spanish conquest, described 800 years of Mayan history using the traditional Long Count dates. It was considered a city favored by the gods, a place of learning and military strength, and Utatlán nobles also ruled many other cities. Tribute was demanded and received from principalities as far away as Soconusco and the frontier with modern-day El Salvador.

At the time of Moctezuma's appeal, Utatlán could produce no one capable of saving the Quiché kingdom from political fragmentation. Population pressures in the western highlands were causing intense competition for land and fierce fighting over the lands rich in cacao and maize on the Pacific coast. Scholars estimate that the population in the zone immediately around Utatlán had increased to 50,000 and Guatemala may have had a population of 2 million, even with the Petén basically depopulated. One of the most powerful groups in the Quiché kingdom, the Cakchiquel Mayans, rebelled in 1470 and founded their own city to the south, naming it Iximché (or "Maize Tree," a meaning that was translated by the Aztecs to "Cuauhtemallan"—the origin of "Guatemala.") Their independence inspired rebellions from other groups, such the Tzutujil from Lake Atitlán.

The constant warfare, starting with the Quiché conquests in the 14th century, caused vulnerable valley sites, inhabited for more than 1,000 years, to be abandoned in favor of fortress cities. Positioned like medieval European castles on mountain ridges and protected by moat-like ravines, these hilltop cities looked over the pine-forested mountains and cultivated valley floors of the highlands. Peasants fled to these citadels, joining the ruling elite and their slaves, adding their numbers to those of the priests, soldiers, and artisans who were already there, and swelling the resident population to at least 15,000. At least three other citadels guarded the sacred capital at Utatlán, with its 140 civic buildings, and others were strategically situated throughout the Quiché kingdom. The conquistador Pedro de Alvarado described Utatlán as well constructed and marvelously strong, and so dangerous to the conquistadores that they were compelled to destroy it.

The Aztec emperors referred to the Quiché as rich and powerful, but war had so weakened these Mayans that by 1510 they were forced to make tribute payments of gold, cacao, quetzal feathers, and textiles to Tenochtitlán. In exchange, Moctezuma, who always preferred to leave local rulers in power in return for their allegiance, seems to have given two daughters in marriage to the Quiché ruler. With such prestige added to the royal lineage, the Quiché readily took on the airs of the great Aztec empire itself: the nobles learned Nahuatl, and even constructed a twin temple complex and an enclosed ball court that echoed those in the religious precinct of the great Aztec capital. The Quichés responded loyally to Moctezuma's request for solidarity, even though the divinations of the priests warned of a Quiché defeat by the Spaniards.

Conquest of Utatlán

> On the day I Ganel [February 20, 1524] the Quichés were destroyed by the Spaniards. Their chief, he who was called Tunatiuh Avilantaro [Pedro de Alvarado], conquered all the people. Their faces were not known before that time.
>
> ■
>
> The Annals of the Cakchiquels (Recinos 1953, 119)

Ruined Mayan fortified city of Mixco Viejo in the Guatemalan highlands. (Photo courtesy Cherra Wyllie)

In 1521 Hernán Cortés and his Tlaxcalan Indian allies conquered Tenochtitlán after a prolonged siege and series of brutal battles. Moctezuma was dead and the great city itself was devastated. Using Moctezuma's tribute list, Cortés sent his captains out to investigate and demand allegiance to the Spanish emperor, and when necessary, to defeat and enslave those who resisted. Within a few years, Cortés had set his sights on Guatemala. He suggested in a letter to Charles V that the Quichés had been stirring up trouble in the Soconusco region, and he would send his loyal captain, Pedro de Alvarado, to resolve the matter. Alvarado would do so with dispatch.

Alvarado was destined to become the single most influential conquistador in northern Central America, not simply for the territories he won for the Crown, but also for his 17-year-long rule as governor. Little is known about his life prior to his departure from Extremadura, Spain, at the age of 25, but both his bravery and brutality are well documented. Fearless and ambitious, he was an ideal conquistador. He had no more than landed in the New World in 1510 when he joined in the

53

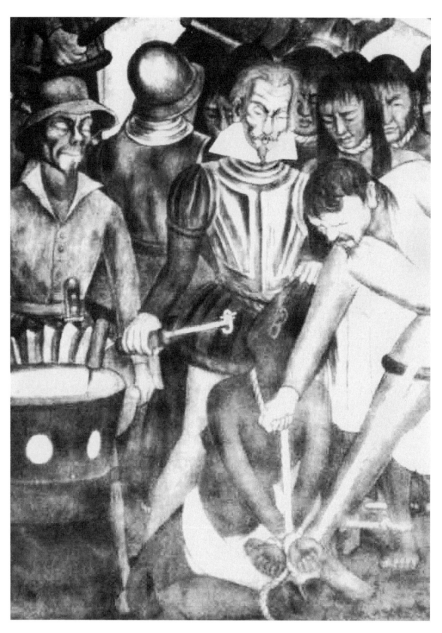

Pedro Alvarado as depicted by the artist Diego Rivera, 1945. No contemporary portrait of
Pedro de Alvarado has survived, but his reputation for cruelty has been preserved in this
20th-century mural depicting the blond conquistador (on the right) branding an Indian slave.
As the Mayans said, "The heart of Tonatiuh [Alvarado] was without compassion for the people
during the war." (The Annals of the Cakchiquels 1953, 120). He even enslaved the Tlaxcalan
and Mexican Indian allies who had fought by his side in the conquest of Guatemala. Yet he
apparently suffered enough remorse for his excesses to order all his slaves freed upon
his death. (Photo by Lawrence Foster)

conquest of Cuba. He explored the Yucatán coast of Mexico with Juan de Grijalva and, having heard rumors of the riches of the Aztecs, he and his brothers readily joined the Cortés expedition in 1519. A good horseman and active almost to the point of restlessness, he engaged in new explorations and conquests until his death in 1541, when his horse rolled over him while he was trying to quash an Indian rebellion. According to the conquistador Bernal Diaz del Castillo, Alvarado was a good talker and frank-hearted. A natural leader of soldiers, he became Cortés's leading captain and most trustworthy troubleshooter. Even Cortés, however, complained about his use of excessive violence—Alvarado massacred unarmed Aztecs in the main temple of Tenochtitlán, for example—and the political unrest it caused. Handsome and something of a dandy with his gold necklace and jewels, the fair-haired Alvarado became known among the Indians as Tonatiuh, the golden sun god.

On December 6, 1523, Alvarado set out from Mexico City for the south with 400 Spanish soldiers, 130 of them crossbowmen and musketeers, and 5,000 to 10,000 Indian auxiliaries. Some were loyal Tlaxcalans, others more recently conquered Aztecs, Mixtecs, and Zapotecs. The costs of the expedition with its 160 horses, 120 horsemen, plentiful artillery and plentiful ammunition, put Cortés into considerable debt, but he expected to be more than adequately recompensed by the "rich and strange lands with many very different people." (Cortés, 316). Within a few months, Alvarado had traveled the 1,100 miles to Soconusco. In February, he left the Pacific slope behind him and ascended the Sierra Madre into the Guatemalan highlands.

The Guatemala he encountered had already been devastated by war and disease. Smallpox had preceded Alvarado's troops by a few years, and the Mayans had died by the thousands. By the time the epidemic had run its course in 1521, more than a third of the highland population was dead; the corpses, too numerous to bury, were left for the vultures. The disease killed without prejudice. The debilitated survivors were left to piece their lives back together. "We were children and we were alone." (*The Annals of the Cakchiquels* 1953, 117).

Greatly weakened, Utatlán nonetheless refused to cooperate with the Spaniards. Alvarado's messengers gave the Quichés a choice: peacefully accept the Crown's dominion or suffer war and, for those who survived the battle, enslavement. The Quichés did not deign to answer. Like Moctezuma, the ruler Three Quej instead appealed for united resistance among the warring Guatemalan factions; and, much like Moctezuma, he would be disappointed in the response. The Cakchiquels already had

TWO CULTURES IN BATTLE

The *Lienzo*, the work of a Tlaxcalan Indian from central Mexico, depicts a mounted and armored Spaniard defeating the Mayans with his Tlaxcalan allies. The Indians described the clamor of the conquistadores' metal armor, the wild eyes of his attack dogs and sweat of his roof-tall horses. They feared the conquistadores' weapons that shot fire and admired the shine of his steel swords. But the fear and confusion were mutual. For instance, Balboa's stranded and hungry soldiers were terrified of poisoned arrows and so took a route into the Darién that avoided the Indians who used them. Columbus noted the lethal

The 1524 conquest of the Guatemalan town now known as Santiago Atitlán. (Drawing by Diódoro Serrano [Chavero, 1892] after the now lost 16th-century original in the *Lienzo de Tlaxcala*)

sharpness of Indian clubs studded with obsidian blades and adorned with feathers and gold. The Indians, some dressed in the costume of their animal spirit or more simply covered in body paint, marched into war calling to their gods with the cacaphonous music of shell trumpets, stone flutes and wooden drums—sounds as maddening to European ears as cannon bursts were to the Indians. Alonso de Aguilar (de Fuentes 1963, 149) said the numbers, noise, and ferocity of the Indians frightened Cortés's soldiers into asking for confession.

Perhaps nothing better contrasts the worlds of the Mayans and the Spaniards than their singularly different descriptions of the same battle outside Quetzaltenango:

> And after I rallied with the horsemen, I turned on them [the Quichés], and here a very severe pursuit and punishment was made. In this affair one of the four chiefs of the city of Utatlán was killed, who was the captain general of all this country. I returned to the spring and there made camp for the night, greatly fatigued, and with several Spaniards and horses wounded.

■

Pedro de Alvarado, 1524 (1972, 58)

> And then Captain Tecum flew up, he came like an eagle full of feathers that grew from his body . . . they were not artificial; he wore wings which also sprang from his body and he wore three crowns. . . . This Captain Tecum came with the intention of killing Tunadiu [Alvarado] who came on horseback and he hit the horse instead of the Adelantado [Alvarado] and he cut off the head of the horse with one lance. It was not a lance of iron but of shiny stone and this captain had placed a spell on it. And when he saw that it was not the Adelantado but the horse who had died he returned to fly overhead. . . . Then the Adelantado awaited him with his lance and he impaled this Captain Tecum. . . . The Adelantado told his soldiers that he had never seen another Indian as gallant and as noble and covered with such beautiful quetzal feathers. . . .

■

Titulo de Nijaib, 16th-century document of Nijaib dynasty of Momostenango, Guatemala (Burkhardt and Gasco 1996, 151)

made their pact with the conquistadores in return for favorable treatment. They assisted the Spaniards in the defeat of their traditional enemies, just as the Tlaxcalans did with the Aztecs. At a critical juncture in the fighting, the Cakchiquels sent 2,000 soldiers "to the slaughter of the Quichés" (*The Annals of the Cakchiquels*, 121). And they would soon regret their actions.

The Quichés prepared for war. Their great captain Tecum organized 10,000 troops from various towns; other captains joined with their warriors. Before fighting, they all readied themselves with seven days of religious ceremonies and war dances in Utatlán. Tecum, seated on a litter like a god, was carried in the ritual directions, adorned with mirrors, precious gems, and quetzal feathers and, as related in Quiché books, given the magical ability to see both before him and behind him. Receiving reports from their spies that Alvarado was approaching what is today known as Quetzaltenango, the Quichés marched into battle behind drummers, conch-shell trumpet players, and 39 flag bearers. Alvarado, his troops and horses tired from the difficult climb from the coast to the highland plain, arrived in the Quiché kingdom and were immediately confronted with what he took to be an army of 30,000.

Alvarado roundly defeated the Quichés on the plain outside Quetzaltenango. As he put it: " . . . our infantry made the greatest destruction in the world" (1972, 59). The Quichés seemed to agree, saying "the day became red because of the great bloodshed." (Burkhardt and Gasco 1996, 151). The Quichés agreed to make peace, and invited the Spaniards to Utatlán to feast. As Alvarado rode toward the citadel and crossed over a ravine on the entrance ramp into the walled city, he sensed a trap. Inside the city, the narrow streets left no room for the Spaniards to maneuver on their horses, and once the ramp was removed, there would be no exit. Making his excuses, Alvarado narrowly escaped with his troops down to the plain below. There, with the aid of his Cakchiquel allies, he fought the Quichés for the final time. He captured many Quiché leaders and burned them alive, and he then burned the city of Utatlán. Alvarado had conquered the Quiché kingdom in just a few months.

> This is enough about the being of Quiché, given that there is no longer a place to see it . . .
>
> ∎
>
> Popol Vuh, Book of the Quiché Mayans (Tedlock 1985, 227)

Alvarado Extends the Conquest

[A conquest] in bits and pieces, revolts and reconquests.

■

Town Council of Santiago de Guatemala (MacLeod 1973, 404)

The defeat of the Quiché did not result in the conquest of Guatemala. Unlike Mexico, where Cortés inherited the organization and vast tribute system of the Aztec empire, Guatemala was politically fragmented. Indeed, the Spaniards would discover that all of Central America, with its diversity of peoples and lack of central authority, required separate conquests and separate negotiations for practically each and every city-state and chiefdom. And once conquered, not every group remained peaceful when the Spaniards turned their attention to the next conquest.

Confronted with this political reality, Alvarado sent out expeditions to the 12 independent Mayan kingdoms in the highlands, often conscripting unwilling, but already conquered, Mayans to fight those still rebellious. To intimidate the Indians, he tortured and burned rulers alive or, at the very least, held them hostage in his own camp. Even when Indians peacefully submitted to the Crown, Alvarado permitted his soldiers to enslave them in total violation of royal decrees and without a thought of their spiritual conversion. When the conquest was extended south toward El Salvador in the region of Cuzcatlán, the Pibil Indians there, rather than risking enslavement, torture, or death, escaped into the surrounding mountains and abandoned their city to the conquistadores. Frustrated by such peaceful resistance, Alvarado tried the Pibils in absentia and condemned them to death for treason against His Majesty Charles V.

Alvarado was frustrated by more than the piecemeal progress of the conquest. The Quiché spoils were disappointing too. In fact, all of Guatemala was disappointing in regard to its wealth, and Alvarado wrote to Cortés complaining about his lack of profit. The large populations, especially in El Salvador, where the city of San Salvador was quickly established in 1525, could produce many valuable slaves, but the vast tons of gold like those discovered in the Aztec treasury were nowhere to be found. So Alvarado, now using Iximché as his capital, stole the lands and enslaved his allies, the Cakchiquels, assigning them in various grants to his soldiers. He then ordered a meeting of the Cakchiquel chiefs and threatened to burn them alive if they didn't hand over their gold. Worrying that they could never satisfy the Spaniards' greed, but not for a moment doubting their cruelty, the Cakchiquels secretly abandoned the city in the middle of the night.

The Spaniards found themselves in the hill town of Iximché without food—or anyone to bring it to them. Forced to relocate to the valley below, they were unable to establish a permanent settlement because of attacks by the Cakchiquels, who not only greatly outnumbered them but who also cleverly devised grass-covered pits to kill the horses. Quiché and Tzutujil warriors were forced to fight by the side of the conquistadores against the Cakchiquels; the situation deteriorated so badly that some Spanish soldiers fled to Mexico. Another two years passed before the region was sufficiently secure for a permanent Spanish settlement. Santiago de Guatemala was founded at the foot of Volcán Agua in November 1527. Alvarado temporarily returned to Mexico to proclaim his conquest of Guatemala. The Cakquichels, however, retreated into the mountains and refused to submit to Spain for two more years. By 1532 the Cakchiquels were laboring as slaves for the Spanish, and Belehé Qat, the former ruler of Iximché, died in servitude while panning gold for his owner.

Conquistador against Conquistador

> ... they plundered and ravaged an area ... that was among the
> most fertile and most heavily peopled on earth ...
>
> ■
>
> Friar Bartolomé de Las Casas, 16th century (Las Casas 1992, 61)

Alvarado was not the only conquistador in Central America. As Cortés extended the conquest into Central America, under yet another royal order to find a passage to India, his captains encountered the upward surge of conquistadores from Panama, some with their own royal orders and others with none whatsoever. Each group contested the territorial rights of the others, and they also fought among themselves. Their unbridled ambition and greed prolonged the conquest of Central America, adding years of chaos and bloodshed to what was already a catastrophic series of events.

Nowhere were such personal ambitions more rawly displayed than in Honduras from 1524 to 1526, where no fewer than six conquistadores clashed over control of the territory. Among them was Cristóbal de Olid, a captain who sailed into the Bay of Honduras under orders from Cortés, but who then quickly declared it his independent fiefdom. To maintain control, he killed his own nephew, captured and imprisoned two other conquistadores, including one sent by Cortés and another with a license granted by the new King of Spain, the Holy Roman Emperor Charles V. Cortés, deciding to teach the rebellious captain a lesson, deserted his capital in Mexico City and set out on an extraordinary overland expedition through the heart of the Petén rain forest; lost and out of touch for six months, he was believed dead. Once in Honduras, he discovered that Olid had already been captured, sentenced, and beheaded. Before returning to Mexico, Cortés rid the colony of a threat from yet another Panamanian conquistador as well as one sent from the government in Santo Domingo. Honduras, was subjected to more political turbulence in 1528, when another Cortés captain, Francisco de Montejo, petitioned the Crown for Honduras after he had failed in his attempted conquest of the Yucatec Mayans. His petition was eventually granted, but Pedro de Alvarado, brought in from neighboring Guatemala to quash an Indian rebellion in 1530, successfully challenged his claims for several years.

PRE-COLUMBIAN AND SPANISH SLAVERY

The Mayans and other Indians conducted their own trade in slaves, but their system functioned somewhat differently from slavery as practiced by Europeans. Mayan war captives became the slaves of those who captured them and thieves became the servants of their victims. Although enslavement was not a life sentence in Mesoamerica—thieves could be freed upon payment of restitution—it certainly could be: slaves might be killed in order to serve their owners in the otherworld, and captives of elite status usually suffered ritual sacrifice to the gods. Mayan slavery was not an inherited condition, because law and custom usually dictated the redemption of children. Slaves could be traded, however, and the rich did purchase orphans to offer for sacrifice during religious ceremonies. Under early Crown regulations, Spaniards could enslave Indian rebels and Indians already enslaved by Indians, but Spanish slaves remained so for life, as did their descendants. Although the Spaniards did not cut out the hearts of their slaves in ritual sacrifice, they did kill them through abuse and overwork. Initially, Spanish policies regulated slavery in order to guarantee the Crown its royal fifth of the income from sales. Only the Crown's officials were permitted to brand slaves, but counterfeit irons were rampant. Branding was eventually outlawed along with the sale of slaves.

Spanish rivalries disrupted other areas of Central America as well. Pedrarias Dávila, the founder of Panama City and governor of the Darién, arranged for the execution of Balboa in order to grab his land and gold for himself. Described as "the cruelest of tyrants," by his contemporary Friar Bartolomé de Las Casas (1992, 31), Pedrarias set a standard of conflict and tyranny that was too often repeated in Central America for years to come. As late as 1550, two of his followers murdered the bishop of Nicaragua and rebelled against Spain in order to keep the wealth to themselves.

Aging and threatened with removal from office, Pedrarias sought to impress the Crown by extending his maneuvers into the north of the isthmus. It mattered little to him that other conquistadores, with legitimate claims to the land, had preceded him. One such person was Gil Gonzáles Dávila, who in 1522, under license from the Crown, had explored the Pacific coast of Costa Rica and Nicaragua up to the Bay of Fonseca in Honduras. He discovered Mesoamerican-style cities and prospering marketplaces unlike the scattered hamlets of thatch-and-wood in the lower isthmus. In Nicaragua, there was even a residential enclave of goldsmiths. Using negotiation rather than intimidation, the conquistador peacefully gained the cooperation of two powerful chiefs in the region: Nicoya, whose name is commemorated on every modern map, and Nicarao, whose name inspired that of Nicaragua. The population was so large—it has been conservatively estimated as more than 1 million—that Gil Gonzáles Dávila was said to have baptized 32,000 Indians in a brief span of time.

The Nicoyan potential for wealth and slaves attracted the avaricious Pedrarias, who sent Juan Vásquez de Coronado and other agents to lay claim to the land. Battles ensued between the two Spaniards, but in the end Pedrarias prevailed in Nicaragua, overseeing the newly founded cities of León and Granada and abusing the formerly peaceful peoples of the region. Looking to expand his empire even further, Pedrarias pushed into Honduras and El Salvador, where he infringed on territory Alvarado already had conquered and claimed as part of Guatemala. Once again, conquistador rivalries led to armed conflict.

So the conquest of Central America proceeded: A series of rash attacks caused by news of riches or densely populated towns, a patchwork of vying conquistador claims that laid the groundwork for a divided isthmus in the centuries to come, a conquest that left in its wake unusually high rates of death and social dislocation even when compared to the conquests in Mexico and Peru.

Slave Trade and Indian Rebellions

The conquest in Central America led to frequent Indian uprisings. Unlike Cortés in Mexico or Balboa in Panama, the Alvarados and Pedrariases of the isthmus were unable to maintain the loyalty of their allies. Similarly, conquered peoples did not remain subjugated, so that the Spanish had to return and fight repeatedly for some of the same territories. Alvarado, for example, quashed a rebellion in the Ulúa valley in 1536, but unrest festered in that region of western Honduras for many years.

The causes of such unrest were clear. Indians suffered from war and epidemics, and they were cruelly treated and killed. Attack dogs were permitted to tear them to pieces. They were uprooted and conscripted to fight the Spaniards' battles far away from their towns. And, in Central America more than anywhere else, the Indians suffered from the depredations of the slave trade.

Nothing demonstrates the unbridled lawlessness of many Central American conquistadores than their trade in Indian slaves. Under Spanish law, they could enslave and brand only those Indians who resisted subjugation, not those who submitted peacefully. During the first several decades of Spanish presence, Indian allies were enslaved and unbranded Indians were shipped off to where they would fetch the best price. Initially, the slaves were sent from the ports on the Bay of Honduras to labor in the mines on islands such as Cuba and Jamaica. When Cortés witnessed such activity in 1525, he was shocked and requested the Crown to order the Indians returned. The only other recorded case of enslaved Indians returning home alive, however, was from Havana, where some Indians stole a Spanish ship and sailed it back to Honduras.

The worst of the slave trade, however, occurred on the Pacific coast of Nicaragua. The large, urban populations noted by the first Spaniards were conveniently situated for easy shipment to Panama and Peru. The slaves were shipped to Panama, where disease as well as Pedrarias's mistreatment of the indigenous peoples had created an acute shortage of porters to carry goods from the Pacific to the Caribbean ports. Operating from Nicaragua in the late 1520s, Pedrarias found it quite lucrative to supply his former colony with the necessary manpower—and womanpower, when that suited a Spaniard's purposes.

Once the Inca Empire was discovered in 1532, the demand for slaves intensified. Slaves served as crew on the ships to Peru; slaves, even when not trusted to fight in the conquest of Peru, functioned as human carriers, miners, servants, and mistresses, until the Inca themselves could be subdued and enslaved. Hundreds of thousands of slaves were sold and exported to Peru; the number is not known with any certainty, but

BARTOLOMÉ DE LAS CASAS: PROTECTOR OF THE INDIANS

The Spaniards have shown not the slightest consideration for these people, treating them (and I speak from firsthand experience, having been there from the outset) not as brute animals—indeed, I would to God they had done and had shown them the consideration they afford their animals—so much as piles of dung in the middle of the road. They have had as little concern for their souls as for their bodies, all the millions that have perished having gone to their deaths with no knowledge of God . . .

■

Friar Bartolomé de Las Casas, 16th century (1992, 13)

Bartolomé de Las Casas (1484–1576), a Spanish landowner and adventurer in the New World, entered the Dominican Order after witnessing a massacre of the native population in Cuba by his fellow Spaniards in 1510. For the remainder of his life, he lobbied ardently for the humane treatment of the Indians. He documented the atrocities committed during the conquest of Central America in order to shame the Crown into outlawing slavery, and he also labored in the land of conquistadores to counteract their brutality. He opened a convent in Granada, Nicaragua, to mitigate the abuses of Indians initiated under Pedrarias, but abandoned this effort in 1536. Then, moving to Guatemala, he was an open critic of Alvarado, but had little impact on policy until 1537, when he convinced the government to permit the Dominicans to pacify, without the use of arms, some rebellious Mayans near the modern city of Cobán. His utopian settlement, called Verapaz, or "Land of the True Peace," was initially successful, but it ended tragically 23 years later when Spanish settlers encroached on Verapaz, causing an Indian rebellion and the massacre of the friars. In 1542, Las Casas wrote A Short Account of the Destruction of the Indies, a book that persuaded the Crown to reform its policies and to issue the New Laws of the Indies that abolished Indian slavery.

some estimate that as many as a half million Nicaraguans and 150,000 Hondurans were exported as slaves. Yet the demand for more remained high; conditions were so wretched aboard ship that in many cases only four in every 20 Indian slaves reached their destination alive; those that did reach Panama or Peru were literally worked to death. The Indian population in Nicaragua proved inadequate to meet demand. Raids for able-bodied adults extended down into the Nicoya Peninsula and up into El Salvador and Guatemala.

Some Indians fled to remote regions in the Nicaraguan highlands or the forested regions of the Caribbean coast and the Petén. Those who remained in their towns had little to lose by rebelling, and they did so from their first contact with the Spaniards. The most famous uprising occurred in Honduras, in the center of the Caribbean slave trade, and was led by Lempira, the legendary chief of the Lenca Indians, who organized 200 towns and successfully coordinated 30,000 warriors against the Spanish in 1537; his success inspired rebellions in most of Honduras. The Spaniards assassinated Lempira during peace negotiations a year later, but rebellions continued to erupt in Honduras, El Salvador, and Nicaragua. Indians along the frontier of Spanish settlements mounted successful guerrilla attacks for years and, in some instances, centuries.

So Few Defeat So Many

From the moment I saw them, I put my men in order, and went out to give them battle with 90 horsemen . . .

■

Pedro de Alvarado, 1524 (Mackie 1972, 15)

The conquest of the Americas leaves a lingering question: How was it possible that so few could defeat so many? It has been estimated that at the time of Columbus's arrival, the population of central Mexico was perhaps as much as 25 million and that of Central America an esti-mated 5.5 million. Yet Cortes's original expedition numbered only 550 Spaniards; Alvarado, in his first battle in Guatemala, defeated more than 10,000 Mayan warriors with several hundred Spaniards; and Balboa took over the Darién with 180 weakened survivors of that mis-guided expedition. How did the conquistadores succeed? Many have suggested that superior European weapons made all the difference. European guns and artillery were certainly superior to Indian bows and arrows, but did they really provide an adequately lethal advantage against such large Indian armies? Steel swords kill more efficiently than obsidian-studded clubs, but they are far from weapons of mass destruc-tion. The cannons and guns, few in number, were notoriously unreli-able at hitting the desired target. The truth is that the Spaniards had two

A MAYAN STRONGHOLD

... the lord [Can Ek] arrived, accompanied by some thirty men in five or six canoes. He seemed very happy to meet me and I, for my part, received him well ...

■

Hernán Cortés, 1525 (Pagden 1986, 375)

They did not wish to join with the foreigners; they did not desire Christianity. They did not wish to pay tribute, did those whose emblems were the bird, the precious stone, the flat precious stone and the jaguar, those with the three magic [emblems].

■

The Chilam Balam of Chumayel, (Roys 1967, 83)

While the conquest wreaked havoc on Central America, especially in its most populous areas, much of the isthmus was too remote to attract Spanish attention, and many Indians escaped to those regions—the Kuna to the San Blas coast on Panama, the Bribri to the Talamanca Massif, and the Mayans to the Petén. The central Petén was once the heartland of the greatest Classic Mayan cities, but in the 16th century it had been abandoned for more than 600 years. The Petén was

secret weapons: disease, often called the "shock troops" of the conquest; and Indian allies who evened the numbers on the battlefield—but who were seldom mentioned in official reports. When the Indians remained united, they often sent the Spaniards packing, as they did to Columbus in Panama and to Montejo in Yucatán. And the Aztecs did defeat Cortés, sending him and his men scurrying across the causeways on the famous Noche Triste ("Sad Night")—only the assistance of the Tlaxcalans enabled him to make a comeback.

Legacy of Conquest

Alvarado's conquest of northern Central America was typical of the entire isthmus. No native empire facilitated the control of large territories. The conquest of the isthmus was long and complicated without adequate financial rewards. The Spaniards, motivated by greed and self-

not completely abandoned, however. In 1525 Cortés, hacking his way through the rain forest in an effort to reach Honduras and its upstart governor, came upon the cultivated shores of Lake Petén Itzá and the island kingdom of Tayasal. The remote Mayan stronghold was ruled by the Can Ek dynasty that claimed to have descended from the kings of Chichén Itzá. These Mayans had heard about the conquistadores and their successes in Mexico, and were well informed about their arrival in Honduras; they must have been intensely curious to see them at first hand. The rugged terrain, rocky ravines, and vast, depopulated forest surrounding Tayasal almost starved Cortés and his expedition to death. Many horses did die, and the few that survived were hardly strong enough to walk. One injured horse was left with Can Ek, and, in later years, missionaries would find the dead horse worshipped as a stone idol called "Tizimín Chak." Cortés's visit would be the last to Tayasal by a Spaniard for another hundred years. Throughout the conquest and colonization of Mesoamerica, however, Mayans retreated from the Spanish-settled areas to Tayasal, swelling its population to 25,000. They created a wealthy kingdom that controlled the cacao trade from northern Yucatán through Belize to the Bay of Honduras along pre-Columbian routes controlled by the Mayans. Iron hatchets were added to its tools and Tizimín Chak to its pantheon, but Tayasal observed the ancient traditions and its scribes wrote in hieroglyphs, while knowledge of such writing disappeared from the rest of the Mayan world. Not until 1697 would Spain finally conquer Tayasal.

aggrandizement, were too often their own worst enemies; they massacred and enslaved the Indians, even those who were their allies, and caused rebellions that persisted for most of the 16th century. They even fought one another, leaving a legacy of divisiveness that would plague Central America throughout its history.

The age of conquest is often said to have ended with Alvarado's death in 1541, a convenient date, but a somewhat arbitrary one because many native uprisings lay ahead and most of the isthmus had yet to be explored. While the absolute end of such an uncoordinated, piecemeal conquest is difficult to determine, the implementation of institutional controls does mark a significant turning point. By the 1540s most of the famous conquistadores, such as Alvarado, were either dead or politically ineffectual, making room for the Crown to assert greater control over its empire.

4

FOUNDING OF THE KINGDOM OF GUATEMALA (1541–1570)

... the land became subject to the Royal Crown and its king ...
and was provided with presidents, judges, and governors to rule
and govern these towns in justice, and sustain the preaching of
the gospel.

■

Friar Pedro de Betanzos, 1559 (Carrasco 1967, 255)

With the end of his conquest, Charles V, Holy Roman Emperor, faced unusual challenges, even for such an august ruler. Spain, a country about the size of the Central American isthmus, and not much more populous, had to govern and settle a vast New World territory that stretched from Peru into what is now the United States. Individual conquistadores could violently grab their booty and move on; Spain had to create an enduring colony atop the trail of death and destruction. For conquest, Indian auxiliary soldiers could help defeat other Indians; for religious conversion, European priests and missionaries, numbering in the hundreds, had the more subtle task of indoctrinating the Indians, who numbered in the millions and spoke hundreds of distinct languages. By the end of the 16th century, despite the 5,500 miles of ocean that separated it from the New World, Spain had created an empire that would endure for 300 years. Its language, religion, and culture are indelibly stamped on what is known today as Latin America.

The Kingdom of Guatemala

. . . the conquistadors are permitted to flout the orders of Your Majesty.

■

Friar Pedro de Angulo, letter to the Crown, 1545 (Bierhorst 1990, 468)

Spain did not trust conquistadores to govern: they were adventurers, not paid soldiers, and as such, they were too independent, too interested in personal fortune, and too indifferent to the religious salvation of Indians. The Crown, jealous of its privileges and suspicious they might be usurped, required everything in triplicate and created a Byzantine bureaucracy in which every administrator was not simply checked, but also double-checked. The conquistadores would not do to govern; only courtly administrators would. Hernán Cortés, a national hero in Spain, was removed as governor in 1528, only six years after conquering the Aztecs. In a telling contrast, Alvarado governed Guatemala for almost 18 years, perhaps because his wife was related to the secretary to Charles V; the tyrannical Pedrarias Dávila was also connected to the royal court and he, too, was left in control of Nicaragua until his demise.

In Central America the prolonged presence of the most powerful conquistadores prevented the Crown from implementing a cohesive government. Spain tried to assert control of Central America, but whether it sent agents from Mexico or Hispaniola, the conquistadores mostly ignored them. In 1530, all of Mexico was centrally administered, yet separate royal orders governed Guatemala, Nicaragua, Honduras, and Panama in recognition of the various claims and disputes of the conquistadores. Independent administrative centers evolved in Alvarado's capital at Santiago de Guatemala, Pedrarias's at Granada, Montejo's in Comayuaga, and, in the oldest settlement of them all, Panama City.

When the Crown finally exerted its control, it experimented with various governmental configurations, first making the entire isthmus an independent administrative unit and then putting it directly under the control of New Spain. It shifted borders, including what is now southeastern Mexico, into Central America. During the shifts and power plays, the capital changed as well, from Comayagua and Gracias a Dios, both in Honduras, to Santiago de Guatemala, now known as Antigua.

In the mid-16th century, Spain settled on the administrative config-uration that would last throughout the colonial period as the Kingdom of Guatemala. The kingdom comprised the provinces of Guatemala (including El Salvador and Belize), Honduras, Nicaragua (including Costa Rica), and Chiapas (now part of Mexico), but excluded Panama, which became an important dependency of the viceroyalty of Peru because of its link between the two seas. The kingdom was adminis-tered by its own *audiencia*, or royal council, nominally under the

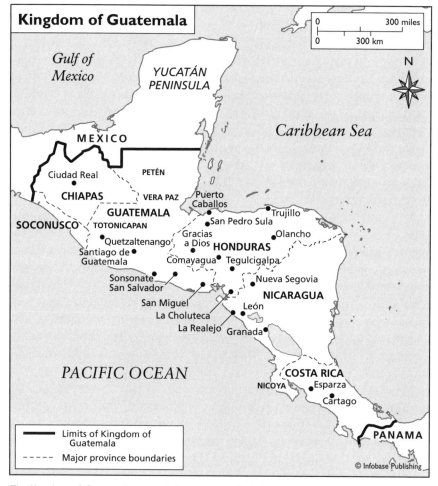

The Kingdom of Guatemala covered the area now divided among the Mexican state of Chiapas, Belize, Guatemala, El Salvador, Honduras, Nicaragua, and Costa Rica, but not Panama. Its capital was Santiago de Guatemala, now called Antigua, before it was moved to the location of present-day Guatemala City.

viceroyalty of New Spain but, in a typical Spanish effort to provide checks and balances, with the right to report directly to the Crown.

After the conquest, a new type of individual arrived in the kingdom, a titled official with royal favor who was usually well educated in the law. These trusted individuals were appointed to the highest governmental offices in the colony, including the supreme position of president of the *audiencia* with its seat in Santiago de Guatemala. In recognition of the separate fiefdoms created by the conquistadores, each province was permitted its own capital and governor; the governor, however, was also appointed by the Crown, and the remaining conquistadores, such as Francisco de Montejo in Honduras, found themselves removed from office. The years of government by conquistadores were ending.

Spain's administration of the isthmus had a lasting impact on its history. For the first time, most of the isthmus was unified into a single political entity; yet it also was carved into provinces that formalized the personal domains of the conquistadores and promoted competition and disunity. Overlapping bureaucracies, so typical of the Crown's desire to divide all but its own power, created jurisdictional disputes and heavy tax burdens. The area of what is now Belize, its coral reefs a natural barrier to Spanish ships, was so ignored that the English could settle there basically unchallenged. Panama, integrated into South America, took a divergent historical course from its isthmian neighbors until the 20th century, when it became independent of Colombia.

Conquistadores to Colonizers

Conquistadores had to be compensated for their services, and they had to be attracted to the conquered lands as permanent settlers. The primary method for accomplishing both these tasks was the *encomienda,* a grant of Indians who were required to provide tribute to the Spaniard in the form of labor and goods. The entire population of a town could be given in *encomienda* to a single conquistador: Alvarado had the labor and tribute rights to the densely populated Mayan villages of Quetzaltenango and Atitlán. Santa Cruz Utatlán, as the former Quiché capital was renamed by the Spaniards, became the domain of one of Alvarado's captains, and other parts of the Quiché central province were granted to other Alvarado favorites. In Nicaragua, Pedrarias claimed half of all the *encomiendas* for himself. Land grants were provided to all Spaniards, but in accordance with their rank: Foot soldiers received about 50 acres of land; horsemen received twice that amount, and neither group received Indians in *encomienda.*

In exchange for this virtual enslavement of Indians, the *encomenderos* were charged with "civilizing" them and instructing them in the Catholic faith. Spain hoped the *encomienda* would accomplish many essentials: payment to the conquistadores, conversion and assimilation of the Indians, and production of foodstuffs to sustain the colony. In regard to their civilizing influences on the Indians, the Crown quickly learned otherwise: as the proselytizing friars said, the Indians could best be pro-

Royal Palace, begun in 1543, in Antigua, Guatemala. The seat of government for the Kingdom of Guatemala was relocated from Alvarado's first capital to Santiago de Guatemala, now called "Antigua," in 1541 when the cone of Agua Volcano collapsed and buried the original settlement in an avalanche of mud. Bartolomé de Las Casas called the disaster "a visitation by Divine Justice" (1992, 61). (Photo courtesy Lawrence Foster)

FAVORITISM IN THE ROYAL PALACE

These officials ... are content to sit in the cool shade and collect their pay ... to win the good will of the Spaniards, and also because they all have sons-in-law, brothers-in-law, relatives, or close friends among them.

■

Alonso de Zorita, 1553 (Keen 1994, 218)

No matter how many well-meaning officials the Crown sent to the New World, they invariably confronted problems in administering the laws exactly as Spain saw fit. One reason was nepotism, something the Crown practiced itself when it failed to prosecute some of the nobility for malfeasance. The Kingdom of Guatemala was rife with nepotism. When Pedro de Alvarado left the capital of Santiago, his brother Jorge acted as governor. After Pedro's death in 1541, his wife, Beatriz de la Cueva, became the first and only woman governor of Guatemala. When she was killed a few days later in the mud avalanche that buried the capital city, her brother succeeded her. Pedro granted the most lucrative land grants and assignments to other relatives as well, and he entrusted them with the conquest of various provinces and, in turn, controlled much of the booty and land from such enterprises. Alvarado favored his relatives and his most trusted captains, many of them from his family home in Extremadura, Spain. His favors made them, as well as himself, the aristocracy of Guatemala: Alvarado's holdings in land, mines, ships, livestock, and slaves generated an annual income of $100,000; the Cueva family, descendants of his brother-in-law, owned the largest *encomienda* in Guatemala in 1549. Nepotism persisted into the first *audiencia* under President Maldonado, who used his position to create the richest cacao *encomiendas* for his family and protégés—a commonly accepted practice in the Spanish Empire, where officials were poorly paid. The practice continued under the second *audiencia*, when President Cerrato, an upright individual who never personally benefited from his office, used his position to help family members. For some, the nepotism extended beyond appointments, and influenced how laws were enforced. Alonso de Zorita, the 16th-century judge, said that nepotism "blinds them." The reliance on trusted familial relationships corrupted the government and became a part of the social fabric of the Kingdom of Guatemala.

tected and Christianized by keeping them in towns separate from those of the Spaniards.

The *encomienda* did not satisfy most of the fortune-starved conquistadores in Central America. Much of the isthmus was not densely populated, so the colonizers, who usually felt manual labor to be below them, could not be granted an adequate labor force to work the land. As a result, entire regions remained unsettled and out of Spanish control, particularly from eastern Honduras into Panama along the Caribbean coast. And even where there were enough Indians to produce food for the colony, some Central American conquistadores found it more lucrative to sell their Indian charges.

Slaves were the biggest export of the early colony. And even when the Indians were not sold and exported, both men and women were carted off from their homes to labor in work gangs panning or mining gold. At the Gracias a Dios mine in Honduras, half the Indians died. Others were forced to travel great distance as *tlamemes,* or human carriers. Alvarado is said to have shipped 8,000 Indians to Ecuador during one of his campaigns in South America. Plundering and enslaving, not colonizing and governing, were what interested the conquistadores, and Central America suffered for it.

The conquistadores remained in Central America while the slaving and mining made them rich. Once the sources of slaves and easily accessible gold were depleted, many of the conquistadores moved on. Alvarado himself spent half his governorship outside Guatemala, mounting expeditions to new lands full of the promise of gold, lands as far apart as Ecuador and Cíbola, in what is now the southwestern United States. Those who remained took refuge in their haciendas, introducing European livestock and crops, particularly wheat. Some made considerable profit exporting raw cattle hides as well as that great American product, cacao. If nothing else, the loss of the adventuring class at least enabled Central American society to become more stable.

American Colonists: The Mestizo

Families were as essential as settlements, but in the early years few women arrived from Spain. Cortés offered bonuses to soldiers who brought wives to New Spain, but many were without the means to do so. Spanish men found their partners, most often ephemeral and too often unwilling, among the Indian women. Bishop Cristóbal de Pedraza reported that all but 10 Spaniards in Honduras had mistresses. An entirely new ethnic group was the result: the *mestizo*—or *ladino,* as they are called in Guatemala—of mixed Indian and European parentage. Luisa Xicotencatl, a Tlaxcalan noblewoman given by her father to Pedro de Alvarado as a peace offering along with a dowry of gold, accompanied the conquistador to Guatemala; their daughter, Leonora de Alvarado, born in a military camp outside Utatlán, was probably the first *mestiza* in Guatemala. The Catholic Church encouraged the conquistadores to marry their Indian mistresses in order to legitimize the offspring and raise them as Christians. Charles V once sent a letter to the bishop of Nicaragua, recommending that a decent Spanish husband be found for Doña Ana, the daughter of an Indian *cacique* (native governor) who was returning from Europe.

Most conquistadores preferred to ignore such advice. Pedro de Alvarado thought it more suitable to marry Beatriz de la Cueva, the niece of the duke of Albuquerque; his mestiza daughter nonetheless lived in a fine house among the Spanish community in the capital city. Some well-born but impoverished Spaniards did find financial rewards in marrying elite Indian women like Doña Ana, especially when the marriage was accompanied by a government appointment. In the period immediately after the conquest, many mestizo children, whether legitimate or illegitimate, were accepted into the Spanish community, but most were absorbed into the Indian towns. In later periods, many found they didn't easily fit into the separate worlds of either the Indian or the Spaniard; the increasing number of mestizo "orphans" in the capital of Santiago preoccupied Bishop Marroquín. By mid-century, more marriageable Spanish women—sisters, cousins, and daughters of the new bureaucrats—had arrived in the colony. Yet the mestizos would multiply in number until they became the largest group in most cities and, eventually, throughout Central America.

The Mendicant Friars

Catholic priests had accompanied Columbus on his fourth voyage and said the first mass in Central America—indeed, the first on the American continents—in Honduras in 1502. The priests smashed idols and baptized Indians; their alliance clearly was with their fellow travelers, the conquistadores. Charles V, however, was a devout monarch who took his role as vicar of the Catholic Church seriously, and after the conquest, he decided to entrust the salvation of his Indian subjects to the mendicant orders rather than the secular, or nonmonastic, church hierarchy. The Dominicans, the Franciscans, and the Mercedarians were

Francisco Marroquín, first bishop of Guatemala. Francisco Marroquín became the first bishop of the Kingdom of Guatemala (1537–63), replacing the chaplain of the army as the preeminent religious figure in the Spanish colony. He requested more Franciscan and Dominican mission-aries for Guatemala—there were so few that no friar was available to instruct Alvarado's first allies, the Cakchiquels, until 1542—and offered to pay for their trips if necessary. He founded a school for orphans in the capital and established the first hospital and college. Marroquín exemplified neither the best nor the worst of the religious. He tried to prevent the most inhumane abuses of the native population and invited Las Casas to pacify the Mayans in Verapaz. Yet he worked just as diligently against the end of Indian slavery, perhaps because of his friendship with encomenderos such as Pedro de Alvarado. Living in Guatemala for 33 years, he became quite powerful and served, for a brief period, as both bishop and governor. (After portrait in Guatemala City cathedral)

given the great task of teaching the Christian faith to the peoples of Central America in the 16th century, and they later were joined by the Augustinians and the Jesuits.

These friars were, on the whole, better educated than secular priests, and their monastic life sustained them, rather than the worldly society of *encomenderos*. They brought idealism and missionary zeal to the New World. Many were millenarians who believed that the conversion of the Indians would bring about the second coming of Christ. They built their churches and convents among the Indians themselves to emulate Augustine's City of God or Thomas More's Utopia. Some were sent to explore the faraway regions others feared—the Grand Canyon and Baja California, the remotest areas of eastern Honduras and Panama's Darién—where they attempted to Christianize and pacify the poor, seminomadic Indians in whom the conquistadores had little interest. Numerous friars lost their lives in the effort, a few by pre-Columbian heart sacrifice; others lived to baptize thousands of new converts.

The contrast between the conquistadores and the friars, many of whom had taken vows of poverty, was emphasized by the first Franciscans in New Spain: Attired in their plain cloth habits, the 12

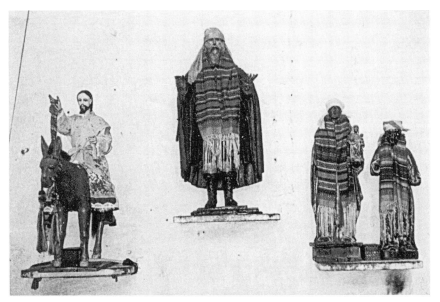

Saints in the Church of Santo Tomás in Santiago, Atitlán, Guatemala, dressed like the Mayan villagers themselves. (Photo courtesy Naomi Smith)

INDIAN MESSIAH

It happened in this kingdom a little after being conquered that, hearing the lives of Christ and Our Lady, John the Baptist, and Saint Peter and others which the friars taught them, that a Mexican Indian came forth, a pseudo-prophet. . . . This caused so much commotion among the Indians that the kingdom was almost lost over it, for they came to imagine that our Holy Gospel told them nothing new.

■

Father Francisco Ximénez, 1700 (Carmack 1981, 301)

Not all Indians accepted conversion. Many of the seminomadic Indians in the southern isthmus refused to remain in the mission villages, where the friars concentrated them. Such new settlements were seldom successful; Bishop Gregorio de Montalvo thought the Indians died of melancholy when far from home (Newson 1986, 242). Along the Caribbean coast, in particular, and in the interior of the Petén and the highlands of Costa Rica, the Indians remained out of reach of both Church and Crown in order "to live as they wished," as one dismayed friar observed after being chased away by angry Indians (Jones 1983, 78). Some native religious uprisings occurred in regions more firmly controlled by the Spanish. At Utatlán, the Quiché priests pointed out the parallels between the religion of their ancestors and that of the Christian friars, casting doubt on any special authority the Catholics claimed. Native priests called for resistance to the friars and, at Utatlán, it all escalated into the uprising related above by Friar Ximénez.

missionaries walked barefoot from the Gulf port of Veracruz to the capital of Mexico City. Devoted to saving souls and protecting the Indians, the early missionaries found themselves in serious conflict with Spanish settlers as well as governmental authorities. Las Casas felt so threatened that, at one point, he considered giving up preaching. Bishop Antonio de Valdivieso in Nicaragua, after defending the Indians against abuses by the governor, was assassinated. Even Bishop Marroquín of Guatemala, who usually sympathized with the colonists, was knifed. Bishop Pedraza of Honduras, who worried about settlers treating him like "a dog in the street," (Sherman 1979,

51) never suffered bodily harm, but in his efforts to protect the Indians he often used the only weapon available to a priest: excommunication. Not all were men apart, of course: Friar Blas de Castillo showed an all-too-familiar trait—greed—when he had himself lowered into one of Nicaragua's active craters, mistaking the lava for molten gold.

The Spiritual Conquest

The friars were overwhelmed by the readiness with which the Indians agreed to be baptized: many hundreds of thousands were converted in New Spain in the first years after the conquest. Initially, the few missionaries were forced to travel throughout New Spain in order to reach as many souls as possible. As late as 1600, there were only 42 missionaries in the province of Guatemala. With native labor and pre-Columbian cut stone, they built churches and convents and set out to remake the Indian world.

The first problem confronting the friars was communication. It is hard to imagine exactly what was communicated during the mass baptisms in the early years. Some Indians were trained as translators, others, usually Mayan nobles, were taught to read and write in Latin characters. Still, the friars hoped to gain better understanding, and so they learned the native languages. Seven Mayan languages were spoken in the Verapaz region pacified by Las Casas; multiple Mayan languages as well as Mexican Nahuatl and Zapotec were spoken in the district around the capital of Santiago. The friars could not learn enough languages, so Indian aristocrats were taught Spanish in the hope they, instead, would properly teach their subjects. Decades passed before the catechism could be properly translated from Spanish into native languages.

The lack of subtlety in communication had very definite consequences. The Mayans, for example, often readily accepted Catholicism because it seemed similar to their own religion—though such similarities were, on occasion, used to resist the Catholic faith. The cross was the form of their world tree, a conduit for otherworldly communication; the story of Christ's sacrifice recalled to them the sacrifice and resurrection of the maize god; and the decapitation of John the Baptist was a familiar form of sacrifice. The annual festival cycle was like that of the Mayans, and religious processions were familiar to the Indians, who also carried their idols in ritual directions and burned incense. The

MESOAMERICAN CATHOLICISM

> . . . the church, rising in solitary grandeur in a region of wilderness and desolation, seemed almost the work of enchantment.

> ■

> *John Lloyd Stephens 1839 (1: 169)*

I n 1578, the year Indian cults were outlawed, the Chortí Mayan town of Esquipulas erected a Christian church over a sacred spring, believed to have curing properties since preconquest times. A few years later the town commissioned a sculpture for the church, which became known as El Señor de Esquipulas, or the Black Christ. The Black Christ quickly became known for his miraculous cures. Stephens reported that 80,000 pilgrims gathered each year in Esquipulas, some from as far away as Peru, and another shrine was established in Chimayo, New Mexico, where miraculous cures were also reported. The Catholic Church officially recognized the powers of El Señor de Esquipulas in 1737, and, in honor of the thousands each year who make pilgrimages to the church, the pope elevated it to the First Basilica of Central America in 1961.

Basilica of Esquipulas. (Photo courtesy INGUAT, Guatemalan Trade Commission)

Indians often embraced these aspects of Catholicism, and the elite willingly headed the *cofradías,* or religious confraternities devoted to a saint, much to the delight of the friars.

Friars as Ethnographers

> *This is the beginning of the Ancient Word, here in this place called Quiché. Here we shall inscribe, we shall implant the Ancient Word . . . We shall write about this now amid the preaching of God, in Christendom now.*

> ■

> Popol Vuh *(Tedlock 1985, 71)*

The friars, eager to detect any reversion to the old religion, tried to learn about the pre-Columbian gods and practices. In their efforts to root out what they perceived as heathen, they recorded ethnohistoric information that is invaluable to us today. A wealth of material was recorded on preconquest religious practices; and missionaries commented on native myths that seemed like alternative versions of Genesis. In 1540, Mayan codices still existed; Las Casas described them as written in "figures and characters" and so sophisticated that "our writing does not offer much of an advantage" (Carmack 1973, 13). Las Casas also states that the friars burned books "because it seemed they dealt with religious matters" (Carmack 1973, 173). Diego de Landa in Yucatán, who did destroy such books, also recorded such extensive information about his Mayan neophytes that he included the key to the decipherment of the hieroglyphs in the 20th century.

The missionaries also used their knowledge of Indian beliefs to facilitate conversion. At schools for Indian aristocrats, such as the one founded by Bishop Pedraza in Honduras, the native lords were instructed in the faith in the hope they would inspire similar devotion in their people. Native origin myths were reinterpreted as biblical stories, and the pre-Columbian sacred calendar was made to follow Christian saint days. Equinox ceremonies were assimilated into those for Easter, and native rituals for deceased ancestors became part of All Saints Day, a custom that continues to the present in Day of the Dead ceremonies. Major Indian pilgrimage shrines became sites of Catholic churches. Both Indians and missionaries dressed their religious practices in a way to accommodate each other and, in the process, they created what has been called "Mesoamerican Catholicism."

Perhaps one of the greatest ethnohistoric legacies of the friars was inadvertent. They taught many members of the Mayan nobility how to read and write Spanish, and the Indians began writing their own languages in Latin script. The Latin script replaced hieroglyphic writing as fewer and fewer Indians could understand the preconquest system. Mayan scribes, who feared that the knowledge contained in their sacred books would be lost, rewrote them in the European script and carefully hid them from the Spaniards. At Sololá, Francisco Hernández Arana, the grandson of the Cakchiquel ruler Jun Ik', recorded most of what is now known as the *Annals of the Cakchiquels;* before his death in 1582, another member of the royal lineage, Francisco Díaz, continued writing the chronicle. Not until the 17th century did the Spaniards become aware of its existence. In the middle of the 16th century, descendants of the rulers of Utatlán also recorded in Latin letters the Quiché words of the famous Mayan book, the *Popol Vuh.* It, too, was kept from Spanish eyes until a priest discovered it in 1701; fortunately, he preserved the great work instead of burning it.

Despite their conquest and religious conversion, many New World peoples tenaciously held on to their traditions. Those who were fortunate enough to live near their ancestral homes remained surrounded by the sacred mountains and caves that had defined their people's identity for millennia; those whom circumstances forced into other regions continued to honor the ancestral deities and life forces that had always animated their world. Today Christianity is devoutly practiced in Central America, from the Mayans in Guatemala to the Kunas in Panama, but it is nonetheless a religion richly embellished with traditional New World beliefs and practices.

Decline in Indian Population

> They [Indians] are the support of that land; and if they perish, it is the end of everything.
>
> ■
>
> *Alonso de Zorita 1553 (Keen 1994, 243)*

> 11 Ahau was when the mighty men arrived from the east. They were the ones who first brought disease here to our land, the land of us who are Maya . . .
>
> ■
>
> *The Chilam Balam of Chumayel (Roys 1967, 138)*

Loss in the Indian population was catastrophic. The population of once thriving pre-Columbian ports, such as Naco on the Caribbean coast, declined from 10,000 male Indians in 1530 to 250 in 1539. Recovery was not rapidly forthcoming: by 1586, Naco had 10 male Indians and was virtually a ghost town.

Slaving, war, and social dislocation had taken their toll. In addition, epidemics swept through the native population wherever the Spaniards went, spreading European diseases in a population that had never before been exposed to smallpox, measles, mumps, or chicken pox, not to mention both pulmonary and bubonic plague, typhoid, and malaria. In 1545 a pandemic of pneumonic plague lasting three years attacked the peoples of New Spain. Known as the Gucumatz plague in Guatemala, it delivered yet another blow to the already devastated populations in the tropical lowlands and substantially reduced the more abundant population in the Guatemalan highlands.

The Gucumatz plague was not the first epidemic, and would be far from the last—another arrived in 1558, and others rampaged the region repeatedly; no preventive measures were taken until 1804, when the Crown attempted to immunize the populace against smallpox. Famine often followed such epidemics because so few people were able to work the land. By the 18th century missionaries in remote regions became so associated with disease that the Indians would keep their distance from the priests and chew tobacco leaves in their presence, hoping it would protect them from infection.

Decline in Indian Population			
		Year	
	1500*	1548	1570
Central America**	5.65 million	n/a	550,000
Guatemala***	1.5 million	n/a	180,000
Nicaragua	500,000	44,500	26,000
Honduras	800,000	n/a	40,000
Quiché towns	50,000	5,000	n/a

* There was no official census until later in the century, when the native population already was decimated, so reconstructed estimates for the time of the conquest vary greatly. Sources for this chart are the moderate figures of Robert M. Carmack for the Quiché towns; William E. Denevan for Central America; Murdo MacLeod for Nicaragua; West and Augelli for Guatemala; and the more generous estimates of Linda Newson for Honduras.
** Figures exclude Panama
*** Figures include San Salvador

Labor abuses in the colony contributed to the decline in population as well. For example, the Mayans and other Mesoamerican peoples transported goods over land on the backs of human porters, called *tamemes* by the Spaniards after the Aztec word *tlameme*. These porters supported backpacks from a tumpline on their foreheads. In a world without pack animals or wheeled vehicles it was the only form of overland transport. The Spaniards corrupted the pre-conquest use of these porters. First, they did not pay them for their labor, but treated them as slaves. And second, they forced the *tlamemes* to carry loads three times heavier than was permitted in pre-Columbian times and over much longer distances from their homes; the change in climate alone, from the highlands to the tropics, killed many. Elderly women and even pregnant women had to climb into the mountains, carrying 75 pounds on their backs. The lack of roads suitable for horses or wagons persisted for centuries throughout Central America, so that although *tlamemes* were officially banned in the 16th century, they did not disappear. Even pack animals, such as burros, failed to eliminate *tlamemes;* the explorer John Lloyd Stephens related in the mid-19th century that it was customary to cross the mountains in a *silla,* "an armchair, to be carried on the back on an Indian" (1969 2, 269).

The human losses profoundly affected the colony, not to mention the suffering Indians themselves. The government needed laborers to build the towns, roads, and ports. The friars and secular priests needed native artisans to build and decorate their churches and others to sing in the choirs and perform household chores in the friary. *Encomenderos* expected Indians to farm their land and supply them with food in their town houses—and they expected them to build the town houses. With the declining population, the slavers found it difficult to round up enough Indians to make a profit, and miners had to resort to paying for African slaves. By 1570 10,000 blacks and mulattos lived in the Kingdom of Guatemala but their numbers were insufficient to sustain the colony because of Crown-imposed limits on the number of slaves permitted and because of cost: an African slave cost 200 pesos, a male Indian slave 15, and an *encomienda* Indian cost nothing.

The demand for tribute labor and taxes didn't decrease with the population, and the growing mestizo population was not subject to tribute at all. As the Indians declined in number, each endured a greater tribute burden: President Cerrato claimed the Indians could not have provided half the tribute even if their numbers in 1548 were doubled. Some escaped the burden by becoming fugitives from their communities; some hanged themselves in despair. Furthermore, the

INDIAN LORDS

He has others to look to his horses, others to fish for him, others to bring him wood for his house . . .

■

Thomas Gage, c. 1630 (1985, 202)

Not all Indians suffered equally. Don Bernabe de Guzmán, a Mayan *cacique* ("lord," or "chief") in Chiapas, lived what seems a surprisingly good life for an Indian in the post-conquest era. Like other Indian aristocrats, he was permitted certain privileges in recognition of his noble status. Only the Indian elites, not their subjects, were permitted to dress like Spaniards and to use the Spanish gentleman's title of *don;* they alone were permitted to own horses and swords and keep title to land as well as the serfs who worked it. They learned Spanish from the friars, and some even traveled to Europe to meet King Philip II. According to the Dominican priest Francisco Ximénez, the power of Juan de Rojas, Quiché king of Santa Cruz Utatlán, remained so great in the 16th century that he was given a receiving room in the Royal Palace in Antigua. Such privileges came with a price. Spain needed the native aristocrats, with their inherited authority and credibility, to control the Indians. Izquín Nijaib, Quiché ruler of Momostenango and war captain against Alvarado, was instrumental in the conversion of his people to Christianity. In exchange for keeping the peace, congregating worshipers at church, and collecting tribute and taxes, these lords were themselves exempted from tribute and taxes. Yet all the native aristocracy lived in reduced circumstances. Even Don Bernabe confronted a daily reality check, for despite all his servants, Gage reported that he "attends and waits on the friar that lives in the next town and doth nothing . . . but what the friar alloweth . . ."

Indian population was not increasing through reproduction. In many provinces Indians practiced sexual abstinence, and in Nicaragua they sometimes practiced infanticide rather than permit their children to live as slaves and slowly starve to death. The birthrate declined, and by the end of the century, the number of Indians in Central America had been reduced by as much as 90 percent: one of the worst demographic disasters in world history.

Resistance to Change

> How can Indian slaves be liberated when the oidor [royal judge]
> himself has two or three hundred slaves? . . . And how can
> tamenes [Indian porters] be taken away by an oidor who has
> eight hundred tamenes in the mines, and when even his dogs
> are carried by tamenes?
>
> ■
>
> Alonso López de Cerrato, letter to the Crown, 1548 (Sherman 1983, 188)

The colonists agreed that something had to be done. Some argued for new conquests and slave raids in Costa Rica and the Petén. Others used their labor force more carefully, particularly in the densely populated highlands where the number of Indians remained substantial despite the high death rate. Bishop Pedraza took matters into his own hands, so that members of the *audiencia* "would not have to strain themselves (Sherman 979, 90)," and reassessed Indian tribute in Honduras. But Bishop Las Casas had the most pervasive impact when he convinced Spain to promulgate laws in 1542 that protected the Indians from abuse and liberated them from slavery. The colonists resisted these New Laws, as they were called, sometimes with violence. As Las Casas observed, the *encomenderos* had no desire to accept any restrictions on their position and wealth. In Chiapas, colonists initially drove Las Casas out of his bishopric; in Nicaragua and Honduras, where slaving and mining abuses were worst, they rebelled against the Crown.

The Crown faced more subtle resistance as well. Alonso Maldonado, the first president of the *audiencia*, engaged in businesses that violated the New Laws, and many of the judges on the council owned mines—and the slaves to work them. Royal officials often shared more than business opportunities with the settlers: President Maldonado, for example, was Francisco de Montejo's son-in-law, and was in sympathy with the *encomenderos*.

Even when personal interests were not involved, officials feared the settlers would abandon the colony if the laws were enforced. Bishop Marroquín, who worried about the lack of new settlers attracted to the region, argued for gradual reforms. His concerns were warranted. The New Laws caused some *encomenderos* to desert their lands in Chiapas and Honduras; a few areas were actually abandoned by the Spaniards in mid-century, such as the frontier outposts in Costa Rica, which remained basically unconquered, and the number of Spaniards in the

capital declined by one-third. Any reduction in the European population of the colony was of concern: in 1570 there were only 15,000
Europeans in the Kingdom of Guatemala.

Mid-Century Reform: President Cerrato

*Soon the washing of gold ceased, the tribute of boys and girls
was suspended. Soon also the execution by burnings and
hangings ended . . . Señor Cerrato in truth alleviated the
suffering of the people.*

■

The Annals of the Cakchiquels (Recinos 1953, 20)

Over the protests of the Spanish settlers, the Crown finally implemented the New Laws by sending the incorruptible Alonso López de
Cerrato to the Kingdom of Guatemala in 1548. For the first time, the
highest-ranking official in the kingdom supported the missionaries in
their efforts to end Indian slavery. Cerrato, an aging and ailing official,
had requested retirement, preferring to return from the Indies to Spain.
Instead, the 60-year-old gentleman became president of the second
audiencia and spent the next seven years of his life, from 1548 to 1555,
enforcing the New Laws with exceptional vigor. His reward was to live
his last years amid great hostility and, unlike most of his colleagues, to
die in poverty.

Cerrato arrived after the worst years of the slave trade, yet what he
witnessed profoundly disturbed him. He estimated that one-third of
the native population had been enslaved, and that the corrupt officials
of the first *audiencia* had done nothing to protect them. He personally
freed 5,000 slaves and aggressively reduced the exploitation of Indian
labor. The practice of using *tlamemes* could not be eliminated in accordance with the law, because there were no suitable roads for overland
transport, but Cerrato did enforce payment for their labor and regulated the loads and distances they could be forced to endure. He
reduced Indian tribute by half. And he cooperated with the friars and
settlers to congregate the Indians in larger villages, where they could
be more easily protected and "civilized." Not all abuses could be eliminated, particularly in the more remote regions beyond the watchful
eye of officialdom. Cerrato did, however, improve living conditions for
many Indians.

Cerrato proved that reform was possible, despite the objections of the settlers. Indian rebellions subsided. Other officials on the *audiencia*, such as the respected jurist Alonso de Zorita, emulated his integrity. Spaniards found their petitions for slave raids into Costa Rica denied or closely regulated; Indians discovered their petitions for relief would sometimes be granted. Progress had been made, however imperfect in its implementation. In the end, the settlers convinced the Crown to replace Cerrato with a less zealous president, and the brief period of idealism ended, but not before royal policy had been enforced and political stability achieved.

Spain Controls an Empire

At the end of the 16th century, Spain had consolidated an empire and expanded it into Costa Rica, where the highland capital of Cartago was founded in 1564. Not every region or corner was settled or protected—or explored. Yet Spain had instituted a government by bureaucracy in place of personal rule, and it had partially enforced the royal laws concerning tribute and treatment of Indians. Tens of thousands of indigenous peoples were Christianized and descendants of pre-Columbian kings were baptized with names such as Juan Cortés and Diego Pérez.

The Spanish governed, replacing preconquest chiefs at the top layers of society. But the 16th-century world below the highest ranks of society owed its existence to the native people. The Spaniards settled where the Indians were most densely concentrated, basically in the Mesoamerican region of Central America: the Guatemalan highlands and the Pacific coast. The world the Spanish controlled existed only through a preexisting Indian hierarchy and through Indian labor—Indian caciques collected taxes, Indian labor built town halls, decorated churches, and supplied the markets with food for the colony. Even the most lucrative trade was conducted over pre-Columbian routes with Indian products, such as cacao, and Indian *tlamemes*.

At the end of the 16th century, Central America was very much a European colony. From the ethnic makeup of the growing mestizo and African-American population to the iron tools and livestock that roamed the savannas, Central America had changed. Indians who had known the pre-Columbian world died out, replaced by children and grandchildren who knew only Spanish rule. The offspring of the conquistadores were also born into a different world from that of their parents, and most would never know Europe. The first excitement of discovery was waning: the priests lost their zeal, and the Crown became more interested in silver than salvation. Even Indian uprisings subsided. The colony was established.

5

LIFE IN THE COLONY

*Without the Indies or its trade, Spain would fall from its
greatness, because there would be no silver for your majesty, for
the ministers, for the private individuals ...*

■

Marqués de Variñas, 1687 (Stein and Stein 1970, 44)

Spain judged the importance of its colonies by their contributions to the royal coffers. As part of New Spain, the Kingdom of Guatemala was part of the most prosperous region of the Americas, and one of the most valued by the Crown. New Spain's capital at Mexico City was the largest city in the Western Hemisphere, with a population greater than 137,000 by the end of the 18th century; it boasted great churches and palaces, parks, and broad streets as well as the first university and the first hospital in the Americas. Fabulously productive silver mines in northern New Spain created new settlements, such as Zacatecas and Taxco; ecclesiastic fervor beautified other cities, such as Puebla. The material wealth of the New World, however, was most often shipped out on the annual galleons to Spain.

The Kingdom of Guatemala, without the resources of Mexico, never attained similar wealth or cosmopolitanism. Yet a casual glance at a map quickly demonstrates the centrality of the isthmus within Hispanic America. Its strategic location between Mexico and Peru made it essential for travelers going to either place, and its Caribbean coast made neighbors of important Spanish possessions, including the great ports for the Spanish trade galleons at Havana, Portobelo (Panama), and Cartagena (Colombia). Nations other than Spain understood the importance of the region, and they coveted it: pirates plagued the Caribbean coast, and Britain grabbed unsettled areas for itself.

A land of promise, but not of bountiful precious metals, the Kingdom of Guatemala struggled to attract Spanish investment and settlers. An

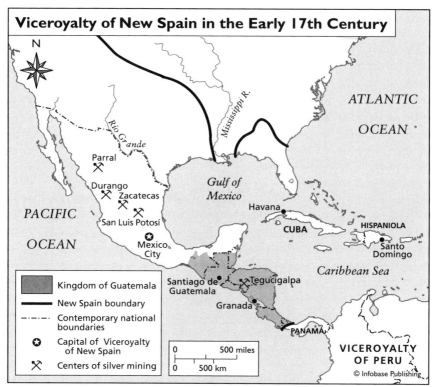

Viceroyalty of New Spain in the Early 17th Century

N

Rio Grande

Parral ⚒

Durango ⚒ Zacatecas ⚒

PACIFIC

San Luis Potosí ⚒

OCEAN

Mexico City ⊙

Mississippi R.

Gulf of Mexico

Havana •

ATLANTIC

OCEAN

CUBA

HISPANIOLA

Santo Domingo

Caribbean Sea

Santiago de Guatemala • ⚒ Tegucigalpa

Granada •

PANAMÁ

VICEROYALTY OF PERU

■ Kingdom of Guatemala
— New Spain boundary
–·–·– Contemporary national boundaries
⊙ Capital of Viceroyalty of New Spain
⚒ Centers of silver mining

0   500 miles
0   500 km

© Infobase Publishing

The Kingdom of Guatemala was at the geographic center of Spain's domain but on the periphery of the wealthy region controlled by Mexico City, the capital of New Spain, and even farther from the fabulous silver mines in northern Mexico. Spanish neglect was the result.

important region of New Spain (unlike, for example, the frontier settlements in Baja California and New Mexico), its strategic location and relatively substantial Indian population were not enough to enable it to flourish. After its early years of profiteering and violence, the Kingdom of Guatemala settled into the rhythms of a provincial colony.

The Capital: Santiago de Guatemala

> But all the while I lived there the noise within the mountain, the smokes and flashes of fire without, and the summer earthquakes were such that with the use and custom of them I never feared anything, but thought that city the healthiest and pleasantest place of dwelling that ever I came into in all my travels.

■

Thomas Gage, 1648 (1984, 184)

The capital of Santiago was one of the finest cities in the New World. Although it could not compare in size and development with Mexico City, given a population just over 25,000 in 1770, it certainly was a capital worthy of one of the most important *audiencias* in the New World. Situated in a fertile valley, the city was as famous for its temperate climate as for the fire flashing from the volcanoes that towered nearby. The edifices of authority—the royal palace, the town hall, and the cathedral—graced its central square. The cathedral, soaring 66 feet in height and lined by eight chapels on each side of the nave, was joined by 18 other churches, 11 chapels, and 18 convents. The royal mint, a printing press, and the Royal and Pontifical University of San Carlos, founded in 1676, the only institution of higher learning in Central America, added luster to the city.

As the seat of civic and ecclesiastic authority, the capital also controlled much of the commerce of the colony. Spaniards and American-born Spaniards maintained homes in Santiago in order to negotiate favors for themselves—grants of land for wheat and cattle and licenses for the trade in sugar and indigo. As the descendants of the *encomenderos* died out, this mercantile and large landowning class became the new aristocracy, and they controlled most commerce in the Kingdom of Guatemala, often to the disadvantage of the provinces. The wealthiest were often European-born—Spaniards, of course, and naturalized Genovese and Portuguese—rather than creoles. Yet some creoles joined the top ranks of the rich: the Aycinena family had the funds to purchase the title of marquis from the Crown, the only such creole family officially raised to the aristocracy in the kingdom. These wealthy merchants and bureaucrats, both foreign and creole, endowed the city with fine mansions and the most glittering social life in the colony.

The Spaniards constituted less than 6 percent of the city's population. Indians, mestizos and blacks, both enslaved and free, could be found throughout the city. Some labored in the mansions in the center of the city, and others lived in the neighborhoods on the edge of town. Initially the Indians, whether allies or captured slaves of the conquistadores, lived in their own separate enclaves. Over time, the neighborhoods became more racially mixed, as did the population. The mestizos became the largest urban group—and the most culturally diverse. Although most were poor and lived in thatched-roof huts, some mestizo residents made a decent living as small shopkeepers and artisans.

Santiago (now known as Antigua) dominated the affairs of the Kingdom of Guatemala and it concentrated much of the wealth of the colony within itself. Its merchants controlled most of the shipping from

SANTIAGO DESTROYED BY EARTHQUAKE

[The earthquake] was so quick, so violent, so fierce . . . Those persons who did not fall, at full speed took the position of lying down prostrate on the ground; the animals did the same—four feet not being sufficient to support them. The trees, those that did not fall, leaned one way or the other with their branches on the ground. The bricks, so bound and tightly joined with cement . . . broke their fittings and cracked.

■

Father Felipe Cádena, July 29, 1773 (Jones 1994, 3)

In 1773, after the second major earthquake in one year severely damaged the capital, the Crown decided to relocate the capital to the current location of Guatemala City. The construction of the new capital was hard on the Indians, who were subject to increased labor drafts. Not everyone was eager to abandon Santiago de Guatemala, or Antigua as it is now known, and the archbishop and other clergy had to be forced to join the civil authorities in the new capital in 1779. In preferring the temperate climate provided by the mountains, the Spaniards built their settlements on a major geological fault line. Earthquakes and all manner of volcanic activity affected their lives. Not only was Santiago de Guatemala forced to relocate, so were such cities as San Salvador and Léon. The civic buildings in the "new" Guatemala City would themselves be destroyed in the earthquake of 1917.

Ruins of Santa Teresa church in Antigua, formerly Santiago de Guatemala. (Photo courtesy Lawrence Foster)

the colony to Spain. The important roads, whether to the Mexican capital or the port of Veracruz, began in Santiago, and the goods from the Caribbean ports on the Gulf of Honduras were shipped into the capital as well, despite the difficult trip this required. The capital of the kingdom was located in Guatemala, the most populous province; over half the population of the kingdom resided in the province and its many Spanish and Indian settlements. These settlements supplied the Santiago market with foodstuffs, spun wool and textiles, pottery, and other items for both local consumption and trade within the kingdom.

Santiago was by far the largest, loveliest, and most powerful city in the kingdom. After a series of earthquakes in 1773 destroyed much of Santiago, the Crown relocated the capital to Nuevo Guatemala, at the site of what is now Guatemala City; its predecessor became known as "Antigua." Whatever its location, the capital dominated the Kingdom of Guatemala.

The Provinces

> ... we began to enter rough and craggy ways ... in all the rest of our journey to Cartago we observed nothing worth committing to posterity, but only mighty woods and trees on the South Sea side [Pacific], very fit to make strong ships, and many mountains and desert places, where we lay sometimes two nights together, either in woods or open fields, far from any town or habitation of Indians.
>
> ■
>
> Thomas Gage, 1648 (1985, 312)

The Spanish were city people. Even when they owned large haciendas, they preferred living in town as long as they had the funds to afford the social life. And they appreciated the sense of security that came with living among other Europeans; as Thomas Gage observed, outside the cities, they were "thinly scattered upon so great and capacious a land" (1985, 215). The number of Spaniards was too small even to sustain many provincial cities: San Salvador, Comayagua, and Granada were the largest, and their Spanish populations in 1620 were little more than 1,000. At that time, there were fewer than 15,000 Spaniards divided among 15 towns, and 40 percent of them lived in the capital. Cartago in Costa Rica, even a century after its founding, had a Spanish population of less than 400.

In such a large territory, the few towns were profoundly isolated. Great distances usually separated the settlements and communication was poor—only burro paths and rivers connected them. Late in the 18th century, officials complained they could not conduct a census ordered by the king, because ill health and, perhaps, death would result from such a journey across the province, with its crude roads, often impassable by horseback, and lack of food and shelter. As scattered as these cities were, they nonetheless were concentrated on the Pacific side of the isthmus. The Caribbean side, except for a few ports and silver boom towns, was less developed.

Each town, like the capital itself, followed a plan laid out in Spain. From a central square surrounded by official buildings, perpendicular streets formed a grid plan for residential lots and stores. Most towns,

View of Tegucigalpa, Honduras. Tegucigalpa, meaning "silver hill" in the local Indian language, was founded in 1578 in accordance with royal decrees regulating town plans. Its Spanish residents were attracted to the remote Honduran region by silver mines that produced a high quality ore, but not in such abundance as to make it an important colonial city. At an altitude of 3,000 feet, Tegucigalpa is typical of the Spanish preference for the benign climate of highland sites: surrounded by mountains, but not volcanoes, the town is unusual in that it has not suffered the catastrophes that destroyed other colonial settlements. (After drawing by E. G. Squier, 1855)

however, lacked the paved streets and the monumental public buildings of the capital, and the residences could be quite modest. Each town had its officials, however, from the royal *corregidor*, who collected tribute from both the town and the region, including the Indian settlements governed by the *caciques*, to the local mayor and, in the provincial capitals, governors and bishops. Spain regulated it all and issued more than 6,000 decrees governing life in the colony.

Despite their uniformity, the cities and the provinces in which they were located varied greatly. San Salvador, for example, was transformed from a densely populated Indian region into one with many African slaves. Prosperous from the Indian slave trade and, later, from indigo, this city, like the mining towns in central Honduras, was able to pay for the import of African slaves. Cartago, the poor capital of a region with few Indians, had little of the ethnic complexity—or labor supply—of other cities. Until cacao smuggling in the Caribbean became a more lucrative alternative, Costa Rican merchants scratched together a living by raising hogs to supply the Spanish galleons with bacon. Granada in Nicaragua was one of the most naturally well-endowed early settlements, with the nearby Pacific slopes, replenished and fertilized by periodic eruptions of Volcán Momotombo, perfect for producing cacao and indigo, the two most valuable export crops of the colony. On Lake Nicaragua, Granada became an important port for transport from the Pacific Ocean to the Caribbean Sea via the San Juan River. Wealthy Granada, however, was not the colonial capital of the Nicaraguan province; Spain bestowed that favor on the rival city of León.

The cities were surrounded by great expanses of countryside and, beyond, wilderness. From Costa Rica to Belize, rebel Indians took refuge in these remote forests and mountains, as did runaway black slaves, who found refuge with them. In the 17th century, the few intrepid missionaries who tried to administer to the Mayans of Belize were expelled. To most Europeans, this distant landscape was too dangerous even to explore, much less settle.

Spanish haciendas, with their herds of cattle and sheep and fields of wheat, were located in the countryside where the Indians had been more successfully conquered and subdued. Some poor mestizos and free blacks were especially attracted to the cattle ranches, where the cowboy life on the open range gave them considerable freedom, especially when the owner resided in the city. During the economic depression that lasted from 1630 to 1680, the Spanish settlers also took refuge in the country, where food supplies were more reliable than in the cities.

PANAMA CITY

It is held to be one of the richest places in all America, having by land and by the river Chagres commerce with the North Sea [Atlantic Ocean], and by the South [Pacific], trading with all Peru, East Indies, Mexico, and Honduras.

■

Thomas Gage, 1648 (1985, 327)

As the only fortified port on the Pacific, Panama City boomed. From Panama City, Peruvian silver and gold were transferred to the Caribbean and the Spanish galleons waiting at Portobelo. Even though it functioned as a port, it didn't function well: the frigates from Peru had to anchor a few miles away. And even though it was the seat of a provincial government, just like Santiago de Guatemala, it was a tropical frontier town more than an elegant capital. The royal palace, the churches and eight convents, and the houses of the richest merchants were constructed of boards and tile, not stone or adobe, which were scarce. Like ports the world over, Panama City had a diverse population and somewhat flexible social structure. Gage reported that African-Americans were among the wealthiest merchants; a census from 1610 counted among the permanent residents 1,007 whites, more than half of them men, 146 mulattos, 148 blacks, and 3,500 African slaves. There was more than enough wine, imported from Peru along with silver but consumed locally, and plenty of prostitutes. As Gage summarized it, "the Spaniards in this city are much given to sin" (1985, 327). In 1671, after its destruction by the English buccaneer Henry Morgan, the city was relocated a few miles farther west.

Spain Regulates the Economy

They adorn us with prices, but keep us naked.

■

18th-century Nicaraguan adage (after Perez-Brignoli 1989, 58)

. . . in this province of Costa Rica . . . we are extremely poor . . . indeed with over one thousand ducates in your treasury here, there is not sufficient to pay the salaries of the governor and the priests.

■

Governor Fernández de Salinas, 1651 (after Perez Brignoli 1989, 45)

97

Without the abundance of precious metals that existed in Mexico and Peru, Central America's economy developed slowly. Although the colony found profitable exports other than silver, such as cacao, indigo, and hides, the economy more often stumbled than flourished. Spain's mercantile policies were meant to generate income for Spain and pre-

EUROPEAN INTERLOPERS

Rival European powers had invaded Spain's New World by the middle of the 16th century. They wanted a share of the wealth. Britain, Holland, and France supported pirates who became national heroes. Francis Drake was knighted by Elizabeth I for his great services to England; Henry Morgan (1635?–88), commander of the buccaneers, was not only knighted but also became governor of Jamaica, which he used as his base for raids on Central America; and Diego el Mulato and Pie de Palo ("Peg Leg") became legends without the help

British Presence in the Kingdom of Guatemala

vent competition with any Spanish industry or commodity. The colonies were expected to provide raw materials, but were seldom permitted to develop the technology to create finished products. For instance, hides were exported, but not leather; dyes, but not dyed textiles. Even when certain industries initially flourished in the New

of titles. They sacked well-fortified Spanish ports and held them in ransom; they lay in wait for the silver-laden galleons, and stripped Honduran ships alone of 930 tons, more than 10 percent of all the merchandise shipped to Spain between 1606 and 1610. They hid on the Caribbean islands and coast the Spanish ignored, and they made daring river raids into the interior of the colony—even Granada was sacked more than once. Around 1630, the British diversified their interests and went into logging, targeting the tropical forests that rimmed the

Sir Francis Drake. (Drawing by Cherra Wyllie after portrait, c. 1590, by Marcus Gheeraerts, the Younger, in the National Maritime Museum Greenwich, U.K.)

Kingdom of Guatemala. On the coast of what is now Belize, a region disdained by the Spaniards and abandoned by the Mayans for the safer interior of the Petén, they established camps for cutting logwood, the source of a purple dye needed for European textiles. Both pirates and loggers traded hatchets, guns, and rum for turtles and fish with the seminomadic Miskito Indians in Honduras and Nicaragua; they formed such a tight alliance that the Miskitos conducted pirate raids for them, traveling by canoe to Costa Rican cacao plantations and, then, into western Panama. By 1670, Spain had granted Britain logging concessions in Belize on the condition that the pirating cease. Britain decided that smuggling would be more lucrative than looting: England's textile industry needed indigo dye, a more profitable and permanent dye than that produced by logwood. Although illegal, trade gradually replaced pirate raids, and both the Kingdom of Guatemala and the European interlopers profited, if not Spain. The British presence took root, and is recalled today in the name of Belize, a corruption of "Peter Wallace," an English pirate.

World—silk in Mexico and wine in Peru—the Crown quickly moved to outlaw their trade or tax them into unprofitability. Whatever Spain manufactured, the Americas had to import, including basic commodities such as cooking oil. In the colonies, costs were high and development low.

Central America became so impoverished that Spain granted permission for some local factories to manufacture goods for strictly local consumption: textiles, shoes, soap, glass, housewares, and gunpowder. Commerce in these items, as well as all others, became increasingly restricted as the 17th century progressed; late in the century, Spain prohibited the various colonies from trading with one another. All trade was through Spain, a stifling policy given that the fleets arrived in the Americas only once a year, and they arrived in the Kingdom of Guatemala even less regularly.

In order to survive, Central Americans learned to circumvent these policies. One way was by tax evasion and fraud. The most important way was by smuggling. Contraband was exchanged with other colonies during much of the 17th century, and by the 18th century, smuggling with European powers, some enemies of Spain, had become commonplace. Initially such smuggling took place clandestinely in isolated Caribbean lagoons, but it became more audacious as a weakened Spain permitted its colony to sink into a prolonged depression from 1630 to 1680.

The colony was so impoverished that some wealthy merchants gave up and returned to Spain with both their families and their capital. American-born creoles retreated to the countryside to eke out a subsistence living. By the end of the 17th century, as the economy continued to stagnate, the Spanish and creole population in the cities had actually declined by 30 percent. Only smuggling could adequately supply the colony and, by the 18th century, revive its economy.

Mining

Spain failed to join the industrialization that swept Renaissance Europe. With so much silver and gold from its American colonies, it could afford to simply import manufactured goods from other nations. After the defeat of the Spanish Armada in 1588, war debts impoverished the empire and made it all the more dependent on American silver. The Crown's demand for precious metals increased during the 17th century and, at times, its need was so great that it deprived the colony of coins. Two-thirds of all the silver received from the colonies went to pay off debts in European banks. More precious metals were needed, yet Spain's policies prevented efficient mining, crippling the modest Central American industry.

Silver mines were discovered sporadically in the Tegucigalpa region of Honduras, in northeastern Nicaragua, and, less often, in the mountains of Guatemala. Although the quality of the ore was often very good, the quantity was modest: one region produced 7,000 measures of silver annually in contrast to 100,000 from Mexican mines in Zacatecas. For the mines to be efficiently exploited, more advanced technology was needed than that required to pan nearby rivers or smelt by fire. Yet Spain refused to advance the capital to invest in the labor or the materials that would have made the mines more profitable. The Crown further hindered progress by its monopoly on mercury—the mercury, which was used to smelt the ore, would not arrive for years at a time and, when it did, it was too costly.

The amount of precious metal produced under such circumstances certainly disappointed Spain; and the regulations just as certainly resulted in the creation of fraudulent schemes for circumventing them. Hondurans, with the complicity of royal officials, often failed to register their mines or pay the royal tax on their ore. Such fraud produced undocumented wealth for some, but there was never enough silver for the number of prospectors: 300 claims were filed for four mines around Tegucigalpa. Silver may have brought settlers to central Honduras, but it never was enough to build gorgeous, baroque cities like those in Mexico, or to profit the Crown.

Cacao and Indigo

Spain's mercantilism encouraged export crops, and the colony produced a variety of them—from sugar and sarsaparilla to tobacco—but only a few ever turned a profit. The kingdom developed an economy that encouraged single-crop dependency. When a crop was in high demand, powerful merchants in Santiago de Guatemala underwrote its production and arranged for its shipping; and landowners devoted their land to it, usually at the expense of subsistence crops. There would be a boom, inevitably followed by the collapse of demand in Europe, or the plants would become blighted and the soil infertile from exploitation. Whichever crop the colony relied on—cacao or indigo—followed this boom-then-bust pattern; only the length of the cycle varied. Ranching followed a pattern similar to the crops: the number of cattle plummeted in the late 16th century and, after decades in which meat had been so plentiful that carcasses were left to rot, there was a scarcity of beef and low profits from hide exports. The economic lows became times of food shortages as well.

Cacao was the first valuable export crop. The chocolate drink of Aztec kings became a favorite of the Spanish court, and spread into 17th-century France when Maria Teresa married Louis XIV. However, Central American cacao was traded mostly within New Spain, where it was used as currency, primarily in payment for Indian labor and Indian tribute, but also when the supply of minted coins ran out. The crop found a world market by the mid-17th century, when chocolate became the rage in Europe and cocoa bars replaced cafés in Britain as gathering places of the intelligentsia. By this time, however, the cacao boom was over in the colony. A native American plant, cacao cultivation in Central America was left to Indian know-how and required year-round Indian attention. By the end of the 16th century, labor was scarce and many plants became infested with insects, lessening the yield. Cacao production in other countries, such as Venezuela, brought competition that made the profits more marginal. By the early 17th century, the land of the Mayans had ceased to be a major producer of cacao. Costa Rica quickly revived the Central American tradition with new plantings along the Caribbean coast, but the production was too small to attract trade more substantial than pirates and, later, smugglers.

Indigo, a high-quality dye that was much in demand for European textiles, was the next major export. In Salvador and Nicaragua, some cacao merchants, worrying about the decline in cacao, started acquiring land and planting the shrub that produced this native blue dye in the wild. Indigo production, unlike cacao, required only a few skilled workers to oversee operations year-round; and, unlike sugar, which could have flourished on the coasts, indigo needed practically no investment in machinery. And, at a time of severe Indian labor shortages, the fact that only small numbers of black slaves or mestizo wage earners were needed to supervise the dye works made the system even more feasible. Labor shortages—and the royal bans on the use of Indian labor in the unhealthy dye works—limited the size of the seasonal harvest, however. Late in the 17th century, when British smugglers made the trade in indigo very profitable, the protective restrictions on Indian labor were increasingly ignored.

Indigo was also attractive to many growers because it could be grown easily along with wheat and other crops. Even more fortuitously, grazing cattle weeded the plots without destroying the plants.

QUICHÉ MERCHANTS

. . . all rich Indians, half-merchants and great workers—I will say, par excellence, for they have 3,000 mules for their work.

■

M. A. Tovilla, 1635 (Carmack 1981, 326)

The Spaniards did not have a monopoly on trade in the colony. Thomas Gage observed that most Mayan towns in the Guatemalan highlands produced a specialty product—salt, honey, pottery, fruits, or textiles—and had traders sell it in town markets. According to Tovilla, the Quiché Mayans in Chichicastenango, whose ancestors founded Utatlán, established a lucrative trade with the coast, bartering or selling highland maize and woven cloth for cacao and cotton. Much of the trade probably followed established pre-Columbian patterns. Even the demand for cacao, which Indians had used for currency and tribute in Mesoamerican times, continued to be used for the same purposes. The cacao fields that enriched Spanish merchants and attracted traders from Chichicastenango were some of the very same ones that the Quichés and Aztecs had fought over. Spaniards and ladinos increasingly took over anything profitable in the colony from the Indians, but even today Chichicastenango remains an important Quiché Mayan market town in highland Guatemala.

Indigo was easily grown on small ladino ranches, in Indian villages, and Tegucigalpa mining settlements, and was profitably sold to the city merchants for processing and export. Despite locust plagues and volcanic eruptions that covered entire farms, indigo became a booming export by the late 17th century, and the shared interest in its production united the cities and farms along the Pacific slope for the first time.

Indigo was perfectly suited to the Kingdom of Guatemala, and it enabled the colony to experience limited prosperity, once markets were developed through smuggling. It continued to sustain the colony until about 1800, when a locust plague, merchant fraud, and wars in Europe ended most of the profits. Despite its marginal profitability, indigo remained the primary export of the region well into the 19th century, when aniline dyes rendered it obsolete.

Ports of Trade

Spain saw the isthmus primarily as a barrier to commerce with the Pacific. Spanish fleets arrived from the Atlantic, but most settlers—and Indians—lived near the Pacific. Not only were there few natural harbors on the Caribbean coast, but Spain never successfully subdued the seminomadic Miskito Indians who lived along the coast from eastern Honduras across Nicaragua, an area known as the Mosquito Coast. (SEE page 98.) Spain required a secure port and easy access to its settlers, but never could find the right location.

The preferred port in the Bay of Honduras changed over time, from little Puerto Barrios to Puerto Caballos and even farther east to Trujillo. Whichever port was used, it required a difficult journey by canoe and burro to the major population centers of the kingdom, whether

PORTOBELO, PANAMA

I wondered at . . . [the droves] of mules which came thither from Panama [City], laden with wedges of silver. In one day I told [counted] two hundred mules laden with nothing else, which were unladen in the public market-place, so that there the heaps of silver wedges lay like heaps of stones in the street . . .

■

Thomas Gage, 1648 (329–30)

The Caribbean port of Portobelo, Panama, was considered impregnable, especially after it successfully fended off an attack by Sir Francis Drake in 1596. Unimpressive except for its fortresses, the port was barely inhabited most of the year because of the malaria and other diseases that festered in the tropics. (Drake himself died here from dysentery and was secretly buried in the bay.) When no fleet was expected, only a few shopkeepers and soldiers remained. But once a year the fleet arrived with eight galleons and 10 merchant ships, and goods from Europe and the American colonies poured off the ships, accompanied by 5,000 soldiers. Ships from Cartagena, Colombia, and other Spanish ports pulled in for the trade fair, and Portobelo was transformed into a vast marketplace, the most important in Central America, filled with the bustle of merchants, soldiers, and royal officials. Even when the Spanish galleons skipped other Central American ports,

Santiago de Guatemala or San Salvador or Realejo, Nicaragua, on the Pacific. As critical as these Honduran ports were to the kingdom, the Spanish fleets often bypassed them entirely. Years would elapse before the galleons came to trade, especially during the depression that followed the collapse of the cacao market: the quantity of goods shipped from Honduras to Seville fell from 9,000 tons (1606–10) to a low of 925 tons (1641–45).

There were a few Caribbean coves near the San Juan River in Nicaragua and what is now Puerto Limón in Costa Rica that were useful for local transport (and smuggling) of goods from colony to colony. The San Juan River, then navigable except for some troublesome rapids, almost connected to the Pacific via Lake Nicaragua and Granada, a fact that was not lost in the 19th and 20th century searches for an easy path

they would anchor at Portobelo to pick up their loads of Peruvian silver. The distance from Panama City on the Pacific was less than 50 miles as the crow flies, but the rugged trail across the mountains was so costly to maintain that Spain would not have kept it open for anything less valuable than silver. The sil-

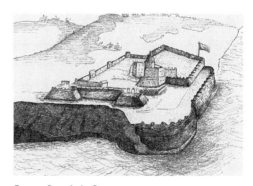

Fort at Portobelo, Panama. (Drawing by Cherra Wyllie after etching by Heredes Homann, Stadt-Atlas, Nurnberg, 1743)

ver shipment required hundreds of burros and massive provisions to sustain it, all of which had to be imported from the ranchers and merchants in the Kingdom of Guatemala. Despite its fortifications, English pirates several times successfully sacked the port: William Parker in 1601 and Sir Henry Morgan in 1688. Not until 1738, however, when Portobelo was again sacked, this time by Edward Vernon, did Spain decide that sailing around Cape Horn might be a safer, and not much costlier, route to Peru. Portobelo was abandoned in 1746, and Panama became a backwater; the commerce it had generated within the Kingdom of Guatemala ended as well, not to be replaced.

between the seas. Unlike the Caribbean, the Pacific coast had decent natural harbors around the Gulf of Fonseca and the Nicoya Peninsula— and they were convenient to Spanish settlements. Although useful for local travel and occasional smuggling among the coastal Pacific colonies from Acapulco, Mexico, to Peru, they were on the wrong side of the isthmus for Spain.

Initially, Spain energetically searched for a port to breach the isthmus from the Atlantic to the Pacific. It hoped for a strait leading to the rich lodes of Peruvian silver, but was forced to consider less desirable options. Some traders in the colony promoted Nicaragua's San Juan River as a transport route, and others encouraged the development of a Honduran overland route to the Gulf of Fonseca. None of these routes, however, replaced or supplemented the narrower Panamanian crossing between Portobelo and Panama City that had been established in 1597, and the Kingdom of Guatemala faced chronic supply and export problems. Spain, financially troubled itself, struggled to send the fleet on a regular schedule. And once the pirate raids intensified along the Caribbean, decades could pass without the galleons anchoring in the Gulf of Honduras. Only the wealthiest Guatemalan merchants could afford to export through Mexico or Panama, and the transportation costs destroyed many businesses.

By the 1630s, the colony was desperate and isolated. Thomas Gage made the mistake of attempting to return to Europe from the Kingdom of Guatemala, rather than from Mexico. It took him over a year, and he explored sailings from every small port. He finally boarded a supply boat from Costa Rica bound for Portobelo along the Caribbean coast. The sails had barely been unfurled before the ship was boarded and robbed by Diego el Mulato and Pie de Palo, and Gage was put ashore to begin his search once again.

Class and Race in Society

In Spain it is a sort of title of nobility to descend neither from Jews nor Moors; in America skin, more or less white, indicates a man's rank in society.

■

Alexander von Humboldt, 1807 (Stein and Stein 1970, 56)

The Kingdom of Guatemala, like all Spanish colonies in America, had a legally enforced system of social caste that was based primarily on

Racial Composition of the Kingdom of Guatemala: Mid-17th Century*			
	Kingdom	Santiago	Cartago**
Indians	540,000	5,600	144
Whites	50,000	6,100	365
Ladinos		24,620	
Mestizos	30,000		16
Blacks	20,000		41
Mulattoes	10,000		12
TOTAL	650,000	36,320	578

* Figures are estimated due to lack of accurate census data.
** Cartago, in the central plateau of Costa Rica, was the only town in Central America with a predominantly white population; ladinos increasingly constituted the urban majority, while the Indians, as a form of Spanish protection, lived primarily in villages separated from the rest of the populace.
Sources: Christopher H. Lutz, Murdo J. MacLeod (1973), and Oakah L. Jones

race. The laws regulated everything from the right to wear Chinese silk to the right to hold civic office and bear arms. The many recognized racial permutations were reflected in a byzantine tangle of regulations that could liberate the children of slaves or force tribute payments on a mestizo.

Given the racial realities of intermarriage in the colony, the theoretical rigidity of such a system was often softened in practice. Elite "white" families could have increasingly destitute Spain certify that all Indian and African blood had been "extinguished" in a family—for a fee. In a society always in need of labor and skills, individual exceptions to these racist laws were not uncommon. For example, Diego de Porres, who was of mixed racial ancestry, was a respected architect in the capital and, in 1707, a member of the infantry. In fact, the ban on arms for all but whites was lifted entirely when the Bourbons improved the defenses of the colony: In 1803, 60 African slaves formed an artillery company. The cavalry, however, remained the domain of whites. Thomas Gage (191) reported that all races go "gallantly appareled" in the capital, and, in rural areas far from the watchful eyes of civic authorities, racially mixed individuals often found they could live just as they wished. There were many exceptions to an oppressive system, yet the caste system alienated the vast majority and left its racist imprint on the colony.

Criollos and Peninsulares

As the ruling class, whites topped the social hierarchy. But even among the whites, there were divisions. The Crown favored the *peninsulares,* Spaniards born in Spain, over the *criollos,* or creoles, who were born in America. Spain distrusted the creoles, as if the foreign soil diluted their loyalty to the Crown. Spain suspected the same would happen to its Spanish-born officials, even those born in Spain, and limited their terms to just a few years in order to prevent them, too, from shifting allegiance. Most creoles were as fair-skinned as the *peninsulares,* and despite the humble origins of many of their ancestors, they were among the elite. Yet they were most definitely lower on the social ladder, and, as might be expected, laws discriminated against them.

Creoles were excluded from the most important, and lucrative, royal and ecclesiastic appointments. They could be elected to lesser offices, and they were sometimes the mayors of towns, which helped a few to improve their situation. (One mayor of Tegucigalpa, his salary less than 700 pesos, used his position to generate an annual income of 8,000 pesos.) The number of positions available to creoles were few, because all royal appointments were reserved for *peninsulares,* including the most powerful religious offices, such as that of bishop, and many lowly provincial ones.

The *peninsulares* used those positions to help their families and friends to prosper. The cacao plantations, indigo dye works, shipping, and other endeavors were most often controlled by *peninsulares.* Not a single creole was among the five richest cacao merchants, all of whom were born in Europe. Royal officials also were involved in some of the most brazen acts of smuggling and fraud. As early as 1630, Thomas Gage noted that both creole clerics and settlers were bristling with the injustice of their treatment.

The colonial economy stalled in the 17th century, and many creoles were forced to abandon town life and take refuge in the countryside. Most did not have great estates. The descendants of the original *enco-menderos* were gradually disappearing, and those who had not invested in land had only the declining tribute of Indians to support them. Most creoles didn't have enough acreage to consider their land a hacienda, and, unlike the *peninsulares,* they didn't have much capital—or political clout—to improve their circumstances. Instead, they often en-

PRESIDENT MARTÍN CARLOS DE MENCOS

On the trade of the coast of Honduras . . . the only solution which was proposed was the tightening of the orders prohibiting trade with foreigners, and the committing of the investigation and punishment, however slight . . .

■

Marqués de Variñas, 1677 report to the king (MacLeod 1973, 360)

A trusted royal servant for 50 years and an admired president of the Guatemalan *audiencia* from 1659 to 1667, General Martín Carlos de Mencos was accused of smuggling 400 cases of indigo and eight bars of silver to Holland in 1663. There was no doubt as to his guilt—witnesses at the port warehouses and jealous merchants had presented evidence against him. The president pleaded extenuating financial circumstances and piety as the cause of his crime: He had arrived in the colony quite poor, he said, having sold most of his possessions to pay for the expensive voyage to Central America. Then, when his wife died from a fever in Portobelo, he had the choice of either honoring her generous bequest to a convent in Spain or depriving the nuns of their funds. To comply with her devout wish, he had engaged in illegal commerce with Holland. What else would the king have him do? He was found guilty, but King Philip IV must have been sympathetic. Not only did he leave the general in office, he also reappointed him for a second term and granted him an *encomienda* to provide him a better income.* The Crown was not usually so forgiving: The Aycinena family of wealthy creole merchants engaged in such illegal commerce and had their indigo seized; others suffered severe fines and even threats of expulsion from the colony. Yet Spain found it increasingly difficult to prevent smuggling as it became widespread, involving most royal officials and naval crews alike.

*After Murdo J. MacLeod (1973, 356–57)

croached on Indian lands in order to find a subsistence living or to invest in a small way in indigo.

Ladinos and *Castas*

Skin color had more impact on status than place of birth, and the Crown was quick to notice every racial variant and to label each. Today, most Central Americans refer to themselves as mestizo, or a racial mix of Indian and European with, perhaps, a trace of African. Then, the colony recognized 16 racial categories in the law, and each was treated distinctly. Among the many *castas*, or persons of mixed race, were the mestizos (Indian and white), by far the largest and best-treated group; the mulattoes (African and white), and the *zambos* and *coyotes* (Indian and African). All *castas*, as well as blacks, were lumped into a category called *ladinos*. Despite the refinement of the colonial labels, the general impact was simple: To the colonists, they were the "other" class.

Being neither European nor Indian, the *castas* had no clearly defined role in Spain's colonial order. Unlike the Indians, they were not protected as special wards, and no edicts prevented them from working in unhealthy situations or ended any African or mulatto enslavement. Yet, also unlike Indians, they did not have to pay tribute and could make their way into new levels of society through the church, the military, and even the university. Upper-middle-class ladinos were priests, teachers, army lieutenants, police officers, lawyers, and doctors.

The mestizos were never enslaved, and in the cities they were the small shop owners and artisans, but in the craft guilds, they were restricted to the apprentice level. (Only whites could achieve master status.) They also were itinerant salesmen, trading in the countryside with some of the Indian settlements. The mulattoes, when free, received special consideration as offspring of Spaniards; in the 18th century, they policed the Indian neighborhoods of the cities, a typical Crown maneuver that pitted the various ethnic groups against one another, rather than against the minority white community. In somewhat the same spirit, ladinos worked in supervisory positions over Indians at haciendas, ranches, dye works, and sugar mills, and they drove mule trains and did some of the dirty work for the colonists, such as illegally recruiting Indian laborers. Some became indigo growers. Others created their own enterprises as cattle rustlers, highway robbers, and smugglers.

The whites had trouble forcing the ladinos to work, unless they were mulatto slaves. Not belonging anywhere—or to anyone—in particular, ladinos could more easily escape the control of local governments than village-based Indians. They could abandon onerous working conditions by moving from province to province, and many of them did. There were attempts to settle them in villages, and attempts to entangle them in jobs through debt peonage, but these were only occasionally effective.

Some ladinos were totally outside colonial control. The Miskito Indians, for instance, intermarried with British pirates and smugglers as well as their African slaves, over time becoming predominantly a colony of *zambos* with a distinct identity, separate from that of their ancestors. "Miskito," in fact, probably is a postconquest name that derived from the English muskets they carried, which were noted with alarm by the neighboring Indians and Spaniards. The Garífuna, though similar to the Miskito in their black and Indian heritage, instead allied themselves with the Spanish after escaping from the British.

Indians

The Indians comprised the largest class of all. In the 17th century they still constituted over 80 percent of the population, and at the end of the colonial period, despite the rapid growth of the ladino class, they accounted for more than half. As wards of the Crown and Catholic Church, they received many protections on paper, and their situation was generally considered better than that of African slaves. They were governed by their own cacique, and they owned community lands. The New Laws also freed them from slavery and regulated the exploitation of their labor.

Yet half a million Indians were forced to work in order to pay tribute to the Crown, the Catholic Church, and the few remaining *encomenderos*; and they labored a specified period of days in *repartimiento,* or labor drafts, for the landowners, cities, and church. In addition, the Indians had to farm their community lands in order to feed themselves and their families. The labor of Indians constituted 70 percent of the colonial resources throughout the 17th century—Costa Rica, with few Indians (only 800 in 1651), was the most impoverished region.

The Indians were poor, and they were exploited in many ways, despite royal edicts that prohibited them from working in unhealthy dye works and mines, or any form of labor that prevented them from working their lands as well as paying royal tribute. Settlers, and even friars and Indian caciques, often ignored these laws in their desperation for labor. Officials, too, frequently accepted bribes to overlook such transgressions. When the Crown sent inspectors, the abusers were duly fined, and this filled the royal coffers even if it failed to end the practice. As Spain itself became impoverished in the 17th century, it was willing to overlook some of the worst offenses as long as its income was boosted. Not until the Bourbon reforms of the 18th century did the Indians increasingly find relief through appeals to the government.

KING MARTÍN: INDIAN PROPHET AND LIBERATOR

Give us a steady light, a level place,
a good light, a good place,
a good life and beginning.

■

Popol Vuh, *a Quiché Mayan book (Tedlock 1985, 170)*

The earthquake that destroyed the capital of Santiago in July 1773 was taken by many Mayans to be a sign of the return of their prophet, Martum. Just before the earthquake, Martín de Mayorga had become president of the audiencia, and the Mayans thought he was the embodiment of their prophet. Martum had promised to free them from tribute by destroying the Spaniards, and he clearly had done so at Santiago. Now, they thought, he would return the land to the way it had been before the conquest. The Mayans rose in rebellion, fleeing from their villages to the site of the new capital of Guatemala City, in order to support their new king, Martín. There were few battles in this uprising and only fleeting hope. The Indians were eventually persuaded to return to their villages.

After Miles L. Wortman 1982, 183

New forms of servitude evolved to replace slavery, the *encomienda*, and even the *repartimiento* labor drafts. Debt peonage was the most pernicious. Indians volunteered for jobs; the money was paid in advance for a set period of labor, and the Indians would work away from home for the designated period of time. Such labor helped them pay tribute and feed their families. But the Indians found they never could work enough to pay off the debt. Forced to buy food and other essential items at inflated prices from the company or hacienda store, their debts increased until their initial commitment became a lifelong job away from home. They died in debt and their children, under Spanish law, were themselves forced into labor. The number of Indians trapped in debt peonage increased throughout the remainder of the colonial period.

In regions where the Indian population had already declined precariously, the Indians found it impossible to retain their ethnic identity under debt peonage. Entire villages ceased to exist as Indians became serfs on haciendas along the coasts and on the valuable Pacific slopes where indigo plants could be grown. Not all Indians worked on haciendas against their will; some chose hacienda life in order to escape the tribute payments and *repartimiento* labor required of Indian villages. Away from their families and villages, the Indians of Nicaragua, El Salvador, and coastal Guatemala and Honduras, became assimilated into a Spanish-speaking peasant class. For all intents and purposes, they became ladinos.

Indians in the northern and western highlands of Guatemala, however, may have been helped by the 17th-century stagnant economy. Their lands were too high, too moist, and too cold for either indigo plants or most Spaniards. Therefore, Spaniards did not settle there, and fewer demands were made on their labor. Even most mendicant friars retreated to the monasteries in the cities. These Mayan Indians were among the few ethnic groups to survive in any number, and their numbers began increasing in the second half of the 17th century, despite sporadic epidemics. At the end of the colonial period, their cultural identity was very much intact.

African Slaves

The first slaves entered the Kingdom of Guatemala with the conquistadores; by 1821, when slavery was outlawed, tens of thousands of African slaves, both men and women, had been legally brought into the colony. At the peak of the trade, there were 30,000 living in the colony—perhaps more, as some slaves were smuggled into Central America, but not in immense numbers, since higher prices could be found at more prosperous American ports. Unlike Indians, black slaves were not royal subjects. Through most of the 17th century, there was no mandate that they even be instructed in the Christian faith. The Bourbons changed that in 1784, when Charles III began issuing a series of more enlightened regulations on the treatment of black slaves so that they might become "useful Christian citizens." No longer could their faces be branded, and their working and living conditions were regulated so as to be more humane.

Yet slavery remained legal. Slaves could be freed by their owners or they could purchase their own freedom. By contrast, the offspring of mulatto (not African) slaves were automatically free. And in a defiant

PUEBLO DE LOS ESCLAVOS

The village of Pueblo de los Esclavos ("town of slaves"), near the Honduran-Guatemalan border was probably founded by the colonial authorities, because no individual slave owners are indicated in the records. The census of 1821 recorded the age, gender, marital status, and occupation of the freed slaves then living in the pueblo. There were 395 women and 376 men ranging in age from five months to 100 years, and six were in their 80s and 90s. There were married couples, widows and widowers, and 69 single men and 47 single women. Seventy-five percent worked as farmers, 14 percent as servants, several were cowboys, and others were day laborers. There were the more fortunate as well: two landowners, two stewards, one sacristan, one carpenter, and a weaver.

After Oakah L. Jones, Jr. (1994, 115)

Spanish gesture toward the British, black slaves escaping from Belize were granted freedom, once they were baptized.

African slaves were a partial, if expensive, solution to the colony's chronic labor shortage. Miners and dye works owners, as well as monastic orders operating sugar mills, repeatedly petitioned for the right to purchase more slaves. But Spanish and creole officials lived in fear of increasing the number of slaves. There had been a number of slave revolts in the 16th century, and revolts had occurred at Honduran mines and in the city San Salvador, where 2,000 slaves had attempted an uprising. Along the Caribbean, they conspired with pirates. The fear of the growing number of runaways, and their *zambo* offspring born of intermarriage with Indians in the rural areas, was so great that in 1671 the kingdom officially refused to admit any more African slaves. Once the economy revived in the 18th century, however, slaves were again imported, but not in great numbers.

The Church and Culture

The Catholic Church introduced the Old World culture into the New. Over the centuries, its churches were constructed and, then, renovated into the European styles of renaissance, neo-classical and baroque art and architecture. Its choirs and organs exposed the populace to sacred music by the likes of Bach and Vivaldi. The latest fashions in art arrived quite late in this outpost far removed from European civilization, and they often took a provincial turn, whether the facade sculptures and cloister paintings were executed by European itinerant artists or Indian and ladino artisans trained from copybooks. Some artists, however, had more formal education abroad, such as the sculptors Quirio Cataño and Alonso de Paz.

Tribute and tithes initially paid for church construction. Indian *cofradías,* cults for Christian saints that Mayans fused with their traditional beliefs, paid more than adequately for the images of saints and the celebrations associated with them. In 1776 *cofradía* funds constituted a third of the total income of the church and exceeded the amount of tribute paid to the Crown. The bequests of other parishioners added to church embellishment.

Indian tribute, bequests, and *cofradía* funds left the religious orders well endowed. In New Spain, the church was rich enough to act as the primary banker for merchants and hacienda owners and it provided emergency support for the populace in times of need. The church owned prime real estate in every town and throughout the countryside, and what it did not own outright it often held in mortgage, as the church was the primary lender of the colony. There were 759 churches in the kingdom by 1700, and 60 percent of them were in Guatemala and El Salvador. Santiago de Guatemala alone boasted a cathedral, 24 churches, 8 hermitages, and 15 convents.

The stately Dominican convent was the wealthiest in the capital. Its revenues from holdings in Guatemala that were bequeathed to it included a water mill for grinding corn, a farm for breeding horses and mules, another for sugar, and even a silver mine. Thomas Gage, a guest at the convent, caustically observed that "those fat friars feast themselves, and have spare to build, and enrich their church and altars." By 1818, the church in the diocese of Guatemala owned and operated 914 haciendas and 910 sugar mills—only the church could afford the investment in equipment and slaves to run the mills.

Given the comforts of the towns, it is not surprising that so many clergy moved from the Indian settlements to nearby towns or cities. By 1750, 1,000 clergy resided in the capital, constituting 26 percent of the population of the city. While the capital had a surfeit of priests, most villages were fortunate to see even one in the course of a year. Those who stayed in rural areas did not necessarily devote themselves to the improvement of their charges: Father Ximénez of Chichicastenango complained that his fellow Dominicans were more interested in their haciendas than in preaching to the natives. Obviously Indians and others living

DON DIEGO VICENTE: A CHURCH DONOR

Diego Vicente (1595?–1675?), a revered cacique of the Quiché Mayan town of Momostenango, was the descendant of Izquín Nijaib, the provincial Quiché ruler who led troops against Pedro de Alvarado. Vicente prospered under Spanish rule, and owned his own haciendas on which grazed herds of cattle and sheep. Although he adopted Spanish privileges, such as riding a horse and wearing spurs and calling himself a "don," he never spoke Spanish and he made the traditional Mayan offerings at the village's ancestral shrines. He had the financial means to travel to Spain in order to legalize his inherited land holdings. On his successful return, he gave boxes of gold and silver in thanksgiving as well as a finely worked silver chalice to the church in Momostenango.

After Robert M. Carmack (1995, 105) and Barbara Tedlock (1992, 16)

DOÑA JUANA DE MALDONADO Y PAZ: A CHURCH DONOR

Like the male convents, nunneries were enriched by their patrons as well, particularly when daughters of the aristocracy joined a cloister and brought their dowries with them. Perhaps the wealthiest nun in the kingdom was the 20-year-old Doña Juana de Maldonado y Paz, daughter of a royal judge of the *audiencia*, who joined the Convento de la Concepción around 1632. Witty, well-educated, and an inspired musician and poet, she spent her years in the cloister in considerable comfort. She built new and spacious living quarters for herself and her six African maids. She had a private garden walk and a chapel hung with paintings imported from Rome, and the many rooms of her apartment were decorated with gilded furnishings as well as an organ, which she played to entertain the bishop. All her possessions became property of the convent upon her death.

After Thomas Gage (1958, 190)

in the country could be, and were, left unbaptized and unmarried—and illiterate. Archbishop Cortés y Larraz complained of the widespread witchcraft and sin of cohabitation that he observed in 1768. Fortunately, the Inquisition, which was instituted in Guatemala in 1572, had little impact in the colony—an average of two cases a year were reviewed during its 110 years—and not a single case concerned Indians, as they were exempt from its authority.

Church wealth and church control of cultural resources became a target of the Bourbon monarchs. The Crown expropriated property in order to generate greater benefits for itself, and, in keeping with its progressive ideas, encouraged secular education and cultural institutions. The Crown curtailed church construction, too, and appointed secular clergy where once the monastic orders had served, particularly in the Indian pueblos. These attempts to limit the power of the church would grow into anticlerical movements after independence.

Schools and Hospitals

The church was expected to educate the populace as well as instruct it in the faith. The Jesuits were most devoted to providing schooling, but the Bourbons expelled them from the colonies in 1767 as part of a political feud with the pope. The Dominicans sponsored the University of San Carlos, the only university in the colony, which granted degrees to an average of 15 students a year at the end of the 18th century. Most religious orders funded *colegios* to instruct young Spanish men in reading, writing, and religion—women were instructed in the arts of sewing and singing. Some orders also endowed orphanages with training programs for mestizos, and others taught Spanish and the catechism to some Indians. (Around 1770 it was estimated that 2,400 to 4,000 Indians, out of a population of 500,000, were in school in the province of Guatemala, and most of them learned only to recite prayers.)

The Bourbon kings ruled that all Indians should be taught how to read and write in Spanish. This honorable ideal was resisted by practically everyone: The Indians did not want their children to speak Spanish for fear they would be assimilated, the towns balked at paying the teachers, and the priests did not want to learn the native languages necessary for proper instruction. There were no secular schools in the Kingdom of Guatemala until the Bourbon reforms, but even then, the churches and priests provided most of the little education there was in the colony.

RAFAEL LANDÍVAR, CREOLE POET (1731-1793)

B orn in Santiago de Guatemala, Rafael Landívar was the most illustrious graduate of its Universidad Real y Pontificia de San Carlos. A Jesuit priest and educator, Landívar was one of the great poets of Spanish America, and perhaps the finest at capturing its landscape in words. In 1767, he was forced from his homeland when King Charles III expelled all Jesuits from the colonies in one of the many anticlerical Bourbon edicts. While living in Bologna, Italy, Landívar wrote his most famous work, *Rusticatio Mexicano*, a 10-canto poem written in Latin that extols the beauty of his Guatemalan birthplace.

> *Hail, my beloved homeland, my sweet Guatemala, hail*
> *delight and love of my life, my source and origin;*
> *How it pleases me, Nutricia, to remember your endowments,*
> *your sky, your fountains, your plazas, your churches, your homes!*
> *I still can conjure the profile of your leafy mountains*
> *and your verdant farmlands gifted with eternal spring . . .*

■

from Rusticatio Mexicano, *1782*
(translated from the Latin)

A number of priests continued the humanistic traditions of the earliest missionaries. Some chose to live in Indian villages and, in addition to providing religious instruction, attempted to protect the Indians from the worst abuses. Friar Diego Macotela was an exceptional priest. From his outpost in Costa Rica, he convinced the *audiencia* in 1690 to stop Costa Rica's kidnapping of Indians from the Talamanca wilderness for work on the cacao plantations. And in the 18th century, Archbishop Cortés y Larraz denounced the illegal exploitation of Guatemalan Indians by the Spaniards and ladinos who lived near them, and he criticized the Indian caciques in charge of them as well. But the most famous benefactor of the poor was Friar Pedro de José, who has been called the St. Francis of the Americas for the hospital he founded in the capital in the mid-17th century. His work inspired the founding of 17 hospitals and several *colegios* throughout the American colonies by the

Bethlehemite Order, the only male religious order originating in Spanish America. The friar was canonized in 2002, becoming the only Catholic saint associated with Central America.

The Spanish Legacy

The colony would undergo some transformation and improvement under the Bourbon kings, but its basic structure—and inherent flaws—had crystallized before their rule began in 1700. Geographically, the kingdom was barely settled; half the isthmus remained unexplored. Few roads or riverine passages had been developed to permit efficient transport along the length of the isthmus, leaving populated regions strangely isolated and resentful of one another. Colonial institutions were established, sometimes for the most humane and enlightened purposes, but nepotism and fraud too often undermined them.

Economically, ports were inadequately developed for commerce and not properly defended against pirates, mining technology was practically nonexistent, and agriculture was oppressively feudal in character. Spanish America encouraged European cattle and native American indigo to coexist and, at the same time, it created a populace that was increasingly racially mixed, despite a caste system that punished such mixing. An underclass was created—and it would endure.

6

THE BOURBONS
AND INDEPENDENCE
(1700–1823)

We possess fertile soil, and we lack profits. We are active and
industrious, and we live in poverty. We pay enormous taxes and
they tell us they are not enough . . . What is the enemy that
devours us?

■

El Editor Constitucional, August 6, 1821 (Bumgartner 1963, 139)

I n 1700 the Bourbons of France took over Spain's monarchy and ushered in the Enlightenment throughout the Spanish Americas. The
empire inherited by the Bourbon monarchs was bankrupted by war and
burdened by corruption and bureaucracy. After the death of the last
Habsburg king, Charles II, who was called "The Bewitched" (1665–
1700), the Bourbons installed several capable monarchs, including the
exceptionally effective Charles III (1759–88). Rationality replaced the
Inquisition; modernization improved the economy. Education and
health became governmental concerns. But the Bourbon reforms, however much they reaped greater wealth for Spain from its colonies,
stirred up deep resentment within the Kingdom of Guatemala and,
especially, in New Spain. The resentments, fanned by enlightened ideas
of self-governance and social equality that had been generated by the
American and French revolutions, led to a resurgence of Indian rebellions, merchant defiance, and creole and clergy complaints. Mexico rose
up in a long, destructive battle for its independence and, in 1821, the
Kingdom of Guatemala, as part of New Spain, found itself free of Spain
with barely a shot fired.

Bourbon Reforms

The Bourbon dynasty instituted a number of reforms to make the colonies more profitable. It sent well-trained and well-paid regional administrators, particularly adept at tax and tribute collection, and it streamlined the bureaucracy, reducing the number of local officials in New Spain by 60 percent, but at the same time giving more local control to the provinces of Honduras and Nicaragua and the new province of El Salvador. The Crown stimulated commerce by opening up new ports and permitting trade between the colonies, and it invested in the Honduran mines and encouraged the discovery of new ones. It improved the trans-isthmian trade routes to facilitate transport, and sent more fleets to the Bay of Honduras to protect it from smugglers.

Above all, the Crown expanded its tax base. Government monopolies were strengthened and new ones created, so that great profits could be reaped from items such as tobacco, alcohol, gunpowder, and even playing cards. Production was increased for many crops, including tobacco, which was planted for the first time in Costa Rica in the late

Cathedral in Guatemala City, the "new" capital of the Kingdom of Guatemala built by the Bourbons in 1773. (Photo courtesy INGUAT, Guatemala Trade Commission)

18th century. (The British had been growing it illegally in the Mosquito Coast area since 1761.) The Crown even attempted to create wage-based Indian labor by accepting only money, not goods, as tribute, and it ended the last vestiges of the *encomienda*. The reforms stimulated the economy and taxed the results. Production increased and, for the first time in the history of the Kingdom of Guatemala, sales taxes exceeded tribute in 1777.

Bourbon Defense

The Bourbons reestablished Spain's prestige as well as its prosperity. The monarchs invested considerable sums in protecting the colony from Indian rebels and securing the frontiers from smugglers and foreign poachers. Russian fur traders were contested in California, Apaches were confronted by an expanded militia in Arizona, and the Dutch were forced to operate more cautiously. After a Dutch attack on Trujillo in 1789, forts were built on the Bay of Honduras and at the mouths of important rivers. Settlers were drafted from Europe and other regions of the Americans in order to occupy critical but remote regions from California to the Mosquito Coast.

The Honduran port of Trujillo, in fact, provides an interesting case study of the times. The port had been sacked so frequently by pirates that it was temporarily abandoned in the 17th century. The Spanish, in order to secure the coast, encouraged new settlers in the region. By the late 18th century, the population nonetheless included slightly fewer than 1,000 mestizos and whites plus several hundred runaway French-speaking slaves from Caribbean islands and 40 English-speaking mulattoes. In 1777 under a Bourbon effort to colonize the Mosquito Coast, 1,300 Spanish settlers arrived from the Canary Islands and other parts of Spain. Most died from disease, starvation, and Miskito Indian attacks, but 500 survivors took refuge in Trujillo.

Added to this unusual mix of people in Trujillo were the Garífuna, or Black Caribs as they are also known for their African and Carib Indian ancestry. The Caribs had intermarried with shipwrecked African slaves in the 17th century, and they developed a relatively prosperous society on St. Vincent Island by trading cotton in the Caribbean. When the British tried to take over the island, war ensued—until the British decided to deport the Garífuna. In 1797 a colony of 1,700 Garífuna escaped to this Honduran port, where the Spanish welcomed them as valuable laborers and expert tropical farmers. In 1804 Ramón Anguiano, the governor of Comayagua, worried they might join the Miskito Indians and the British to make trouble for the Kingdom of Guatemala. Some did, and others worked for the British loggers in Belize. In fact, their numbers increased and their settlements spread along the Caribbean coast from Stann Creek (now Dangriga), Belize, to Nicaragua, where approximately 80,000 of their descendants continue to live today. Yet many were loyal to the Spanish and repeatedly fought for the Crown. Colonel Pedro Gregorío, a Black Carib, commanded an all-Garífuna garrison at the San Felipe fort on the Bay of Honduras in 1819, and others fought in militia units in both Guatemala and Honduras. They fought for the Crown even after independence was proclaimed in the colony.

Captain General Matías de Gálvez. (Photo courtesy Ministry of Education, El Salvador)

Bourbons and the British

Spain tried to defend its frontiers everywhere and against everyone and, in Central America, it succeeded—at least temporarily. In 1777 Spain doubled the size of its militia in the colony and sent more artillery. Under military leaders such as Captain General Matías de Gálvez, president of the *audiencia* from 1779 to 1783, the Kingdom of Guatemala was strong enough to dislodge the British from much of its territory, but success required repeated battles against smuggling bases on Roatán Island and the Mosquito Coast. In the Treaty of Paris in 1783, Britain agreed to give up its settlements in these areas in return for the logging concessions in Belize, yet Spain had to fight once again to remove the English and their slaves from settlements on the Mosquito Coast like Bluefields. For over a decade after Spain flexed its military might, Britain did not attempt to reoccupy these regions. Spain's accomplishment was marred, however, by Britain's successful

FRONTIER SETTLEMENTS

THE ENGLISH IN BELIZE

The English Settlers, with their Wives Children and Domesticks, live on St. George's Key, where there is an exceeding good Harbour . . . although this Key is the general place of residence of the Settlers, yet they have Plantations they visit occasionally, where they employ their Slaves in raising provisions cutting Logwood . . .

■

Letter to Governor Dalling, 1779 (Bolland 1977, 30)

St. George's Caye, Belize, was the preferred settlement of the British on the Central American coast. The first settlers, known as Baymen, were former pirates who found logging less dangerous than piracy. Of the 3,500 residents in the 18th-century colony, 3,000 were slaves. Although Spain had forced the British out of most of Central America and had, in fact, captured St. George's Caye in 1779, it granted them concessions in Belize. Yet the British never really pulled out of other areas on the Caribbean, and attempted to assert their control there almost into the 20th century. In 1798, with Spain and Britain once again at war, Spain attacked the settlement at St. George's Caye. Spain lost and never again attempted to forcibly remove the British from Belize. The British loggers, however, encountered new resistance in the late 18th century as the European demand for mahogany carried them inland on rivers that encroached on the retreats of the Mayans. For the next few decades, Mayan attacks on the logging camps were so ferocious that British troops were required to protect them. By 1820, the Mayans had retreated even more deeply into the rain forest. Disputes between loggers and Mayans would continue, however; In 1996 Malaysian loggers working in the Columbia River Forest Reserve sparked protests from the Mopan Mayans.

smuggling operations and the raids by its Miskito Indian allies on Costa Rican cacao plantations that continued well into the 19th century. Nonetheless Bourbon Spain had revived the colonial economies and gained greater control of its frontiers. Wars in Europe would soon undo much of what had been accomplished.

THE COSTA RICAN DIFFERENCE

*... the freedom of a man born in the mountains who has lived
independent of authorities and social obligations. . .*

■

Carlos Monge Alfaro (Edelman and Kenen 1989, 2)

Scarce Indian labor and its remote location, far from the power centers of the colony, kept the Meseta Central, the fertile highland valley of Costa Rica, and its capital, Cartago, impoverished. In 1720, in all of Costa Rica there were only 3,500 Spaniards and mestizos and fewer than 1,000 Indians, many of whom remained fiercely independent. The Spaniards were forced to work—even the governor had to farm his own land in order to feed his family. With so few Indians, the church presence was quite limited as well. Costa Rica became a society of laboring creole peasants. Although some of the cacao growers and royal officials formed a small elite class—albeit an impoverished one—the feudal class distinctions and elaborate church hierarchy so typical of the rest of Spanish America never became so entrenched in Costa Rica. Some 20th-century historians, such as Rodrigo Facio and Carlos Monge Alfaro, have argued that this colonial reality is the foundation of modern Costa Rica's democratic institutions—institutions notably absent in the history of other Central American nations. With Bourbon encouragement, the highland settlers planted tobacco in addition to wheat, and new Spanish and mestizo settlers arrived to farm the land. The region experienced a population boom, with a spillover to the new towns of Alajuela (founded in 1706) and San José (founded in 1736), where the Crown established an office for its tobacco monopoly. In Cartago there were fewer than 100 Spaniards for almost a century; by independence, the Meseta Central had more than 100 people per square mile. Yet the economy of the region remained so undeveloped that cacao was used as currency throughout the colonial period. And its continued remoteness meant news of independence did not reach Costa Rica until a month after it was declared.

Bourbon Backlash

The reforms initially succeeded in improving Spain's finances, but they took a toll on the colony. Creoles and ladinos became disgruntled; many were impoverished. Indians were provoked into rebellion, and a crisis was created in church relations as the Crown tried to curtail the church's power and wealth. When Spain regulated the consumption of liquor in 1756, riots broke out in Santiago de Guatemala. More riots followed in 1766 after taxes increased and the tobacco monopoly was established. The policies of the Crown encouraged exports, but did little to benefit the majority of citizens, who produced foods and goods for local markets. The improvements in infrastructure had not facilitated communication or trade among the various provinces.

Initially many elite merchants of the capital were adversely affected by the strong presence of the Spanish fleet, as it hindered smuggling, and they bristled at the new port taxes. They were somewhat mollified, however, by their official elevation into a *consulado,* or merchants' guild, with its own tribunal, founded in 1792 to resolve commercial conflicts. They also were granted some responsibility for improving commerce in the kingdom.

The guild merchants, mostly *peninsulares* but also some creoles, were among the wealthiest and most influential in the colony. Spain's empowerment of them through the *consulado* aggravated relations with the rest of the kingdom—and even with the more progressive creole merchants in the capital who wanted free trade. The guild merchants enriched themselves at the expense of the provincial creoles and ladinos; they improved roads, for example, but only along routes that favored their investments and exports through ports on the Bay of Honduras and with merchants in Spain. The merchants kept most of the indigo profits in their pockets, forcing into debt the small family farms, owned mostly by ladinos, that produced two-thirds of the total crop. The impoverished state of Honduran miners also was blamed, in part, on the fraud and excessive profit-taking of the merchant elite.

Increased taxes and more efficient collection affected both the colony, in draining it of capital, and its residents. Bourbon efficiency meant fewer public offices, and creoles sometimes found themselves displaced from the few appointments they had been permitted. The streamlined bureaucracy upset the corrupt practices that had benefited so many in the past. And it directly affected Indian villages, too, as tribute collection was taken from the native caciques and overly diligent officials tried to collect overdue payments for past tribute. The church bristled when the Crown ended its Indian tribute and both clergy and Indians bristled over the taxing of the *cofradia* funds, which constituted the Mayans' hard-earned money and one-third of church funds.

Mayan Uprisings

The [Mayans] do not want anything Spanish, neither religious doctrine, nor customs."

■

Archbishop Pedro Cortés y Larraz, 1770 report to the king
(Carlsen 1997, 71)

As the economy bustled, the demand for Indian lands and labor meant an increase in confrontations. The mendicant friars, having come to a peaceful accommodation with Indian ways, were replaced by the harsher scrutiny of the secular priests, who had less tolerance for native worship of sacred ancestral mountains and feast days full of drinking and traditional dances. Confrontations often ended in bloodshed. The Tzeltal Mayan Revolt in 1712, fomented by Spanish suppression of a native cult based on the Virgin Mary, was one of the fiercest Indian rebellions in the colonial period and lasted for two years. Not all rebellions were so violent and long-lasting, but they were frequent in the last years of the colony.

The Quiché Mayans of Momostenango repeatedly required the attention of *audiencia* officials and the militia alike. Described by Bishop Cortés y Larraz in 1770 as both pagan and bold, rebel Momostecans clashed with officials over everything from village governance and land to nude bathing practices. Nothing, however, provoked them more than tribute payments and religious meddling. When secular priests attempted to change their religious observances in 1785 by requiring attendance at mass and prohibiting traditional dances, the militia had to be called in to reestablish order; in 1803 a new priest provoked a similar situation and had to be removed. That very same year, the Mayan cacique refused to pay tribute, the tax on the silver chalice donated to the church by Diego Vicente especially rankled him (SEE page 114). The cacique was jailed and shackled for two months, but this did not stop a repeat the next year or in subsequent years even though 50 lashings were added to the punishment. When liberals in Spain argued for the abolition of tribute, independence issues fused with Momostenango's ongoing protest, and the entire village rose up in rebellion in 1810 and liberated the imprisoned Quiché cacique, Juan Vicente. The outbursts continued, and, in 1820, 600 men and women from Momostenango joined other villages in a nativistic uprising in the western Guatemalan highlands. They fought the Spanish militia—unsuccessfully, as it turned out—under the newly crowned King of the Quiché, Atanasio

JOSÉ DEL VALLE, CREOLE INTELLECTUAL

America shall not lag a century behind Europe: it will stride as an equal first, and lead later; it will, in the end, be the most illuminated by the sciences just as it is most illuminated by the sun . . .

■

José del Valle, El Amigo de la Patria, 1821 (Pérez Brignoli 1989, 64)

José Cecilio del Valle (1776–1834), an important member of the intelligentsia in the capital during the independence era and early republic, was born in the Choluteca ranching region of Honduras to wealthy creole parents. Valle's family moved to Guatemala City in 1789 so that he could receive a university education. At the University of San Carlos, his professors included some of the most enlightened thinkers of the age, such as Friar José Liendo y Goicoechea, a Costa Rican creole who applied scientific reasoning to the economic and social problems of Central America. In an age that valued science and the study of politics, Valle graduated with a degree in physics and then took another in law in order to pursue a career in government. He wrote articles on science, education, and democracy for the liberal newspaper *Gazeta de*

Tzul of Totonicapán. At a time when most of the colony only discussed resistance to the Crown, Quiché Mayans challenged its authority and continued to do so until independence.

Growing Discontent

. . . already the springs fill the rivers to overflowing, already people enliven the streets already a fertile and anxious peace settles on my country . . .

■

Rafael Landívar, 1781 (translated from Rusticatio Mexicana)

The seeds of revolt grew at the end of the 18th century. Newspapers, such as the weekly *Gazeta de Guatemala* (published from 1793 to

Guatemala, and had some influence on the intelligentsia regarding free trade, free expression, and democratic principles. As a creole, long treated as a second-class citizen in the Spanish kingdom, he took particular pride in the uniquely American character of his birthplace, its natural beauty and pre-Hispanic civilization. Yet Valle, like many creoles in the bureaucracy, remained loyal to the Crown; he was even secretary to the despised and autocratic José de Bustamante, conservative president of the *audiencia* from 1811–18, and in that capacity, he censored the *Gazeta de Guatemala* for the government. Although the foremost spokesman for the conservatives, in 1820 Valle began arguing for independence in his newspaper,

José Cecilio del Valle. (After portrait c. 1825, anonymous, in the Museo de Costa Rica)

El Amigo de la Patria, and drafted Central America's declaration of independence in 1821. Throughout the early decades of independence, he was one of the new nation's foremost statesmen. In 1834, he was elected president of the Federation of Central America, but died before the votes could be tallied.

1816), spread the ideas of Voltaire and Rousseau among the intelligentsia, and Enlightenment institutions, such as the Sociedad Económica de Amigos del País (chartered in 1794), became meeting places to discuss free trade and limits on the monarchy. Faculty and graduates of the University of San Carlos agitated for a curriculum that included the scientific study of politics and the economy. Creoles also were becoming increasingly proud of their American identity: Poets like Rafael Landívar lovingly described the beauty of the land, and intellectuals wrote histories of the region. The creole aristocracy in the capital, having benefited greatly from Spanish rule, nonetheless wanted reforms that would treat them as equals with the *peninsulares.* Yet their appeal in 1808 for a creole to be appointed as the archbishop in Guatemala City fell on deaf ears. The colony was restless, but among the most influential creoles, there was no consensus for independence.

The economy contributed to the growing dissatisfaction with Spain. After the French Revolution, Spain became involved in the nearly continuous Napoleonic Wars. Unable at times to send its own ships, it permitted the colonies to trade with foreign but neutral powers, especially the newly independent United States. Central America found a number of new export partners from Boston and Philadelphia as well as its former smuggling partner, but now Spanish ally, Britain. This trade in indigo, silver, and cacao was not easy for the colony to relinquish in 1800, when Spain rescinded its permission. Nor did the colonies easily accept the "patriotic loans" forced on their treasuries to pay for European wars.

To compound the discontent, another economic depression settled in during the early 19th century. The market for indigo collapsed, and official exports fell from 1 million pesos in 1810 to half that amount in 1820. Merchants foreclosed on the small farmers indebted to them; cattle ranches, too, were lost. At the same time, an expanding population—reaching more than 1 million by 1825—created land conflicts among all groups, including Indian versus Indian. Crop failures and an overcommitment of land to indigo resulted in widespread food shortages. Many provincials came to believe that the interests of the colony and Spain no longer coincided.

Spain in Turmoil

From 1808 to 1821 Spain did little to improve the economic situation in the colony. Napoléon invaded Spain and forced the abdication of the Bourbon king, Ferdinand VII, in 1808. With Ferdinand exiled, Napoléon installed his brother, Joseph Bonaparte, on the Spanish throne in Madrid. The Spaniards, not about to be ruled by a usurper, established a junta to govern in Ferdinand's absence and declared war on France. The colonies, still ruled by Bourbon appointments, swore their allegiance to the junta. In Guatemala City General Antonio González, president of the *audiencia* from 1804 to 1810, decided the tumultuous situation called for an unusual open meeting of concerned parties. He invited all the power brokers in the kingdom: the judges of the *audiencia* were joined by the city councilors, the archbishop and members of the ecclesiastical council as well as representatives from some of the convents, the rector of the University of San Carlos, captains of the militia, and directors of the merchant guild. Together they voted to support the junta.

The governing junta turned out to be far more liberal than the Bourbon monarch and his colonial administrators had been. It recommended—persuaded, perhaps, by demands for independence in Mexico and other colonies—that the Americas should be represented in the government, although not proportionately (the Indian population was not included in the calculation), and no longer exploited as colonies. Dr. Antonio de Larrazábal, a professor at the University of San Carlos, was one of the few delegates selected to represent the Kingdom of Guatemala in the constitutional congress in Cádiz, Spain. He departed Guatemala on November 23, 1810, but given the nature of colonial transportation, he didn't arrive until August 17, 1811, after many of the deliberations had been concluded. In March 1812 a constitution was promulgated that established free trade, limits on the church, and a constitutional monarchy that shared power with a representative parliament.

The Constitution of 1812 incorporated some of the noblest principles of the Enlightenment, but Ferdinand VII believed in the absolute power of the monarchy, as did his more conservative followers in the colonies. When Ferdinand was restored to the throne in 1814, he immediately repealed the Constitution of 1812. The liberals, however, had grown accustomed to a more representative government. Internal strife culminated in a revolt that forced the king to accept the constitution in 1820.

In the Kingdom of Guatemala these same conservative and liberal ideologies divided the ruling class, pitting the royal bureaucracy against locally elected city councils, the protectionist merchant guild against the free-trade indigo growers, and the *peninsulares* and church against newly wealthy creoles and provincial elites. These conflicting ideologies would define two opposing political parties, fuel civil war, and eventually destroy the independent republic.

Independence

In Mexico and South America the liberals fought for their independence from Spain; war swept the continents in 1810, as mestizos and Indians joined battle against the royalist forces that had so long oppressed them. Under Simón Bolívar, Colombia (including Panama) defeated Spain in 1819. Mexico gained its independence in February of 1821. In the kingdom, independence was most on the mind of provincial groups; El Salvador bristled under the arrogance of the *peninsulares* in the nearby capital, and Nicaragua and Honduras witnessed protests too. Rebellions flared on occasion but lacked widespread support and so were easily suppressed, such as one led by a priest, José Matías

Delgado, and his nephew, Manuel José Arce (who would become the first president of an independent Central America) that was quickly put down in San Salvador in 1811.

Surrounded by wars for independence, the Kingdom of Guatemala remained relatively quiet during the crisis years of 1808 to 1821. One reason may have been the provincial character of most of the territory, and the isolation of the towns and provinces from each other. Another reason independence did not sweep the kingdom was José Bustamante y Guerra. President of the *audiencia* (1811–18) under the 1812 constitution, Bustamante was doggedly conservative. He believed liberals were decadent and needed to be firmly controlled by *hierro y fuego*, as he said, or "iron and fire." This uncompromising monarchist was joined by an equally conservative archbishop, Ramón Casaus Torres y Plazas, who thought liberal priests were heretics.

Bustamante used iron control to prevent any agitation against Spain. Aristocratic creoles who had supported the Constitution of 1812— quite legally, of course—found themselves stripped of their usual privileges; some were removed from office and jailed. A special police force "prevented" crimes against the public order; meetings in private homes were broken up, and the militia was sent to the border with Mexico to block any spillage of revolutionaries into the colony. The liberals in Spain mandated a free press and free trade, but just as Bustamante ignored many of the constitutional provisions, he censored the *Gazeta de Guatemala* and interfered with foreign trade, which he equated with smuggling.

His firm hand stirred resentments and united natural enemies against him. Everyone from the noble Aycinenas to more radical creoles attempted to remove him from office. A coup was planned for Christmas Day, 1813; Bustamante learned of it, however, and arrested the conspirators. San Salvador then attempted a revolt. Once Ferdinand was reinstalled, Bustamante executed many of the rebels, both priests and members of the lesser nobility. But the creoles eventually won: Despite Bustamante's unswerving support of the absolute monarchy, he was removed by Ferdinand VII.

End of Spanish Colony

America has a hemisphere to itself.

■

Thomas Jefferson, 1813 (Whitaker 1954, 29)

By the time of Bustamante's replacement in 1818, independence could no longer be forestalled. The Spanish bureaucracy was in disarray. The conservative Ferdinand VII inflamed the liberals. The 1820 reaffirmation of the Constitution of 1812 disgusted conservatives, who preferred what they saw as the grand traditions of the absolute monarchy. Although the liberals wanted independence and free trade, the conservatives wished for gradual autonomy and trade protections. In addition, there was a growing fear of a people's revolt, like those already realized in some of the Quiché villages. By 1821 the elites, despite their differences, thought independence—and subsequent elections—would give them the relief they sought.

Late in the summer of 1821 Mexican troops appeared on the Guatemalan border, demanding that the kingdom, as part of New Spain, join independent Mexico. Any remaining Central American hesitation over independence vanished. Without the slightest resistance by either the settlers or Spanish officials, the Kingdom of Guatemala declared its independence from Spain.

> . . . independence from the Spanish government is the general voluntary will of the people of the [Kingdom of] Guatemala
>
> ■
>
> *Act of Independence, September 15, 1821*

7

THE FEDERATION
OF CENTRAL AMERICA
(1823-1839)

*This magnificent location [Central America] between two great
oceans could in time become the emporium of the world. Its
canals will shorten the distances throughout the world,
strengthen commercial ties with Europe, America, and Asia, and
bring that happy region tribute from the four corners of the
globe. Perhaps some day the capital of the world may be
located there, just as Constantine claimed Byzantium was the
capital of the ancient world.*

■

Simón Bolívar, 1815 (Haggerty 1990, 7)

*But to reach ... the pinnacle of power, it will be necessary to
climb rugged heights.*

■

José del Valle, 1821 (Pérez-Brignoli 1989, 67)

Independence arrived before the Central American provinces had
determined the shape of their future, but they optimistically discussed the many political options at hand. The lack of a sustained
struggle for independence, however, seemed to deprive the isthmus of
a national identity or sense of solidarity. At first it remained part of the
new empire of Mexico, just as it had been part of New Spain. Then, its
provinces united into a federation of states, but the provincial frictions
and political imbalances created during the three centuries of the
Kingdom of Guatemala proved impossible to overcome. Each phase of
this early period of independence was fraught with conflict. Provincial

and ideological differences materialized in the shape of armies, and ideals were achieved only through the bloodshed of opponents. The federation disintegrated, but not the ideal of a united isthmus.

Annexation to Mexico

My object is only to manifest to you that the present interest of Mexico and Guatemala is so identical or indivisible that they cannot constitute themselves in separate or independent nations without risking the security of each ...

■

Emperor Agustín Iturbide, November 27, 1821
(Bumgartner 1963, 163)

The new Central American nation was independent of Spain—but not of Mexico. Mexico, in its declaration of independence, had annexed all the provinces of New Spain within its newly formed empire. Central America understood the threat behind Mexico's request that it proclaim itself part of the empire. Without the resources to offer resistance, Central America accepted its neighbors' troops in Guatemala City under the authority of a Mexican governor, Brigadier General Vicente Filísola. The Central Americans, fortunately, benefited from many provisions in the new Mexican constitution, including the abolition of all slavery and tribute and the establishment of free trade.

Central America was not of a single mind in regard to Mexican annexation, although many interest groups and regions found it an attractive option. Most town councils favored it and elected deputies to represent them in the Mexican congress; the respected José del Valle was the most illustrious of the deputies. Many conservatives favored annexation, because they thought it would preserve their privileges just as they had been under Spain—only the crown now was worn by a creole. Many believed that Mexico's homegrown emperor, Agustín Iturbide, would provide the central authority necessary to avoid the provincial conflicts that threatened to divide the isthmus. Others hoped that Mexico's wealth would help to strengthen the Central American economy.

The issue failed to touch the vast majority of Indians and rural poor. Yet some groups in the western highlands, such as the Quichés of Momostenango, actively supported annexation and were loyal to Filísola, who permitted the rebel Mayans to control local affairs. Costa Rica proclaimed its neutrality on the matter. A few important cities,

Tegucigalpa and Granada among them, and the most ardent liberals, such as Pedro Molina of Guatemala and Miguel José Arce of El Salvador, opposed annexation. San Salvador, daring to declare its intention of attaching itself to the United States rather than to Mexico, was quickly occupied by the Mexican army in San Salvador to quell any chance of insurrection.

Filísola successfully annexed El Salvador in 1823, but Mexico was in no position to sustain the fight for Central America and could not even pay the troops stationed in Guatemala City, much less force compliance in Granada or faraway Costa Rica. Iturbide proved more of a buffoon than a monarch. Soon after the Salvadoran uprising, the emperor was deposed. Not knowing what else to do, Governor Filísola convened a Central American congress that was mandated by the Mexican constitution. On July 1, 1823, the congress convened and immediately declared its independence from Mexico. Chiapas, the only province to dissent, remained part of Mexico. To get rid of the unpaid Mexican troops in the capital, however, the residents of Guatemala City had to raise thousands of pesos to pay for their trip north.

The Federation Created

Once independent, Central America was confronted with true independence—and the tug of disparate interests. With no king and an empty treasury, the former colony faced the choice between unity and division into five autonomous states: Guatemala, El Salvador, Honduras, Nicaragua, and Costa Rica. (Belize theoretically remained part of Guatemala even though the British occupied its coastal regions; Panama was part of Colombia.)

Filísola's congress, transforming itself into a constitutional assembly, optimistically declared the new sovereign nation of the United Provinces of Central America under the banner of God, Unity, and Liberty. This vote reflected the hopefulness and experimentation that marked the first years of the republic. Full of the idealism of the Enlightenment, the Central Americans engaged in lively debates about the best direction for the future. Most recognized that the individual provinces were too small and too weak economically to survive as sovereign states, so the fractious liberals and conservatives seriously negotiated with one another to avert such a fragmentation of the isthmus. Despite the Conservative Party majority in the assembly (46 to 13 Liberals), a liberal constitution was agreed upon on November 22, 1824, based on the federal principles of the United States of America.

And to put some money in the treasury, a five-million-peso loan was negotiated with a bank in London.

One problem confronting a unified government was the distrust the provinces had for the vested interests in Guatemala City. This was such a persistent issue that the federal capital was eventually relocated to San Salvador. A further serious obstacle to representational government was the imbalance in population and physical size of the member states. Guatemala, already despised for its concentration of power, accounted for 40 percent of the population. When the federal congress convened in 1825, the number of delegates for each province reflected the problem: 18 for Guatemala, 9 for El Salvador, 6 each for Honduras and Nicaragua, and 2 for Costa Rica. The Senate, with two members from each state, equalized matters, but the preponderance of Guatemalans in the legislature remained a problem in the view of the more provincial areas.

Boundaries between states were redrawn, and in some instances the changes were peacefully accomplished. Guatemala gave Sonsonate, part of its fertile Pacific coast, to El Salvador, and contemplated carving a

Population of United Provinces of Central America				
	Federation[*]	Guatemala	Nicaragua	Costa Rica	Guatemala City
Indian	836,869	358,484	20,814	7,800	n/a
Ladino	399,122	n/a	146,339	n/a	n/a
Spanish/creole	51,500	n/a	6,960	n/a	n/a
TOTAL	1,287,491	512,120	174,213[**]	60,000[***]	23,334[****]

[*] Population statistics vary for the period. As the observer E. G. Squier said, "The statistics bearing on the subject are imperfect or wholly wanting" (1855, 52). The 1825 population total for the federation is based on a census, as is the size of the Guatemalan population. Most historians agree on the relative size of the various ethnic groups, and most believe the population became less dominated by whites as the 19th century progressed, except in Costa Rica, where the creole population always predominated. Nicaragua had the highest percentage of ladinos (84 percent) in 1823; Salvador, also with a high percentage, had 54 percent. As of the mid-19th century, more than half of the Honduran population was Indian. Mestizos dominated urban populations; most Indians lived in rural areas. Guatemala's Indian population remains a near majority even today.
[**] 1823 total based on Sarabia (Squier 1855); estimates as to ethnic distribution.
[***] 1823 estimate (Torres Rivas) based on delegate distribution; it was the smallest province of the federation; the percentage of Indians is based on an 1836 report (Torres Rivas), which indicated that most lived dispersed in the jungle.
[****] 1825 census.

sixth state called Los Altos out of its western highlands (SEE map below). Los Altos would have had Quetzaltenango, the second largest town in Guatemala, as its capital, and thus a population of more than 200,000, greater than any state other than Guatemala. The final decision to create Los Altos, however, was delayed from fear this Quiché region might secede (which it did anyway, but only for a brief period, 1838 to 1839). Costa Rica officially separated from Nicaragua and annexed Nicaragua's region of Guanacaste, including the Nicoya

The Central American federation lost Chiapas to Mexico, and its interior borders shifted to carve out El Salvador and Costa Rica and, briefly, an entirely new state, Los Altos, from the larger states of Guatemala and Nicaragua. With half the isthmus remaining unexplored at the time of independence, the federation's effort to delineate boundaries for the member states (boundaries which would not be fully adjudicated until the 21st century) involved considerable guesswork. As E. G. Squire, a 19th-century North American traveler, observed: " . . . the early maps of [Central America] . . . can only be characterized as geographically absurd . . . the interior geography has remained as obscure as it was a hundred years ago." (1855: viii)

Peninsula. Other state borders, however, were disputed well into the 20th century, especially in the areas of British interests, such as the Mosquitía and Belize. Part of the problem was not simply territorial, but also ignorance about the geography of the isthmus. Although demarcations between the member states were not all resolved and the imbalances were barely corrected, the federation proved that important compromises could be made, just as they were in the drafting of the constitution.

States vs. Federation

> ... the ignorance of the people, the local rivalries, and the lack of public funds . . . provide obtacles for the Superior Government ...
>
> ■
>
> Juan Lindo Zelaya, congressional deputy 1824
> (Bumgartner 1963, 211)

While the constitutional assembly was attempting to shape the future of Central America, more provincial interests continued to fester. Except in Costa Rica, long-held antagonisms between elite families and neighboring townships rose to the surface and the contenders vied with one another for power under the new government. Comayagua, the capital, and Tegucigalpa, the bustling economic center, fought for control of Honduras; the fighting did not cease until they agreed to alternate the capital between them every other year. León, a liberal Nicaraguan city and home to the second university in Central America, bitterly fought Granada, the aristocratic economic stronghold. In Guatemala, the expanding center of the western highlands, the conservative interests in Quetzaltenango undermined liberal ones in Guatemala City. Everywhere turf battles as old as the early struggles among conquistadores were fueled by the lack of an established central authority.

The weakness of the national government was starkly revealed in Nicaragua when war broke out between León and Granada, a conflict that would not truly be resolved until a neutral capital was created at Managua in 1857. The federal government wished to send a negotiator, but El Salvador wanted to send in its own troops in clear defiance of the constitution. El Salvador acted unilaterally and, unfortunately for the federal government, successfully brought about a temporary peace in January 1825.

PATRIOTISM AND MAYAN RUINS 1834

. . . the history of the state shall be ennobled with the descriptions of the monuments and antiquities.

■

Federal Decree, 1834 (Chinchilla 1998, 380)

. . . we followed our guide, who . . . conducted us through the thick forest . . . to monuments . . . in workmanship equal to the finest monuments of the Egyptians. . . . The only sounds that disturbed the quiet of this buried city [Copán] were the noises of monkeys moving among the tops of the trees . . .

■

John Lloyd Stephens, 1839 (1:103)

While the federation struggled to unify the isthmus, Guatemala undertook to embellish its identity. The liberal head of state, Mariano Gálvez, commissioned historians to write about the former colony, and he also underwrote some of the earliest archaeological expeditions in the Americas. Believing the pre-Columbian heritage of Guatemala would give it an ancient and admirable past comparable to those of European nations, he paid for the exploration the Mayan sites of Utatlán and Iximche by Miguel Rivera Maestre in 1834. At the same time, Colonel Juan Galindo was sent to explore Copán. When Galindo published his account in a Paris journal and John Lloyd Stephens published his travel journals about the marvelous Mayan ruins, the international recognition brought to pre-Columbian civilization reinforced local patriotism. The respect for preconquest civilization did not usually translate into respect for the living Mayans. As Stephens observed, the

Taxation, too, was an ongoing problem. The national congress would not grant the government enough authority to function without fiscal reliance on the states. The tobacco monopoly, for example, was given to each province to administer on the condition that a percentage of the revenues would be paid to the federal government; most states neglected to comply. Deeply suspicious of the central authority, the

Vista of a fortress at Utatlán. (Lithograph by Julián Falla after a field drawing of Rivera y Maestre, 1834)

situation of the Mayans had so declined that some doubted they could have been the builders of such monumental cities as Copán. The liberal constitution, however, did grant the Indians equal status as citizens with creoles and mestizos. The expropriation of Mayan heritage by creole politicians marked a historic moment when the shaping of a new nation's identity was critical. No further archaeological investigations would be funded by the state until the 20th century.

After Oswaldo Chinchilla Mazariegos (1998)

states seemed willing to bankrupt it. And it became transparently clear that most congressional deputies held the narrow interests of their home states, not those of the republic, dear.

The congress also maneuvered to control the first presidential election. By promoting numerous candidates, it hoped to take a majority away from the certain victory for statesman José del Valle. With the election then given to congress to resolve, the conservative deputies planned to choose the candidate they could most easily control. Valle won a popular majority nonetheless, but the congress disqualified the vote on a questionable technicality. The congressional choice was Manuel José Arce, a supposed liberal from El Salvador, who garnered more votes from the conservatives than did their conservative colleague Valle. The first election of the United Provinces of Central America defied the popular will, and the first president of Central America was compromised before he was even sworn into office. The republic was in the hands of the deputies and local interests, and the federation was beginning to look more like a loose confederation of small independent nations than a single republic.

Civil War 1827–1829

Law. Law. That is what saves nations from the most imminent dangers.

■

José del Valle, 1826 (Bumgartner 1963, 256)

Petty feuds and regional rivalries soon dominated Central American affairs. Arce was no sooner installed by the conservatives as the first president of the federation than new elections resulted in the liberals taking control of congress. Party ideology had little to do with the conflicts that ensued, however. Instead of attending to the important matters confronting Central America, each faction—the deputies, the president, the states, and the church—tested the limits of its power. The deputies issued counterorders to the military commander, undermining the presidency. Guatemala intervened in the affairs of the federal government on the pretext that state laws took precedence over federal laws, and President Arce responded by trying to move the capital to San Salvador. The bishop of Honduras allegedly organized an assassination attempt on Dionisio Herrera, the governor of that province. The lieutenant governor of Guatemala was killed in a mob uprising in Quetzaltenango organized by the church and conservatives.

Conflicts between Guatemala and the other provinces, between central and provincial authorities, and between the church and state would afflict Central America in the decades to come. The rule of law and order was lost in the struggle for power, as the factions refused to respect the constitutional authority granted to the various branches and levels of government. Civil war was the result.

142

Honduras and El Salvador conspired to remove Arce as the federal president. Arce sent troops to Honduras to arrest Herrera in March 1827; in retaliation, Salvadoran troops marched on the federal capital. The civil war was under way. It would spill over into Nicaragua, but leave Costa Rica untouched. Costa Rica offered to negotiate a peace, but

General Francisco Morazán (1792–1842). Morazán was born in Honduras to a landed creole family that made its money in mining. He worked in a law office as a clerk, and then, after independence, joined the army of Tegucigalpa. He quickly worked his way through the ranks until the liberal governor Herrera appointed him secretary general of Honduras. He fought to keep the federation alive from 1829 until his death in 1842. When conservative forces dismantled the federation in 1837, he fought to keep it together even though El Salvador was the only remaining member state. He was defeated in 1840 and forced to live in exile. Yet he returned to Costa Rica to restore the federation, but faced a firing squad instead and died in San José in 1842. His liberal principles were by then so despised by the conservatives that they would not permit his burial in Central America. (Portrait courtesy Ministry of Education, El Salvador)

the extreme conservatives, financed by the church, refused. The fighting continued.

In April 1829, Guatemala City, the last conservative stronghold, fell to the liberal army of Francisco Morazán. The conservatives had forced a military solution on the liberals and they would pay the price for their recalcitrance. Morazán had the leaders arrested and sentenced to death as traitors. A general amnesty was declared that substituted exile for execution. The church, too, suffered for its active support of the conservatives, the archbishop and 40 Guatemalan priests were exiled and legislation confiscating church properties was quickly passed. The possibility of reconciliation was lost in the drive for retribution.

Liberal Victory

> How can one govern without taxes, without strength, without authority?
>
> ∎
>
> *José del Valle, 1833 (Bumgartner 1963, 264)*

The liberals won the civil war and, in 1829, congress reconvened and scheduled a presidential election for the end of the year. This presidential election, however, would be between two of the most popular politicians in Central America, both of them Hondurans: José del Valle, the conservative statesman, and Francisco Morazán, the triumphant liberal general. Fresh from his battlefield victories, Morazán won.

The liberals had an ambitious program—too ambitious, thought many conservatives, for a country that was so poorly developed and whose population was overwhelmingly illiterate. And for a nation without any money in its coffers, liberal hopes for mass education and economic development were very ambitious indeed. The liberals were undaunted, however, and they even promoted a new legal code in Guatemala that provided for such foreign procedures as trial by jury—in a state where half the population spoke Mayan languages, not the Spanish of the judicial system. Nowhere were these progressive ideals implemented more diligently than in Guatemala under the governorship of Mariano Gálvez (1831–38).

Gálvez did much to stimulate Guatemala's economy, including improving the roads and developing exports, such as textiles, indigo, and cochineal, another indigenous dye. He diverted commerce from the poor ports on the Honduran coast to the British-built port at Belize City and, thinking Spanish colonialism had hampered Guatemala, he encouraged investments from the more capitalistic English-speaking world. He also invited foreign colonization projects into his country as another way of modernizing the economy; public lands were devoted to such projects, including one for a "New Liverpool" settlement in the Verapaz region, where, two centuries before, Bartolomé de las Casas had hoped to create a Mayan utopian community. Within two years, from 1834 to 1836, Gálvez doubled the volume of trade. For a few years, Guatemala progressed, but the lack of capital and increasing government debts hampered further improvements.

Gálvez also ardently pursued one of the most divisive items on the liberal agenda: the separation of church and state. He expropriated church properties and implemented other anticlerical laws, such as the secularization of education—the University of San Carlos became the Guatemalan Academy of Sciences—and the creation of civil registers for births, marriages, and deaths, all areas that the church had formerly controlled. The church resisted the changes, and the government retaliated by exiling any priest who used the power of the pulpit to defy its orders.

Not content with taking on a rich and powerful church in a devoutly Catholic country, the Guatemalan liberals also tried to disband the old merchant guilds in order to create freer trade and more commercial opportunities. And they idealistically thought the Indians would be grateful for equal citizenship and the westernization of their culture; instead, the liberals were seen as interfering in the affairs of the most traditional Mayan villages by ending the special laws that had governed them for three centuries. In truth, the liberal policies that replaced Spanish law permitted a handful of mestizos and creoles to intervene in new ways in Indian affairs and even to buy their communal lands. On top of this, the federal government instituted a head tax that struck the Indians as the same old Spanish tribute they thought independence had eliminated. These liberal policies guaranteed the alliance of Indian groups, such as the Quiché Mayans in the Guatemalan highlands, with the conservatives.

Liberal vs. Conservative

Although most states were not as aggressively liberal as Guatemala, their agenda nonetheless offended conservatives who preferred emperors to elected presidents and church to secular control of education and morality. The conservatives also wanted the old protectionist laws for their commerce and thought that the colonial paternalistic policies toward Indians fit with the natural social order by keeping them subservient. The former Spanish colony was viewed as superior to the progressive policies represented by Protestants in the United States and Britain—in fact, many Central Americans developed a xenophobic dislike of the non-Spanish foreigners who lived in increasing numbers in their land, encouraged by the liberals.

Except in Costa Rica, where Governor Juan Mora Fernández (1829–33) practiced a more consensus-based form of government, the liberals nearly always managed to stir up the the most powerful groups: the wealthy creole merchants and the church. These conservative forces convinced the Indians, the most populous group, that an alliance would protect their traditional, separate societies. The three groups—in combination with mestizo peasants—would eventually combine to unleash forces that would undermine the government and usher in nearly half a century of conservative and dictatorial rule.

The union was threatened by conservative forces from within and without. The conservative leaders did not accept their exile quietly after the civil war. Arce attempted to invade from Mexico, but was defeated. Even Spain threatened the peninsula, and in 1832 pro-Spanish forces attempted to hold one of the forts on the Bay of Honduras. Not to be outdone by the politicians, nature matched the violence afflicting the republic: In 1830, the worst earthquake since the destruction of Antigua rocked Guatemala and two others damaged San Salvador in 1831, causing its residents to flee. In 1835, Volcán Cosiguina, in Nicaragua, exploded with such violence it was heard 800 miles away in Jamaica. The eruption, the largest in Central American history, changed the course of rivers, caused earthquakes throughout the isthmus, and spewed ash as far away as Colombia and Mexico.

Like the constant rumblings of earthquakes, the state governments shifted back and forth between conservative and liberal control, and conservative changes brought periodic surges for greater state autonomy. Costa Rica was the first to secede from the federation; it retained its independence for almost a year before yielding to the federation in May 1830. El Salvador, always leaning toward independence, attempted to secede in 1832, and the federal army quickly intervened. The relocation of the capital to San Salvador further integrated that recalcitrant state into the federation. Honduras, too, had to be subdued. And in 1833, an Indian uprising in central El Salvador, caused by dissatisfaction with liberal polices and forced army conscription, terrified the creoles. Anastasio Aquino, a laborer on an indigo hacienda, successfully led several thousand rebels against Salvadoran troops. His victory was brief; the Salvadoran army regained control the next day with the help of Morazán. Aquino was executed, but Indian rebellions continued to disrupt the region until the end of the federation.

Given such tumult, General Morazán may have been the best possible president for Central America at the time. But he also was a radical liberal and incapable of promoting the compromise necessary for peace with the conservatives. Instead he used military force to fill the political vacuum caused by the lack of a generally accepted central authority. José del Valle was a voice of moderation that may have united the less extreme factions, but history would never have a chance to render the final verdict on his performance. Valle died on the eve of his election to the presidency in 1834; Morazán, placing second in the vote, automatically took Valle's place. Although Morazán was able to maintain the peace for a number of years, the federation disintegrated in 1838 just before the end of his term. Federal reforms that would have improved the commercial infrastructure and the educational system never were implemented. Before the federation ever really had a chance to gain a firm foothold, it was destroyed.

Upheaval 1837–1840

. . . masses . . . threaten the honor of the families, property, civilization and all that is sacred and worthy in society.

■

*Guatemalan citizens' petition to President Morazán, 1838
(Woodward 1993, 86)*

The federation had financed its armies and policies by forced loans on the church and wealthy aristocrats. When these occasional levies proved inadequate in 1836, new taxes were implemented that affected not just the elite, but also the middle class and poor masses. Mestizos and artisans were taxed directly. A land tax affected creole and ladino alike. The Indians already were angry about what they considered a demand for tribute. Political dissatisfaction and unrest were widespread—even the liberals disliked the taxes.

In 1837, a cholera epidemic broke out in the Guatemalan highlands. Gálvez sent medicine to the villages to treat the water, and the priests told the Mayan and ladino peasants that the government had poisoned the wells. The unrest turned into uprisings in at least 30 Indian villages, and the revolts spread to other provinces in the federation from the Mexican border to Costa Rica. The church fanned the hysteria caused by disease, and a battle cry of *"Viva Religion"* (Long Live Religion), "Death to the Heretics," and "Death to Foreigners" resounded in liberal ears.

The most vitriolic backlash to the liberals occurred in Guatemala. Guatemala City was taken over and looted by a mob of armed peasants. Mariano Gálvez was forced to resign—due to "public opinion," as the state legislature phrased it. To appease the insurgent peasants, anticlerical laws were repealed, government support of the church was reinstated, and policies favoring foreigners were suspended. Adding to the chaos, various regions, among them Los Altos, seceded from Guatemalan authority, so most of the state was either at war or claiming independence.

The liberals had controlled previous outbreaks, but instead of taking concerted action against the spreading insurrection, they fell to squabbling among themselves. The most radical liberals in Guatemala, for example, attempted to ally themselves with the rebels. And for the first time, the conservatives found a charismatic leader to fight for their causes: Rafael Carrera.

Carrera, an illiterate ladino pig farmer in eastern Guatemala, led a successful attack on the local government with the encouragement of his parish priest. The success inspired other villages, including parts of El Salvador, to rise up under Carrera's leadership. Government troops retaliated; they sacked and burned villages, and they destroyed Carrera's house and, allegedly, raped his wife. Carrera, hanging pictures of saints on his cotton fatigues and taking the religious hymn "La Salve Maria" as his battle cry, vowed never to lay down his arms until he eliminated all liberal officers from the land. Repeatedly wounded, but fearless, the fanatical Carrera inspired his peasant guerrillas into acts of incredible bravery and sacrifice. Conservative elites tried to exploit Carrera for their own purposes, but they soon discovered Carrera was leading a mass uprising of Indians and ladinos against all privileged whites, both liberal and conservative.

From 1837 to 1840 anarchy ruled Central America. For once, both liberals and conservatives in Guatemala City looked to the federal president, Francisco Morazán, to restore order. But while Morazán fought Carrera, the federation fell apart. The insurgent demands were identical to the conservative agenda, and led to the increasing empowerment of conservative politicians. In July 1838, Congress, led by the conservative Marqués de Aycinena, recognized the individual provinces as sovereign states. In that same year, new conservative governments in

AN EYEWITNESS ACCOUNT: CARRERA'S ARMY

John Lloyd Stephens (1: 231–32), traveling in Central America in 1839, related an eyewitness account to the invasion of Guatemala City by Carrera's rural guerrillas on February 1, 1838:

> . . . Carrera's hordes were advancing . . . Among his leaders were Monreal and other known outlaws, criminals, robbers, and murderers . . . A gentleman who saw them from the roof of his house . . . saw the entry of this immense mass of barbarians; choking up the streets, all with green bushes in their hats, seeming at a distance like a moving forest, armed with rusty muskets, old pistols, fowling-pieces . . . sticks formed into the shape of muskets, with tin-plate locks; clubs, machetes, and knives tied to the ends of long poles; and swelling the multitude were two or three thousand women, with sacks . . . for carrying away the plunder. Many, who had never left their villages before, looked wild at the sight of the houses and churches, and the magnificence of the city . . . Carrera himself, amazed at the immense ball he had set in motion . . . afterward said that he was frightened at the difficulty of controlling this huge and disorderly mass.

Nicaragua, Honduras, and Costa Rica seceded from the federation. Congress ended its term without arrangements for the next elections, and the legally constituted federal government simply ceased to exist at the end of Morazán's presidential term in February 1839.

While Morazán fought to defeat Carrera and keep the federation together, Nicaragua, Honduras, and Costa Rica formed an alliance under General Francisco Ferrara of Honduras to defeat the federation and its liberal constitution. Morazán fought Carrera in Guatemala, and almost defeated him, and then he fought the alliance in El Salvador and Honduras. But once General Ferrara convinced Carrera to join forces with the conservatives, Morazán—and the federation—no longer had a chance. War ravaged the countryside. Sentinels shot innocents abroad in the capital after dark. Atrocities escalated. El Salvador was invaded by just about everyone; foreigners were threatened and murdered just about everywhere. The isthmus was bankrupted as Central America succumbed to a reign of terror. By 1840, when Morazán fled to Panama after a decisive defeat by Carrera, the federation had come to a humiliating end, and it would not be revived.

The Last Federation

The first decades of independence witnessed unity in Central America. Yet the United Provinces of Central America would be the only internationally recognized political union in the postcolonial history of the isthmus. Nicaragua would lead an attempt to reunite the isthmus in 1840, but no states other than Honduras and El Salvador joined the federation, which lasted, off and on, just a few years (1840–45). All other attempts failed to unify the small nations. In 1839, John Lloyd Stephens arrived as the new U.S. consul to the federation, but he could not find

FREDERICK CHATFIELD, BRITISH CONSUL

Despite the conservative and liberal rhetoric concerning foreign interests, both parties relied on foreign agents for assistance. The foreign representative most involved was Frederick Chatfield, who had represented British interests in Central America since independence. Some historians have argued that he played a pivotal role in the collapse of the federation, because he found it easier to promote his nation's interests in a weakened and divided isthmus. Yet Chatfield was a strong supporter of Morazán and the federation until 1839; by then, the Central Americans themselves had already done so much to undermine the federation, it is difficult to attribute its collapse to the actions of a foreign consul. In the last year of the fighting, however, after Morazán tried to force loans on British concerns. Chatfield did throw his support to the Marquis of Aycinena and the conservatives in Guatemala City. He published circulars denying the existence of the central government. And his behind-the-scenes collaboration with the conservatives—all in the hope of gaining Belize, Roatán, and the Mosquitía for Britain—assured Carrera that he would have adequate ammunition in the decisive battles against Morazán. Chatfield was not finished; he would manipulate Central American affairs until Britain, internationally embarrassed by his increasingly aggressive actions, withdrew his commission in 1851. Such diplomatic interference in Central American political affairs became the norm in the decades to come.

the government. The most honest advice he received was to present his credentials to each state individually.

The provinces never achieved a national outlook, nor could they reconcile the conservative interests of an elite class with liberal concepts of a democratic republic. Under Spain, the class hierarchy had been rigid; wealth and power had been retained by only a few. And politically, the Kingdom of Guatemala had failed to integrate the various regions, leaving them isolated instead to evolve into separate fiefdoms focused on major cities. Surrounded by expanses of unexplored territory and connected only by burro paths, these small domains could not transcend their own desire for power or their long-standing distrust of one another—even when it would have been to their advantage.

The political turbulence experienced under the federation—only Costa Rica, remote from the political center, had much stability— would make it harder for the provinces to unite in the future. Ironically, the federation did achieve clearer, if somewhat disputed, boundaries for its five member states, boundaries that then defined them into separate nations. The isthmus, once the great connector of continents, was broken into fragments not only by rugged mountains but also by parochial attitudes. After expressing so many lofty and progressive ideals upon the independence of his native land, José del Valle watched it disintegrate into rival factions. A year before his death, he concluded:

> Politically, America is the same as it is physically: the land of earthquakes.
>
> ■
>
> José del Valle, 1833 (Bumgartner 1963, 263)

8

CONSERVATIVES AND FOREIGN PROFITEERS (1840-1870)

The old families, whose principal members had been banished or politically ostracized, and the clergy, were elated at the expulsion of the Liberal party, and their return to what they considered their natural right to rule the state; they talked of . . . making [it] . . . what it had once been, the jewel of Spanish America.

■

John Lloyd Stephens, 1839 (1:200)

The conservatives ruled Central America throughout the mid-19th century. For 30 years they kept the individual Central American states under their iron control, but failed to unite them in another federation. Guatemala's power and size had been an issue in the federation, but ironically, that nation continued to dominate the isthmus even as the individual countries attempted to assert their independence. The conservatives recognized the need for a united isthmus, and they organized congresses to plan such a union. But local interests, often made irresistible by foreign promises, prevailed. Unionism became an excuse to invade a neighboring nation or, as in the case of the William Walker episode (SEE page 167) to expel a foreign interloper. Occasionally liberals would gain power and try to revive the federation, but as long as Rafael Carrera ruled in Guatemala, they never could succeed. The conservatives, helped along by foreign interests, created a Central America divided into five separate and autonomous states—and one British colony. And so the isthmus would remain.

The aristocratic conservatives tried but failed to replicate the Spanish colony that had so greatly benefited them. They were forced to ally themselves with a new kind of dictator who was often illiterate and usually mestizo. And the creoles, who had dominated politics after independence, found that they were dependent not only on mestizos, but also on the industrial world for trade and economic development. Foreign profiteers and foreign diplomats, whether looking for an efficient route between the oceans or investing in export crops, intruded on the isthmus and changed Central America forever.

Conservatives

> *Carrera . . . at first more dreaded by the [Conservatives] than the Liberals . . . suddenly, and to their utter astonishment, placed the former nominally at the head of government.*
>
> ■
>
> *John Lloyd Stephens, 1839 (1:199)*

With the collapse of the federation, Central America no longer was a land ruled by republican principles. The conservatives ushered back the laws of the Spanish colony, reinstating separate laws for the Indian villages that protected their communal lands and customs and eliminated the head tax. Monopolistic powers were granted again to the elite creole merchants who, then, controlled much of the economy. Church privileges were restored; priest-politicians became policy makers; and some church lands (not all—the conservatives had profited from their sale as much as the liberals) were returned.

Government expenditures contracted—indeed, there was no additional federal layer to support, only individual state governments—and in Guatemala, for example, salaries of state officials were reduced by more than 25 percent. With education left to the priests, no funds were needed for the massive liberal public education programs; instead, church tithes were reinstituted, proving the greater power of the church over the needs of the state. Customs duties and taxes on alcohol and tobacco were deemed adequate to cover state expenditures, and they satisfied the conservatives, who had an aversion to direct taxation. The armies, however, became a burden, sometimes constituting more than half the state budget; special war taxes to support the military were not unusual, nor were forced loans on merchants. Overall, though, the tax burden was reduced.

Taxes and the Capital

... the number of fine Churches; and the trees and gardens ... give Guatemala a very handsome appearance when viewed from a short distance; but on entering the city the illusion is dispelled ...

■

Robert Dunlop, 1847 (78)

With limited taxes, municipal services in the capital of the Republic of Guatemala were, of necessity, restricted. The police department in 1847 consisted of four officers, despite a high homicide rate. (Although a city ordinance banned the carrying of firearms, the Englishman Francisco Crowe noted that "every native wears in his belt a large sharp-pointed knife—most frequently of British manufacture—which is encased in a leathern sheath, more or less ornamented" [1850, 295]). The wealthy had to hire their own security forces; in fact, an ordinance made citizens responsible for policing their property. In 1843 the merchants' guild paid to have the streets paved, but the installation of street lights could be achieved only with a special city sales tax—.06 U.S. cents on a measure of flour or a pound of cinnamon, and even more on liquor, vinegar, and oil. Even so, the city relied on a system of candlelight until 1862, when gaslights finally were installed. Education was a task returned to the church and no longer a government responsibility; the secular university established by the liberals once again became the church-run University of San Carlos and schooling was mostly limited to the male elite. Health care, too, except for special vaccination programs during epidemics, was left to the church; San Juan de Dios Hospital, the only formal one in Central America, was run by nuns and supervised by a board of wealthy citizens. The merchant aristocracy could easily arrange for the services the government failed to provide, just as they could afford the imported pianos, carriages, silks, and chandeliers they bought in city shops.

Caudillos

This [horsewhip] is the constitution I govern by.

■

Justo Rufino Barrios, c. 1870 (Burgess 1926, 134)

The conservatives, having witnessed the chaos of the preceding decades, believed Central America simply was not ready for democracy.

QUICHÉS UNDER CONSERVATIVE RULE

T he restoration of the Laws of the Indies reinforced the separate traditions of the Mayans in the Guatemalan highlands. Because different laws applied to them, the Mayans had to be identifiable as Indians, but skin color no longer differentiated Europeanized Guatemalans from Indians; language and dress did. Each Mayan village had a traditional and distinctive form of dress and retained its Mayan language, and many of these costumes and distinctive Mayan languages persisted into the 21st century. The Momostecans, like most Mayans, were loyal supporters of Rafael Carrera, and they were permitted direct access to the president of Guatemala whenever they had complaints against mestizo and creole officials. After the liberals in Los Altos tried to secede from Guatemala in 1848, the Momostecans rebelled with the support of Carrera. Mestizos became so threatened by the Quiché Mayans that most abandoned Momostenango, leaving only nine families who dared to live among the 5,000–6,000 Mayans in 1849. The Momostecans no longer experienced pressure to assimilate European ways. They were free to celebrate feast days in accordance with their native Catholicism; just as important, they were permitted to adjudicate local matters by their own customs. The grateful Mayans, in return, supported the conservatives.

Left: A Mayan woman from Santa Cruz del Quiché. Right: a Quiché Mayan cofradía member in Chichicastenango, 1989. (Photo courtesy Naomi Smith)

Instead, a firm hand was needed, they argued, to guide their small nations into the future. The governments, unhampered by any democratic sentiments, became streamlined: presidents became dictators, and the checks and balances of a republican government—or even of constitutional law—became superfluous. Nonetheless each state proclaimed itself a republic.

The Central American states were ruled not just by conservatives, but by caudillos—military dictators like General Rafael Carrera in Guatemala and General Santos Guardiola, nicknamed "the Butcher," in Honduras, men who were themselves the law. These caudillos, who often used government as the means to personal enrichment and social mobility, came to epitomize Central American governments, both conservative and liberal ones, for the next 100 years. The caudillos, in their own way, continued the well-established tradition of nepotism and influence that had prevailed in the governance of the Spanish colony; these new politicians, however, provided favors and positions not just to the conservative elite, but also to an entirely new class of official—the mestizo. The mestizo dominated the military in particular, and relatives often held advisory positions closest to the president.

The caudillos varied in the rigidity of their policies and the firmness of their control. Braulio Carrillo pronounced himself Costa Rica's dictator for life in 1841, yet was deposed a year later. The Honduran Santos Guardiolo (1856–62) and the Salvadoran Francisco Malespín (1840–46) were both assassinated, but Trinidad Muñoz (1845–51) of Nicaragua, who had only a tentative hold on power, managed to leave office alive. The decade-long term of Juan Rafael Mora Porras (1849–59) of Costa Rica was more typical, and in conjunction with the long reign of Carrera in Guatemala, Central America experienced the political stability that was in such contrast to the warring years of the federation.

Rafael Carrera of Guatemala (1839–65) was the caudillo par excellence. No one ruled longer or had greater influence in Central American affairs. Not content with controlling Guatemala, Carrera installed conservative dictators in neighboring nations, among them General Francisco Ferrara (1839–47) and Guardiolo "the Butcher" in Honduras, and Malespín in El Salvador. He financed the destruction of liberal gains in Nicaragua in 1854. And he invaded El Salvador in 1863 and overturned its liberal president, General Gerardo Barrios, who had been so progressive as to institute educational reforms—and so intrepid as to bury the remains of Francisco Morazán with state honors. Carrera knew how to wield his power intelligently as well as ferociously, and for most of the many years

RAFAEL CARRERA: CAUDILLO

. . . so young, so humble in his origin . . . with honest impulses, perhaps, but ignorant, fanatic, sanguinary, and the slave of violent passions, wielding absolutely the physical force of the country . . .

■

John Lloyd Stephens, 1839 (1:249)

Rafael Carrera (1814–65) was born in the crime-ridden slums of Guatemala City. His father was a mule driver, his mother a domestic servant and, later, a vendor in the market. Indian in appearance, poor and uneducated, he began his military career as a drummer boy in the federal army, and then worked on a cochineal hacienda, where he was fired for gambling. He was a drifter before settling in eastern Guatemala in 1832, and becoming a pig farmer. His life reflected the lot of many poor mestizos—but that would soon change. After leading the antiliberal uprising, he became the most powerful man in Guatemala. Just 25 years old and barely able to write his name, General Carrera became a skillful manipulator of political events, equal to the intrigues of his supporters, the conservative aristocrats and clergymen. A succession of epithets and official titles succinctly summarizes his career, from "robber and assassin" (1838) to "general" (1839) and, then, "Worthy Leader and General in Chief" (1844) to "President for Life of Guatemala" (1854)—in the same year, the pope conferred on him the Order of Saint Gregory (1854)—and, finally, "Founder of the Republic of Guatemala" (1866), a posthumous title inscribed with his bust on silver coins. He died a rich man.

Rafael Carrera (1814–65). (Portrait courtesy Ministry of Education, El Salvador)

of his rule, he enjoyed popular support. By the mid-1850s, Carrera was the strongest of Central America's strong men. His power was such that his rule endured six years after his death when his handpicked successor, General Vicente Cerna (1865–71), was finally overthrown.

Conservative Policies

From poor and aristocratic families alike, these despots all were supporters of the church and elite economic interests, but they varied in their style of governance and concerns. Frutos Chamorro, from a patrician ranching family in Granada, made sure the 1854 Nicaraguan constitution limited individual liberties and privileges only to the "worthy"—those of property, of course, as well as those of virtue and merit, however those two qualities might be measured. Other caudillos were more responsive to the concerns of the peasants who had brought them to power. Carrera mediated Indian land disputes himself and ordered the development of irrigation systems in rural areas; he was so popular with the lower classes they nicknamed him "Angel." Carrillo gave away small plots of land in Costa Rica in order to encourage the cultivation of a new export crop, coffee. And while some instituted reigns of intolerance and terror, Mora's policies in Costa Rica were, on the whole, quite moderate, and the Honduran, Juan Lindo Zelaya, permitted the unthinkable: the peaceful succession of a liberal to the presidency in 1852.

The Economy

The economy could not fail to improve after the devastation of the federal years. Free trade, however, was a liberal concept not entertained by the family oligarchies now in control of the economy; instead, protectionist policies were revived. Central America in the 1840s was, in fact, not a very different place from the time it had gained independence. The import of cheap goods from industrialized nations, such as textiles from Britain, slowed with the renewal of tariffs, and the major exports remained natural dyes, both indigo and cochineal; hacienda owners continued to graze cattle to supply the domestic market. Using burro paths and Indian porters to transport these goods to Caribbean ports, the colonial products used the same old colonial infrastructure for most of the conservative period. The main commercial road from the Caribbean port at Izabel to Guatemala City, which was often traversed by merchants from Paris and London, could take 10 hours to travel just 12 miles.

The social structure based on this colonial economy remained quite the same as it had always been in Guatemala and El Salvador and the Granada region of Nicaragua. The lack of economic vitality meant that not many demands were made for Indian labor, which was fortuitous given the conservative alliance with the indigenous peoples during the civil wars. Honduras, with a collapsing mining industry, fell into considerable poverty and disarray during the conservative period, a situation worsened by the British presence on the Bay Islands and in the Mosquitía. Nicaragua, too, suffered from British attacks along the Caribbean and the ongoing civil war between the liberals based in León and the conservatives in Granada, but the discovery of new mines in the Chontales region contributed to modest economic progress there.

By the middle of the century, renewed effort went into improving the economic infrastructure. Foreign investments and, in particular, exclusive agreements with foreign countries propelled many projects forward, although conservatives in Guatemala were so wary of relying on foreign monies that railroad construction lagged behind such countries as Panama (SEE page 165). Nonetheless, a Belgian company received the contract for telegraph service in Guatemala and a British firm contracted to build a bridge. British and Belgian ferry lines were commissioned to service the Caribbean coast, and they transferred both passengers and exports from the small ports to the transatlantic deep sea port at Belize. Many development schemes never went beyond the survey stage; others were only partially completed.

On the whole, transportation improvements were few except to the primary ports. Yet the first stagecoaches and carts appeared on the most important roads for commerce, and transportation costs were reduced. Exports became more profitable and the Central American economy actually expanded, particularly in Guatemala and Costa Rica—except in those years that locust plagues destroyed the crops.

A LOCUST PLAGUE

The insect which is most dreaded is the . . . locust, which at intervals afflicts the entire country, passing from one end to the other in vast columns of many millions . . . destroying every green thing in its course. I once rode through one of these columns which was fully ten miles in width. Not only did the insects cover the ground, rising in clouds on each side of the mule-path as I advanced, but the open pine forest was brown with their myriad bodies, as if the trees had been seared with fire, while the air was filled with them . . .

■

E. G. Squier, 1855 (201)

In 1856, aniline dyes were invented, and those countries that relied on the profits of indigo and cochineal were forced to restructure their exports. Although natural dyes remained the primary export product of Central America for much of the 19th century, the profits from these exports declined as synthetic dyes gained popularity. The price of cochineal in 1858, for example, was 42 percent less than in 1846. Guatemala successfully supplemented its cochineal exports with cotton, the export of which during the U.S. Civil War grew from .1 percent of total exports (1862) to over 19 percent (1865). Some nations experimented with sugar. But the product of the future would be coffee.

Great Britain

The order and stability brought to Central America by the caudillos was much appreciated by foreigners—and the fact that business could be accomplished directly with the all-powerful presidents attracted many investors to the region. Britain, the great maritime power of the day, was the most formidable presence in the Caribbean and Central America. In 1840, 20 percent of Guatemala's imports came directly from Britain and another 60 percent came via the British-controlled port at Belize. Under the guise of collecting the five-billion-peso debt incurred by the federation in 1824, and now owing from the individual states, Britain entangled itself in the finances of the Central American governments. Subsequent loans to pay off the original debt worsened the financial dependency of the states: In 1856 Guatemala had to pledge half its customs revenue to pay off one such loan.

Britain used the debt to bully the new nations into accepting its territorial ambitions on the isthmus. When Nicaragua persisted in protesting England's aggression in the Mosquitía, a naval blockade, officially justified as necessary to force repayment of the debt, was the result. When Honduras protested British actions on the Bay Islands, the ships lined up in the Bay of Honduras—all under the subterfuge of protecting British business interests.

Gunboat diplomacy was only part of Britain's strategy in the region. Consul Chatfield made sure that the nations did not trouble or embarrass Britain about its violations of their sovereignty. When Britain attacked the Caribbean port of San Juan de Nicaragua, for example, and then renamed it "Greytown" and incorporated it into the Mosquitia, the Central American nations recognized that they must unite in order to protect themselves. Frutos Chamorro, a Nicaraguan conservative, spearheaded a drive to create the Confederation of

Central America in the early 1840s, but Chatfield outmaneuvered him. The consul's promises to Guatemala and Costa Rica kept those two nations out of the alliance—and left Britain to control much of the Caribbean coast.

British Honduras

One of the most lucrative government agreements seems, at first glance, to have been Carrera's 1859 grant of Belize to the British in exchange for a road from Guatemala City to the Caribbean. Belize became British Honduras, but the road was never completed. The British hoped to end the road within its own territory, so that Guatemala would be forced to use its ports. The Guatemalans objected, and the project was never completed. Although Britain gained Belize, the colony was soon to lose much of its value, the world market prices of mahogany and logwood were falling, and once Central America shifted its trade to the Pacific in the 1860s, Belize lost more than 60 percent of its trade and became a backwater. When it became clear the road would not be built, Guatemala reclaimed Belize as its own. Wars between the two erupted sporadically. Not until 1991 did Guatemala concede that Belize was not part of its territory, and by then it had been an independent nation for a decade. Border disputes between the two nations continued into 2007.

Britain was able to operate with international impunity well into the 1840s. European powers were not in a strong position to protest, although France had significant business interests in the region (17 percent of all imports into Guatemala were French), as did Germany and Belgium, on a lesser scale. Spain maintained trade relations through Cuba, but did not recognize Central American independence until 1863. The small Central American nations were left to fend for themselves, and Chatfield's intrigue as well as the self-interest of the caudillos meant the isthmus remained divided and weak.

But in 1848, the nearest power, the United States, won its war with Mexico and turned its expansionist energies to the south. Under the Monroe Doctrine of 1823 that celebrated the independence of Latin America from Spain, the United States had claimed the Western Hemisphere for its citizens only. For the first time, it was ready to flex its muscle against Great Britain, a world power and formidable force in Central America.

Chatfield soon met his North American match in E. G. Squier, who was sent in 1849 by the U.S. government and business interests to

THE KINGDOM OF MOSQUITIA

. . . it is probable they [the Miskito Indians] would have disappeared from the earth without remark, had it not suited the purposes of the English government to put them forward as a mask . . .

■

E. G. Squier, 1855 (245)

Since the 17th century, Britain had tried to legitimize its infringement on Honduran and Nicaraguan territory by creating what it called the "Kingdom of Mosquitia" and claiming it a British protectorate. The British governor of Jamaica duly installed the king, and though the monarch never was taxed by any administrative responsibilities for the basically egalitarian villagers of the Miskito "kingdom," the fiction was useful in maintaining Miskito separateness from the Spanish colony. The fiction, however, had fallen into disuse for half a century—until a trans-isthmian canal became a matter of world interest. One proposed crossing was via the San Juan River in Nicaragua, next to the Mosquitia. Maneuvering for control of any project connecting the seas, Britain reasserted its claim to the region in 1843 and crowned a new Miskito king, who received the remarkable honor of British warships to enforce his rule over a population of a few thousand. Britain tried expanding Miskito territory by raiding and taking over San Juan del Norte, a port on the San Juan River, and renaming it "Greytown." It published maps that showed the Mosquitia covering one-third of Central America. Unlike its eventual success in Belize, the fiction did not serve Britain for long. The United States, testing its muscle in world politics, insisted on a limited British presence in Central America and negotiated the Clayton-Bulwer Treaty with Britain to that effect in 1850.

survey the San Juan depression in Nicaragua for the construction of a canal. While Chatfield maneuvered to keep the Central American states divided, Squier argued for their union. When Chatfield spread fear about U.S. ambitions in Central America after its annexation of half of Mexico, including Texas, Squier responded with the slogan of the Monroe Doctrine: "America for Americans." The political maneuvering erupted into battleship confrontations as the need for a trans-isthmian crossing became more urgent.

Britain was finally forced to officially cede the Mosquitia to Honduras in 1859 and to Nicaragua in 1860, although it did not completely evacuate the area until almost the 20th century. The kingdom did give the English-speaking Miskito Indians a spirit of independence that endures to the present day, often to the dismay of Honduras and Nicaragua.

A 20-year-old Miskito chief (seated, center) with his advisers from British Jamaica, 1893. (Photo *Popular Science Monthly*, June 1894)

Passage Between the Seas

. . . by means of the canal, the republic would be transformed within a few years into the richest, most populous and happiest nation on the globe.

■

Alejandro Marure, historian, 1837 (after Woodward 1985, 122)

Since the time of Christopher Columbus, explorers and pirates, kings and presidents had dreamed of an efficient passage between the Atlantic and Pacific Oceans. Central Americans believed the strategic position of the isthmus for such a passage would convert it into a great power. The individual republics discussed the development of overland passages and canals with foreign governments, Nicaragua especially, but also Honduras—even Costa Rica pursued its own dream with a French company.

A new impetus came in 1848. The United States, as a result of its war with Mexico, now reached from the Atlantic to the Pacific, and the fastest and safest route from New York to California (until the transcontinental railroad was opened in 1869) was over the narrow land barrier known as Central America. The California Gold Rush of 1848 made Central America even more critical to U.S. interests.

After Britain's aggression in the Mosquitia, Nicaragua was eager to seek the protection of the United States, and in 1849 it granted exclu-

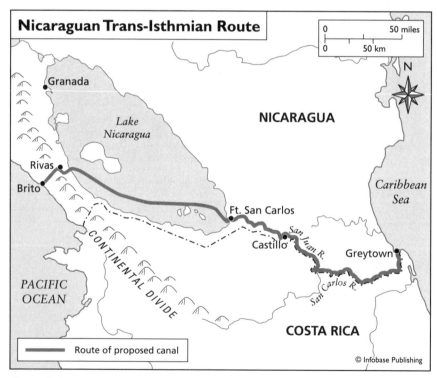

Route of Nicaragua Canal as proposed by U.S. Isthmian Canal Commission. (Photo *National Geographic Magazine,* January 1901)

sive transit rights to the United States—or any company of its choosing—for an ocean-to-ocean passage across that country. The Río San Juan was the perfect route, from Greytown it coursed through a natural depression that was 31 miles wide and only 165 feet above the sea, before emptying into Lake Nicaragua near the Pacific. Although the crossing from the Caribbean to the Pacific was somewhat longer than in Panama, the route was more convenient to the Gulf of Mexico and, in fact, made the trip between New York and San Francisco 500 miles shorter and two days faster.

There was much maneuvering by both Britain and the United States to monopolize this interoceanic passage. Chatfield encouraged Costa Rica to claim Greytown as its own, and then, without the permission of his government, commandeered a strategically located Honduran island that had already been ceded, through Squier, to the United States. An international incident resulted, forcing Britain to sign the Clayton-Bulwer Treaty with the United States in 1850. The treaty prevented either nation from having the exclusive control of a canal, and purported to limit Britain's activities in Central America; more important, it signified Britain's acknowledgment of the growing power of the United States in the Caribbean. The incident also forced Chatfield's recall in 1852, but the conflict continued to fester and flare, and the U.S. Marines shelled Greytown the following year.

Despite the crises in foreign affairs, plans continued for a route between the seas. The urgency of the prospectors was such that there was no time to construct a canal or railroad. Cornelius Vanderbilt's Atlantic & Pacific Ship Canal Company quickly developed an alternative passage by 1852; small steamships carried passengers on the Río San Juan and across Lake Nicaragua, then a 12-mile stagecoach ride between the lake and the Pacific completed the crossing of the isthmus. Vanderbilt's company also provided the steamships linking New York and San Francisco with Nicaragua.

British gunboat diplomacy in the Caribbean was as self-defeating in Panama as it was in Nicaragua. At mid-century, Panama, then part of Colombia, feared Britain would attempt to incorporate its Caribbean coast into the Mosquitia. Colombia turned to the United States for a guarantee that the region would remain neutral; in exchange, it granted the United States transit rights across the Panamanian isthmus. Between 1850 and 1855, a U.S. company constructed the Panama Railway.

Vanderbilt's company faced serious competition from the Panamanian route. Prices for first-class passage from New York to San Francisco plummeted from $400 to $150. But until the Panamanian

Photo entitled "Lake Nicaragua Steamship on Nicaragua Canal Route, Controlled by the U.S."
(From a stereoscopic photo taken at the end of the 19th century)

railroad was completed in 1855, most passengers crossed by way of Nicaragua because it was a quicker, more comfortable route. Vanderbilt made a profit from the sheer volume of travelers; by 1868, a total of 68,000 had crossed Nicaragua on their way to California, and another 57,000 had made the return trip.

The Nicaraguan route faded from importance, however, and was abandoned in 1868. Once the transcontinental railroad was completed in 1869, travel across the United States became the most efficient route between its two coasts. The Panamanian railroad, though, provided a three-hour crossing of the isthmus by steam locomotive and was critical to Central American development: it encouraged the trend toward Pacific ports, not Caribbean ones, and it greatly facilitated the export of coffee. The dream of a constructing a canal persisted, and foreign powers surveyed 30 possible interoceanic routes between 1850 and 1900.

The William Walker Episode

Adventurers, much like smugglers, had attempted to establish their personal domains on the isthmus since colonial times. In 1820, for example, the Scottish profiteer Gregor MacGregor purchased 70,000 square miles in Honduras from the Miskito Indians for a few kegs of liquor and some bolts of calico. Like most such schemes, the effort was abandoned after the 200 colonists suffered too many hardships. But in 1855, a very different kind of adventurer appeared in Central America, one who took over the presidency of an entire nation and, as a result, succeeded in uniting the Central American nations where everyone else had failed.

William Walker, born in Tennessee, was a filibuster, one of many soldiers of fortune in the United States who believed land conquest was a good way to spread democracy—and slavery—just as the United States had fulfilled its "manifest destiny" by taking over the west from Mexico. In 1855, Nicaraguan liberals, as part of the ongoing civil war in Nicaragua, contracted with Walker and his army of 57 mercenaries to remove the conservatives and install a more republican, and Liberal Party, government in their country. Walker, financed by investors who hoped to take control of Vanderbilt's Atlantic & Pacific Ship Transit Company, agreed to help them in exchange for land and power.

Initially, the liberals suffered defeats, but Walker won a few battles and became commanding general of the liberal army. When he took control of the conservative stronghold at Granada, the conservatives negotiated a coalition government with Patricio Rivas, a conservative, as figurehead and the mercenary Walker as chief of the armed forces and the true power in Nicaragua. The unusual hybrid government instituted some liberal reforms, and the U.S. government formally, and too hastily, recognized it in 1856, despite protests from other Central American nations. Later in 1856, when Rivas resigned, Walker became president of the largest country on the isthmus.

The National War

. . . now I am preparing to continue the campaign, flattering myself with the hope of being able to say to you very soon that filibusterismo no longer exists.

■

President Juan Rafael Mora, April 15, 1856
(Edelman and Kenan 1989, 35)

Rumors spread throughout Central America that the United States intended to annex Nicaragua as a slave state. The arrival from the United States of some 2,500 mercenaries and southern slave owners, who joined Walker's army in exchange for generous grants of Nicaraguan land, gave credence to the rumors. And when Walker legalized slavery and made English the official language of Nicaragua, few doubted his intentions.

In an unusual expression of unity, the conservatives of Nicaragua and the four other nations formed an army in 1856 to expel Walker. Carrera argued that he would be most useful raising funds and ammunition (both from British coffers) and troops for what would become the National Army of Liberation. The leadership of what became known as the "National War" was left to Carrera's close Costa Rican ally, President Juan Rafael Mora. The fighting lasted a year, devastating much of Nicaragua: Granada, the colonial jewel of the nation, was burned. But it was simply a matter of time before the Central Americans would succeed. A British blockade prevented supplies from reaching Walker, and an angry Vanderbilt conspired to give the Costa Ricans access to his steamships. When Mora offered the mercenaries amnesty and free passage home (paid by Vanderbilt), most deserted. Walker, left with only 200 soldiers and facing a better-supplied Central American army, surrendered. The United States sent a ship of mercy to carry him home in 1857. Yet Walker tried returning to Nicaragua, but the U.S. Navy stopped him at Greytown. He attempted another invasion in 1860, but this time he was captured by the British and turned over to the Honduran president, Santos Guardiola, who executed him.

The consequences of the Walker episode were substantial. Liberal support for Walker consolidated conservative control of the isthmus. William Walker—and, by association, the liberals—were viewed as such a threat to Central American autonomy that no republic elected a liberal government until a new generation of politicians arrived on the scene. The United States, too, was tarnished and so distrusted by Central Americans that Nicaragua took the precaution of granting canal rights to a Frenchman. Above all, the National War proved the effectiveness of Central American unity, but that unity lasted only the one year it took to expel Walker.

Conservative Legacy

The conservative era ended with the isthmus divided—and thus weakened—into five nations and the colony of British Honduras. Each nation was too small and too undeveloped to defend against the invading armies of another, much less those of the more powerful, industrialized nations. Foreign debts and foreign concessions of territory were the price paid for each nation's independence.

Conservatives ruled until the 1870s, and in Nicaragua, where the Walker episode discredited an entire generation of liberals, they ruled until 1893. The caudillo-style dictators, and the militarization of the state they brought with them, outlasted the conservatives well into the next century.

With the completion of the Panamanian railroad, the two seas were efficiently linked for the first time. The control of the trans-isthmian railroad was not local, and those who benefited the most were usually not Central Americans. The railroad, however, radically changed the commercial focus of the isthmus, making the Pacific ports more convenient than the harbors of the Caribbean. Honduras suffered from this, and Belize became a backwater, but most Central American governments found their cities and areas of production more conveniently located to the ports. The groundwork had been laid for a transition from the colonial economy to the new one based on the export of coffee.

9

THE MAKING OF THE COFFEE REPUBLICS (1870-1900)

The liberals took over Central America in the 1870s. They brought with them promises of modernization and capitalistic reforms, and they ushered in the boom years of the "coffee republics" that endured through the last decades of the century. World influences and capitalistic investments sped along the economic and social change of the period. Foreign investments—German, British, and, increasingly, North American—supported the modernization and development of each country, but by the beginning of the 20th century such indebtedness led to inordinate foreign control of local economies and policies, giving rise to "banana republics." The liberal era ended with railroads and telegraph lines crisscrossing each Central American nation, and a new, but not more equitable, social and economic order. Government remained in the hands of military dictators.

Liberal Takeover

In the 1870s the liberals overthrew the conservatives. Armed struggles in Guatemala and in El Salvador in 1871 placed liberals in power, and these liberals then fought to put others in charge of Honduras and Nicaragua—and to keep them in charge. Mexico was interested in the outcome as well; Justo Rufino Barrios of Guatemala, for example, defeated Carrera's successor with the support of the Mexican liberal president Benito Juárez and ruled from 1873 to 1885. The liberal period was marked by the presence of a strong military, but political stability remained most often an unfulfilled promise—except when compared to the chaos of the preceding 50 years. Military coups and border conflicts continued to characterize political succession and regional relations.

With unemployment increasing from declines in the market for indigo and cochineal, Central America was ready for a change. The power and wealth of foreigners had been impressed on the populace during the conservative era, and many Central Americans thought it was time for progress. More openness to capitalism and modernization was the result. Change was also spurred by the positivist philosophy of the French thinker, Auguste Comte, which was taught in the University of San Carlos along with Herbert Spencer's Social Darwinism. A generation of graduates became imbued with the "scientific" ideas of social evolution and material progress through what Comte called "republican dictatorships." Two of these university graduates became presidents: Barrios of Guatemala and Marco Aurelio Soto (1885–90) of Honduras.

The New Liberals

Peace, Education, and Material Prosperity

■

liberal slogan, 1870s

The new liberals believed church and educational reforms were imperative, and they encouraged foreign investments and colonization as the means of bringing new technology and development to Central America. But unlike the Morazán liberals of the Federation, the positivist generation was more pragmatic than progressive. Democratic principles were all well and good, but they believed Central America had not sufficiently evolved for such political principles to be appropriate. Indians, from the positivist viewpoint, need not be treated equally, as they were deemed inferior. It was economic progress that required immediate attention, not social justice.

Although the liberals drafted new constitutions, their governments functioned as they had under conservative caudillos: by military dictatorship. These liberal dictators, better educated than their predecessors and committed to modernization, gave a new style to Central American politics. This style was best exemplified by the professional armies that replaced the peasant guerrillas on whom the conservatives had relied. Their grip on national affairs, however, was just as firm as that of the conservative caudillos, who would have envied their tenacity: Rafael Zaldívar led El Salvador for 11 years (1876–85); Tomás Guardia governed Costa Rica for a dozen years (1870–82); José Santos Zelaya

(1893–1909) ruled Nicaragua for 16 years; and Manuel Estrada Cabrera (1898–1920) controlled Guatemala for a record 22 years of uninterrupted rule.

The liberal governments did accomplish unfinished business left from the federation. They successfully curtailed church power, and took control over many civic matters formerly left to the clergy; when the priests protested, they were exiled. Liberal free market policies challenged the economic privileges of the conservative elite, and gave monetary control to the first banks on the isthmus, many of which were owned by coffee entrepreneurs. Liberal labor policies once again stirred resentment among the Indians and rural poor, and land reforms dramatically affected the old social order. Both land and labor policies were driven by the desire to develop a profitable cash crop: coffee.

UNIFICATION REVISITED

. . . divided and isolated we are nothing.

■

Justo Rufino Barrios, 1885 (Pérez Brignoli 1989, 87)

The new generation of liberals did not give up on the idea of a federation, although few were as strongly committed to the concept as President Barrios of Guatemala, who envisioned himself the head of such a union and unilaterally proclaimed himself the supreme military commander of the new federation. The governments of Nicaragua, El Salvador, and Costa Rica, with the encouragement of Mexico and the United States, joined forces against the Guatemalan strongman, and he was killed in the Battle of Chalchuapa in 1885. The next strongman to try his hand at unifying the isthmus was José Santos Zelaya of Nicaragua, but only the three middle states—El Salvador, Honduras, and Nicaragua—ever got so far as promulgating a common constitution, which they did in 1898. This Greater Republic of Central America lasted less than a year, and future efforts were thwarted when Zelaya's ambitions worried the United States. The late 19th century was marked more by consolidation of national identities than strides toward unity.

Costa Rican Coffee

The coffee plant arrived from Cuba in 1796, but it was not until 1830 that Costa Rica began cultivating coffee, which flourished in the temperate climate and volcanic soil of its highland valleys and Pacific slopes. By 1845, Costa Rica was in the business of exporting beans to England. And just as important, it shipped the beans from the Pacific in order to avoid the longer and more difficult jungle routes to the Caribbean. Costa Rica also implemented policies to encourage the cultivation of coffee. It distributed uncultivated land to those who had no land at all, and to make the small family farms more profitable, it eliminated the church tithe on coffee and other agricultural products.

By mid-century, England was buying up Costa Rica's coffee crop and investing in its commercialization. New transportation networks were developed connecting such highland Central Valley cities as Cartago and San José to the Pacific port of Puntarenas, from which the beans were shipped to Chile and then around Cape Horn to Europe and the United States. With the completion of the Panamanian railroad providing a 47.5-mile crossing to the Atlantic Ocean, shipping to Europe and North America became more efficient, and the longer route around South America was abandoned.

The Coffee Boom

Costa Rica's coffee experiment was noted by the other nations. Guatemala, El Salvador, and to some extent Nicaragua started cultivating coffee by the 1850s. In 1860 coffee represented 1 percent of total exports in both Guatemala and El Salvador, but by the 1870s it had grown to 50 percent. Although some conservative governments encouraged this initial phase of coffee cultivation, the conservative elites were slow to abandon their indigo and cochineal production. The first coffee growers were not part of the old elite; they were more interested in free trade and other liberal policies. Some liberal coffee producers, such as Justo Rufino Barrios, led the overthrow of the conservatives.

The liberal dictators—most of them coffee producers like Barrios—created the economic conditions for the cash crop to dominate Central America exports. Following Costa Rica's example, they created incentives for the cultivation of coffee, eliminating church tithes and granting loans to producers, and they, too, improved transport to their most convenient Pacific ports. Costa Rica's success was quickly matched in El Salvador and Guatemala. The liberal commitment to the new agricultural export was well rewarded; throughout the last decades of the 19th century the world market for coffee expanded and prices increased. In El Salvador, the value of coffee exports increased 1,100 percent from 1880 to 1914.

Central America produced 14 percent of the world's coffee in the 1880s. With national infrastructure developed for the cultivation and export of coffee, its production increased and drove the Central American economy until the U.S. depression of 1929. Not every country experienced the coffee boom, however. Nicaragua, under the political control of conservatives until 1893 and, like Honduras, preoccupied with the mining of silver and gold, never invested as intensely in coffee. When these two nations did start exporting more significant amounts of the new crop, they did so considerably later and, in Honduras, not until after World War II.

Coffee exports incorporated Central America into the world market and provided a much-needed stimulus for economic growth and mod-

Chontales gold-mining company in Honduras. Coffee was not the primary export of every Central American nation during the liberal era. Silver and gold bullion constituted 75 percent of Honduran exports in the 1890s, and silver remained the leading Honduran export until 1915. In Nicaragua, cattle ranching and mining remained extremely important; the discovery in 1890 of Nicaragua's rich Pis Pis deposits of gold and silver gave the mining industry a boost that made it profitable into the post–World War II era. (Drawing by Thomas Belt, 1874)

ernization. Although coffee profits were not taxed, they brought in foreign currency and made imported goods affordable. Imports increased and customs duties swelled government coffers. During the last decades of the 19th century, for example, import duties constituted nearly 60 percent of El Salvador's revenues.

The heavy reliance on a single agricultural export subjected Central American nations to price fluctuations caused by capitalistic forces out of their control. Brazil and other nations started exporting coffee as well, and the competition forced down the Central American share of the world market to less than 5 percent in the 1930s—even though domestic production had increased. In 1929, Costa Rica's population was producing an average of 94 pounds of coffee per inhabitant (1 percent of world production) and El Salvador 91 pounds (2.6 percent of world production). Even after the 1929 depression, coffee was the largest single Central American export commodity, and it remained so during the 20th century.

Land "Reform"

The liberals' concern to maximize growth through agricultural exports led them to convert what they saw as unprofitable land use into cash crop production. Another top liberal priority was curtailing the power of the church. The two concerns dovetailed into a massive confiscation of monastic properties that were then redistributed. In Guatemala, where Justo Rufino Barrios expropriated 958,143 acres of church property, and in El Salvador, these properties were transformed into coffee *fincas* (farms). The land was sold to people linked to the new liberal

Coffee Production in Central America			
Per 1,000 Pounds			
1885	1900	1930	1940
Costa Rica	19,842	35,715	51,809	41,227
El Salvador	20,062	48,943	143,301	140,788
Guatemala	47,620	66,947	97,224	132,013
Honduras	3,307	2,646	3,527	3,704
Nicaragua	9,700	19,842	33,731	29,013
TOTAL	100,531	174,093	329,592	346,745

Sources: *The World's Coffee* (1947) and Torres Rivas (1993)

governments—army officers, politicians, and merchants. Once the liberals distributed church lands for cultivation, they continued reassigning other lands they believed were not adequately producing a profit; public lands were next.

The land redistribution created a new mestizo class that replaced many conservative aristocrats in influence and wealth. Central Americans were the greatest beneficiaries of the land grants, but so were foreign investors as well as German, French, Italian, and English immigrants. Germans cultivated coffee in Guatemala and in El Salvador; the English were involved in coffee production in Costa Rica. All nations granted land and resources to foreign entrepreneurs in exchange for modernization projects such as telegraph and electrical lines, docks, and railroads. These foreign grants and loans would become a problem within a few decades for most Central American republics.

Ecclesiastic and state lands were not the only properties redistributed. The liberals also turned their attention to communal, or *ejido,* lands. Even before colonial times the *ejidos* had been reserved for subsistence farming by Indians, but such lands, viewed in purely capitalistic terms, were unprofitable compared to their potential, if used for cultivating export crops. Coffee growers were permitted to rent such lands from the Indians, and the Indians seldom were permitted to refuse. The rent often went unpaid, and when the Indians complained to government officials, they received little sympathy.

Land disputes usually ended with the government surveyor redrawing the boundary to the advantage of the grower, even when the Indians were sophisticated in the ways of ladino politics. In 1883, for example, the Vicente family of Momostenango tried to forestall the taking of their cornfields by mestizos; these elite Quiché Mayans bribed President Barrios 1,000 pesos and offered the mestizos 1,000 cut stones, 60 sheep, and a bull to leave their land alone, but to no avail.

Indians were increasingly alienated from communal lands, and eventually liberal laws forced the sale of the lands. Justo Rufino Barrios started his coffee *fincas* by renting Mayan *ejido* lands; after he was president of Guatemala, he took title to them. Nowhere were such policies more thoroughly implemented than in El Salvador, where the Extinction of the Ejidos Law was promulgated in 1882. The community lands were sold to private individuals, and many small landholders had their properties seized as well.

Land was thus concentrated in the hands of a few. As the price of coffee increased during the late 19th century, more land was devoted to its production. Old crops, such as indigo and cochineal, were basically abandoned. Coffee replaced food crops, too, and foodstuffs had to be imported—at higher prices. In the more densely populated regions, food shortages caused peasants to migrate in the search for land. Indian and ladino peasants alike, especially in El Salvador, had difficulty sustaining themselves.

The Coffee Elite

By the late 19th century, Central American nations were ruled by coffee growers—or, at the very least, by the interests of the coffee growers. The class structure of Central American society changed little, but liberal policies and the coffee economy created a new ruling class. The Meléndez-Quiñónez family were among the Salvadoran coffee elite. President Carlos Meléndez of El Salvador, for example, and Jorge, his brother who succeeded him, and Alfonso Quiñónez Molina, Jorge's successor and brother-in-law, ruled that nation as a family domain from 1913 to 1927.

Coffee profits were of both personal and national concern to liberal dictators, so that the economic interests of the state and the coffee growers coincided. The resulting web of political, military, and economic power was tightly woven, and excluded all but the wealthiest. In El Salvador, the oligarchy is said to have included merely 16 families, although a few historians have claimed that wealth and power were distributed among anywhere from 40 to 100 Salvadoran families.

The coffee elite came to power in the liberal era and continued to control much of Central America into the 21st century. Oscar Arias Sanchez, the president of Costa Rica elected in 1986 and again in 2006, descended from two of the three wealthiest coffee families—and the third wealthiest family included his business partner. The elite families occasionally reached out to others and intermarried with foreign investors: Alfredo Cristiani, for example, the president of El Salvador in the 1990s, descended from an Italian coffee-producing family that married into the oligarchy. And the colonial aristocracy, through intermarriage and economic diversification, was not left out of power for very long: Oscar Arias Sanchez is a descendant of prominent coffee growers and of the conquistador Juan Vásquez de Coronado. The Chamorro family of Nicaragua gained its wealth initially from cattle ranching in the Granada region, and although not part of the original liberal coffee elite, the family now owns coffee *fincas* and produces political leaders as well, including President Violeta Barrios de Chamorro, who served 1990–96.

THE QUICHÉ MAYANS

Mayan communities, located in the Guatemalan highlands 4,500 feet above sea level, had a climate too cool for growing coffee. As a result most traditional villages survived the liberal land reforms, even though they lost their farmlands located at lower altitudes. But the liberals nonetheless infringed on even the highland *milpas*, granting them to their political friends. In Momostenango, for example, mestizo militia officers received grants of Quiché Mayan lands. These losses occurred at the very time the Indian population was doubling due to greater control of epidemic diseases such as smallpox with the result that by 1894 only 20 percent of the Momostecans could live off their fields. The lack of sufficient lands meant many Mayans had to import maize and beans for subsistence and rely on commercial activities, such as the weaving and sale of blankets, to survive. Momostenango became the most important center for woolen textiles in Guatemala. But even this activity was disrupted by forced seasonal migrations to harvest coffee. Although Momostecan Mayans remained fiercely protective of their cultural separateness, commercial activities led some men to abandon traditional dress and, in increasing numbers, to learn Spanish. They did not share the liberal interest in capitalist accumulation of wealth, however, but instead used any extra monies to sponsor religious celebrations.

Market Day at Momostenango, 1920. (Photo A. W. Anthony, Latin American Library, Tulane University)

Labor Reform

You should therefore see to it . . . that the Indian villages . . . be forced to give the number of hands to the farmers that the latter ask for, even to the number of fifty or a hundred to a single farmer . . .

■

President Justo Rufino Barrios, 1876 (Woodward 1993, 427)

The resident worker doesn't know the flavor of coffee

■

Luis Sam Colop, Refuges Sentimentales (from Handy 1984, 55)

With coffee production increasing, labor shortages became acute. The liberal dictators did everything they could to turn peasants into wage laborers. They instituted antivagrancy laws and the police strenuously enforced them. They intimidated peasants and the urban poor into accepting salary advances, and then permitted the growers not to pay them at all, or to pay them with goods from the company store in lieu of cash. Unemployed peasants were forced to accept any wage offered, and during the harvest season, even peasants fortunate enough to own land were forced into seasonal migrations to work on the coffee *fincas* for one to three months at a time. The Indians also were forced into "volunteering" their labor for road construction and other liberal projects. Less than a century after independence, the caudillos had essentially recreated the colonial system of debt peonage and labor tribute. Only Costa Rica, with its family farms, avoided a repetition of the feudal system.

By the end of the liberal period, wages had declined and malnutrition increased. In Guatemala, for example, the daily wage in the period from 1900 to 1917 could buy only 2.5 to 4.5 pounds of maize, in contrast to the more protectionist conservative period (1853–66) when wages could buy 7 to 12 pounds. Abusive labor practices led to unrest. In 1876, the Mayans of Momostenango, upset by the land reforms, attacked Guatemalan troops and joined a conservative movement to assassinate President Barrios. A few years later, the city of León, Nicaragua, was threatened when Indians in the Matagalpa region of Nicaragua rebelled over the exploitation of their labor for road construction. Such incidents were not unusual. Military presence was increasingly focused on domestic unrest, rather than the protection of national borders, and such

THE COSTA RICAN DIFFERENCE

... No one shall be harassed or persecuted for holding political opinions unless a person commit or conspires to commit criminal acts.

■

Article 8, Law of Individual Rights, 1877

C osta Rica, underpopulated and underdeveloped even for 19th-century Central America, had plenty of vacant land to distribute. With only a small and dispersed Indian population, all Costa Ricans had farmed the land themselves since colonial times. The government simply needed to make coffee profitable for them, and that was enough to encourage cultivation of the new crop. The result was many family farms on which family members themselves harvested the crops. The nation, like other Central American countries, was unified by coffee production; unlike other Central American countries where tenant farmers and Indians were displaced from their communal lands and forced into debt peonage, most Costa Ricans benefited from coffee. Social differences existed, but such differences were not based on race, as the population was overwhelmingly white. Some landowners, after consolidating their holdings, became the exporting elite. Yet small growers remained numerous even in the 1990s, when there were 65,000 to 100,000 coffee-producing farms. Costa Rica's more inclusive economy expedited democratic reforms and welcomed the enlightened leadership of General Tomás Guardia. Although a military dictator himself (1870–82), General Guardia convinced the wealthy coffee growers that coups d'état were bad for business and gained their support for placing the military under civilian controls. He promulgated the Law of Universal Education to develop a trained labor force and implemented a far-ranging system of public education. In addition, he instituted the Law of Individual Rights and eliminated capital punishment. By the end of the 19th century, Costa Rica was still not free of dictators, yet it had distinguished itself from other Central American nations by checking the power of the military and conducting peaceful elections between conservative and liberal candidates.

unrest escalated in the first decades of the 20th century. El Salvador created a National Guard in 1912 for the sole purpose of providing security on the coffee *fincas*; the growers, to guarantee the soldiers' loyalty, supplemented their salaries.

A Honduran Investment: Bananas

Bananas diversified Central America's exports in Guatemala, Nicaragua and Costa Rica—and, for that matter, British Honduras and Panama, too—but they became the primary export in Honduras. The commercialization of banana production at the end of the 19th century resulted in an exaggeration of the worst aspects of coffee production. Once again, governments created incentives for investment and conditions for a profitable agricultural export. But this time the incentives were given not to Central American landowners or merchants, or even to some individual foreigners, but rather to foreign companies.

This generosity resulted, in part, from a desire to develop the Caribbean region. The region had been largely ignored in colonial times, and the situation worsened after the development of Pacific ports by coffee exporters. Foreign corporations had the capital and means to develop banana plantations in formerly malaria-ridden territory and to connect these plantations by railroad to Caribbean ports.

Honduras was especially eager to be generous. Surrounded by other nations on three sides, it had been buffeted by border disputes with Nicaragua, political interference from Guatemala, and conflicts with El Salvador, all of which had destabilized its government and resulted in countless coups d'état. During the coffee boom, it remained predominantly rural, poor, and undeveloped; even Tegucigalpa, the capital of Honduras since 1880 and located near the most lucrative mines, had no municipal water supply before 1891. At a time when coffee wealth was adorning Central American cities with belle epoque buildings—Costa Rica constructed a $2 million opera house in San José, the most costly in all of Central and South America—Honduran cities remained pitifully undeveloped. In the early 1870s, the nation had no newspapers or libraries. The combined value of all Honduran exports was worth less than the value of Guatemala's coffee exports alone. The situation improved somewhat under the liberals, but lack of revenues left Honduras far behind the coffee republics.

. . . caught the first sight of Tegucigalpa, the "City of the Silver Hills," capital of the Sovereign and Independent Republic of Honduras. It was no very astounding sight; merely what in other lands would have been considered a large village, a chiefly one-story place with a white-washed church, filling only a small proportion of a somewhat barren valley . . .

■

Harry A. Franck, 1916 (363–64)

UNITED FRUIT COMPANY

The government concedes to the company 800,000 acres of uncultivated state lands, along the railroad or at any other place in the national territory of the company's choice, including all natural resources within, in addition to the land necessary for the construction of the railroad and required buildings . . . and two lots of land . . . in Limón harbor . . . all without any cost.

■

Costa Rican contract with Minor Keith, 1883
(Edelman and Kenan 1989, 61)

Banana exporting began almost accidentally. U.S. steamers plying the Caribbean picked up bananas from Honduras as early as the 1870s and sold them in New Orleans. Eventually they added those from Belize, too, a very poor and overlooked British colony that soon found its commerce with New Orleans more profitable than any with the British West Indies. The commercialization of the banana export business did not really get under way until 1878, when Costa Rica granted Minor Keith, a U.S. citizen, an immense tract of land—approximately 7 percent of Costa Rica—in exchange for the construction of a railroad from Puerto Limón to San José, a segment of track that would give Costa Rica a trans-isthmian railroad from the Pacific to the Caribbean. Long before the railroad was completed in 1890, Keith started transporting bananas on the finished track to Puerto Limón and packing them onto his supply ships returning to the United States. Demand for the tropical fruit became quite substantial, and he was soon making a fortune out of bananas. He

With profits from its mining industry waning at the turn of the century, Honduras saw banana exports as its chance to catch up. Foreign monies—in the case of bananas, U.S. money—were necessary for the refrigerated transport, railroads, and fast freighters that made the commercial export of the fruit possible. In return for company investments and the development of a railroad system uniting the country (which was never constructed), Honduras practically gave away its national economy. Land grants put the most productive part of the economy in the hands of foreign companies, not Honduran citizens. By 1910, North American companies owned 80 percent of the banana crop and the best lands on the Caribbean coast; even the ports, such as Puerto Cortés and

A U.S. steamer loads bananas from the Caribbean coast of Nicaragua, 1893.
(Photo *Popular Science Monthly,* June 1894)

joined together other small banana companies from Honduras to Colombia and, in 1899, he merged his company with the Boston Fruit Company to create the United Fruit Company. Keith failed to cultivate most of the land under the agreement, so he was forced to return it to Costa Rica; he nonetheless became so rich and powerful that some called him the uncrowned king of Central America.

Trujillo, functioned like company towns. The companies paid a set export tax—and by 1925, bananas constituted 88 percent of Honduran exports—but no taxes were paid on their profits.

The banana companies did employ Honduran workers, but workers were forced to buy in company stores that sold imported, not Honduran, goods—and the goods, carried on company steamships and sold in Honduras, were exempted from customs duties. Chronic labor shortages—most Hondurans did not want to relocate from the highlands to the disease-ridden Caribbean—also meant workers were brought in from the English-speaking West Indies, reinforcing the long-standing preference for English on the Caribbean coast and the dominance of the foreign English-speaking companies. The banana companies became more influential than the Honduran government. Although Honduras was the world's largest banana producer from 1925 to 1939, it remained sadly undeveloped. While railroads connected banana plantations to the ports, Tegucigalpa was the only Central American capital without train service, and it would remain so until 1980.

Five National Identities

Liberal policies developed national economies that reinforced the independence of each state. Railroads ran from the Pacific to the Caribbean—or, given the interests of the foreign investors, from coffee *fincas* and banana plantations to the ports—but they did not cross national borders, nor did they unite the isthmus. Telegraph lines and roads linked once isolated provinces with the cities and pulled the countries together for the first time. National agricultural exports also served to unify countries, giving both cities and rural communities a common economic purpose.

The liberal era consolidated each Central American nation, and each emerged from the positivist age with a distinct national identity. Even the three major coffee republics developed different social and political characteristics. Costa Rica laid the foundation for a democratic republic and a national economy that relied on small family farms. El Salvador did the opposite; by eliminating the small landowner, it created a coffee oligarchy unparalleled in other Central American nations. Guatemala's coffee elite, a more expansive class than in El Salvador, nonetheless ruled quite similarly in its collusion with military dictatorships and dominance over a peasant population. Guatemala, however, was unique among all Central American nations in that its population remained predominantly Indian and culturally removed from mestizo society.

Honduras and Nicaragua were subject to far more political turmoil than were the three coffee republics. Despite liberal reforms of the church and efforts to develop their mining industries and agricultural exports, they did not force systematic land and labor reforms in the manner of Guatemala and El Salvador. The two nations confronted unusual foreign obstacles to their internal development. Honduras permitted foreign companies to control its mines and banana production, and in the process lost its political independence as well. It was too poor to develop elite classes like those in the other nations. Although Nicaragua was more assertively independent and its diversified economy sustained a substantial elite class of about 5 percent of the population, its internal development was ultimately forced to take second place to foreign interests.

Liberal Legacy

The liberal dictators changed Central American society, placing wealth and power in the hands of coffee producers and merchants instead of the colonial aristocracy, but they left the militarized political structure of the conservatives intact and the arbitrariness of dictatorial rule unchecked by anything other than rubber-stamp legislatures. Coffee integrated Central America, particularly Costa Rica, Guatemala and El Salvador, into the capitalist world market, but at the same time the export-driven economy failed to develop other aspects of the domestic economy, such as industry or consumer markets. It did, however, create a large, powerless class of rural workers that would trouble the isthmus in the decades to come.

The liberals modernized their countries to unprecedented levels. The improved roads, railroads and telegraph lines unified them internally, if not across national boundaries. The Central American nations emerged from the period with individual identities, despite their shared history, geography, and economy. But they paid the price for modernization in massive land grants and debts to foreign institutions, and they would pay quite dearly in future decades as well.

10

DOLLAR "DIPLOMACY" AND THE DICTATORS (1898–1944)

The United States is powerful and great.
When it shivers there's profound earthquake
that occurs in the immense spine of the Andes . . .

■

Rubén Darío, Ode to Roosevelt
(translated from Cantos de Vida y Esperanza, *1905)*

Central American dictatorships grew increasingly repressive during the first half of the 19th century. Even as their modernization and educational programs changed Central American society, the oligarchies provided few opportunities other than the military for social mobility. Social unrest and border conflicts worried foreign businesses and their governments, who meddled in local affairs and, in the case of Nicaragua, occupied entire nations.

U.S. companies eventually replaced European creditors, and U.S. Marines replaced British gunboats. After the Panama Canal was completed in 1914, the United States considered Central America and the Caribbean sufficiently critical to its economic interests and security that it needed to police the region. Intervention in Central American affairs became frequent. By the end of World War I, U.S. companies and the U.S. government controlled more of the Central American economy— and, often, more of its politicians—than the Central Americans did.

The Mexican Revolution (1910–17) gave hope to the growing class of intellectuals and laboring poor in Central America. Labor movements and opposition parties contested dictatorial power, but the pockets of unrest caused by the depression of 1929 were quickly and ruthlessly suppressed by the military. The creation of international tri-bunals and organizations, such as the Pan American Union, provided forums for Central Americans to be heard above the gunboats, but the desperate need for economic and political reforms would not be addressed until after World War II.

Central American Society

Liberal regimes grew more tyrannical as they became accustomed to unchallenged control of every aspect of national life. Declaring martial law, that great exception clause to constitutional rights, they suppressed free speech, censored the press, and exiled or imprisoned the opposi-tion. Political corruption was rampant and government concessions were granted to those privileged citizens and foreign investors with the money to pay for them. The military expanded, as did national police forces; military coups multiplied. Costa Rica, which honored freedom of the press and opposition political parties, was the exception to oppressive dictatorial rule, and it was the only nation that spent more for education than for the military.

At the same time, Central American society had changed quite radi-cally because of liberal policies. Reorganized postal services meant a let-ter no longer took two months to travel between Costa Rica and Guatemala. Improved public health services and mandatory vaccinations controlled epidemics such as smallpox and cholera. Foreign corporations in the Caribbean region used sanitation, modern medicines, and com-pany hospitals to control malaria and other tropical diseases. The result was an increase in population: In 1945 the population numbered 8 mil-lion, in contrast to 2 million in 1855. For the first time population levels in Central America exceeded those at the time of the Spanish conquest.

Some Government Expenditures in 1913*					
	Guatemala	Honduras	Nicaragua	El Salvador	Costa Rica
Public Works	220,000	287,000	902,000	600,000	695,000
Education	180,000	152,000	159,000	354,000	635,000
Military	520,000	720,000	410,000	1,600,000	627,000

*In U.S. dollars
*After Munro, 1918, 286

Given their emphasis on education, the liberal dictators could have accomplished more than they did: Only 150,000 of 5.5 million Central Americans (excluding Panama and Belize) could read and write by the 1920s. Nonetheless, that was an improvement. The number of schools had increased markedly, especially in Costa Rica, where universal education laws had been enacted. Even in impoverished Honduras, there were 851 schools by the beginning of the 20th century in contrast to 275 in the 1870s, and President Zelaya's reforms in Nicaragua put 20,000 more students in the classroom. Costa Rica had enacted compulsory education laws. Each republic, not just Guatemala, had at least one university and

RUBÉN DARÍO, FOUNDER OF MODERNIST POETRY

It is our America that has had poets
since the ancient times of Netzahuacoyotl . . .
that since remote moments in its life
has lived on light, fire, perfume, love,
the America of the great Moctezuma, of the Inca,
Christopher Columbus's redolent America,
Catholic America! Spanish America! . . .

■

Rubén Darío, "Ode to Roosevelt," 1905
(translated from Cantos de Vida y Esperanza 1948, 49)

Rubén Darío (1867–1916) is considered one of the great poets of the Americas. Born in a village near León, Nicaragua, Darío was initially educated at a Jesuit school, but at the age of 14, he educated himself in the classics of Spanish literature at the national library in Managua. His exceptional talent was recognized early—he wrote his first verses at age 13—and he was chosen to accompany diplomatic missions throughout Latin America, eventually serving as President Zelaya's ambassador in Madrid. Like most cosmopolitan Central Americans of the era, he looked to Europe for cultural inspiration and spent much of his life abroad. He established a residence in Paris, where he was influenced by French symbolist poetry. His poems, such as *Cantos de Vida y Esperanza* (Songs of life and hope), expressed his concerns about the future of Spanish America. He was a founder of *Modernismo,* a literary movement that revolutionized Spanish poetry, especially in Latin America.

a national library, which contributed to the growth of an intellectual class in urban areas. As limited as these public institutions were, they inculcated a growing sense of nationalism and greater social awareness.

Central American society also had taken on a more foreign cast during the liberal era. Germans owned 10 percent of the coffee *fincas* in Guatemala. Costa Rica's foreign residents constituted almost 10 percent of its population. The Caribbean coast, with the influx of West Indian workers for the banana companies, added African-American, English-speaking residents in great numbers. Banana plantations and American-dominated ports became enclaves within Hispanic Central America, each with company-owned schools, stores, and clinics, as well as Protestant churches and English-language newspapers.

Not only was the population more diverse than ever before, but it was increasingly influenced by more industrialized and wealthier cultures, through the growing number of newspapers, radios, and movie theaters. Cigarettes became more fashionable than cigars; baseball more popular than bullfights. Cars ran alongside mule-drawn trolleys. Paved streets, parks, indoor plumbing, and ornate public buildings transformed the colonial capitals. The cities, however, remained provincial compared to those in Europe and the United States.

The liberal era increased the government bureaucracy as well as the number of white-collar workers, and, in Costa Rica, a middle class began to emerge. Yet most Central Americans were increasingly impoverished; they filled sprawling slums that were the result of export policies. The upper class, rewarded by coffee profits, remained small, although foreigners, often the wealthiest and most influential members of society, were added to their number. Foreigners controlled the natural resources; they owned the railroads and the telegraph lines they had built, along with the shipping lines and, often, the banks; in some instances, their governments actually collected customs receipts—all as their price for modernizing the republics and lending them funds. These powerful foreigners within the republics caught everyone's notice, including the dictators who were beholden to them.

Dictators Clash

... they cannot be happy and prosperous unless they maintain order within their boundaries.

■

Theodore Roosevelt, President of the United States, 1905 (Le Febre 1993, 38)

Foreign investors desired stability and cheap labor. At the beginning of the 20th century, cheap labor was in plentiful supply, thanks to the policies of liberal dictators, but peace was not. Honduras was especially subject to coups and revolutions—it had three different leaders in a single year (1903)—partially because of standoffs between other dictators on the isthmus. Two of the most powerful dictators were Manuel Estrada Cabrera (1898–1920) in Guatemala and José Santos Zelaya (1893–1909) in Nicaragua.

Zelaya had brought Nicaragua, geographically the largest Central American nation, to an appropriate position of power on the isthmus. He guaranteed domestic peace by building up the neutral capital of Managua at the expense of the feuding cities of León and Granada. When he confronted British warships in 1894 and forced England completely out of the Mosquitía once and for all, he became a hero to all Central Americans in addition to his own people. He meddled in the leadership of neighboring countries, a power move formerly the domain of Guatemala, and even when he was not actually invading another nation, he supported exile groups in Nicaragua that could do the fighting for him. Nationalistic and increasingly worried about foreign intervention in Central America, he advocated unification—with himself as head of the federation, of course.

Zelaya's rise to prominence was an affront to Guatemala, the most populous nation in the region and the most powerful since colonial times. President Estrada Cabrera, like many Guatemalan dictators since independence, had isthmus-wide ambitions of his own, so much so that Mexico supported Zelaya in order to hold Estrada Cabrera in check. The squabbles led to coups and invasions. In 1906 Zelaya organized El Salvador and Costa Rica against Guatemala, and invaded it. Guatemala retaliated. Honduras was caught between the two great dictators and became the battleground for the first Central American conflict employing machine guns, introduced by Zelaya. The instability worried U.S. investors, now backed by President Theodore Roosevelt (1901–09), who had no tolerance for the byzantine feuds of Latin American politicians.

U.S.A.: World Power

As in their several ways England and France and Germany have stood, so we in our own way are beginning to stand and must continue to stand toward the industrial enterprise of the world.

■

Elihu Root, U.S. Secretary of State, 1906 (La Feber 1993, 36)

QUICHÉ WAR HEROES

A bugle was blown to signal the advance, and the fierce Momostecans charged with daggers drawn.

■

A Momostecan military officer (Carmack 1995, 209)

Momostenango provides an interesting glimpse into the militarization of Central America and, in particular, Guatemala during the liberal era. In that village, the official mestizo militia governed the town and occupied its only two-story building. The militia, somewhat miraculously, managed to absorb the rebellious Quiché Mayans into what would become the largest and best fighting unit in the entire country. All Indians were forced to serve in the military, but the success of the Momostecan militia was its preservation of Mayan lineage organization in special fighting units, led by Quiché officers. Mayan shaman priests also were absorbed into this system as special spiritual advisers in charge of the militia's patron saint, Santiago (St. James). In 1906 the Momostecan Mayans became national heroes when they fought courageously against the Salvadorans during a power struggle between President Estrada Cabrera and President Tomás Regalado. The Quichés killed the Salvadoran dictator on the battlefield, and brought home a victory for Guatemala. After their defeat of the Salvadorans, Quiché soldiers were honored with medals, promotions, and land grants. Five hundred of them became the trusted palace guards for President Estrada Cabrera as well as the tyrant, President Ubico (1931–44). While they lived in the presidential palace in Guatemala City, they were permitted to construct ancestral shrines where they celebrated Mayan rituals, burning incense and sacrificing chickens.

After Robert M. Carmack (1995) and Barbara Tedlock (1982).

By the turn of the century, the United States had become a world power and an industrial giant. Having won the Spanish-American War of 1898, the United States "liberated" Cuba from Spanish control, effectively eliminating any remnants of Spain's power in the New World. It substituted its own naval bases on Caribbean islands and as far away as the former Spanish possession of the Philippines.

With a sphere of influence that stretched from the Atlantic to the far Pacific, the United States required a canal through the isthmus of Central America for its navy. Yet the Clayton-Bulwer Treaty with Britain in 1850 prevented its exclusive control of such a canal and reduced the U.S. government to idle blustering about the Monroe Doctrine as the French company of Ferdinand de Lesseps started digging a canal in Panama in 1882. Yellow fever and engineering obstacles bankrupted the French effort in 1889, keeping U.S. options open. In 1901, Britain agreed to release the United States from the treaty; in the same year, a U.S. commission recommended that the United States construct a canal through Nicaragua. The possible construction, and control, of a canal intensified U.S. involvement in Central America and raised concerns about maintaining the security of such an investment.

Business interests represented a major ingredient in the expansionist policies of the new world power. U.S. capital invested in Central America was growing at a phenomenal rate, from $11.5 million in 1897 to $76.9 million in 1914. Investments surpassed those of many longtime investors in the region, such as Germany; by 1913 the U.S. was catching up with the $115 million peak level of investments made by Great Britain, until then the most powerful nation in the region. The United States also helped local governments refinance their loans to European powers, making Central America even more dependent on its neighbor to the north.

U.S. investments not only outstripped other foreign investments in magnitude, they frequently were different in their nature. North Americans preferred productive enterprises such as banana companies, mines, shipping companies, and railroads, not the government securities in which England had invested. As a result, U.S. investments prac-

Direct U.S. Investments in Central America (in millions of dollars)				
	1897	1914	1919	1929
Guatemala	6.0	35.8	40.0	58.8
El Salvador	n/a	6.6	12.8	24.8
Honduras	2.0	9.5	18.4	80.3
Nicaragua	n/a	3.4	7.8	17.3
Costa Rica	3.5	21.6	17.8	20.5
TOTAL	11.5	76.9	96.3	201.7

Source: UNECLA, *El Financiamiento externo de América Latina* (Dec. 1964, 13)

Central American Commerce, 1913*		
	Exports	Imports
To & From U.S.A.	17,500,805	20,519,159
To & From Britain	7,861,577	6,154,025
To & From Germany	11,820,866	5,239,729

'In U.S. dollars.
Source: After Munro 1918 (1967, 274–77)

tically monopolized the economies of Honduras and Nicaragua and transformed all the others; in Costa Rica, for example, North American tropical fruit companies by themselves nearly matched all British investments there. The impact of U.S. investments was quickly revealed. By 1913, the United States already dominated Central American commerce and after World War I disrupted trade with Europe, U.S. dominance was guaranteed. Between 1913 and 1929, Nicaragua's exports to the United States increased 100 percent, Guatemala's 150 percent, and Honduras's, an astounding 600 percent.

The Natural Protector

Intervention is justified when it's made necessary to guarantee the capitals and markets of the United States.

■

U.S. President William Howard Taft, 1912 (Handy 1984, 77)

As the 20th century began, political personalities, canals, and an expansionist U.S. foreign policy all conspired with business interests to create an aggressive North American presence in Central America. Honduras and Nicaragua, with the largest U.S. investments, took the brunt of the United States declaration that it was the "natural protector" of the Western Hemisphere.

Long disdainful of Latin America and even racist in attitude toward the people he called "dagos," U.S. president Theodore Roosevelt decided to put an end to the incessant political feuds and coups. Turning the Monroe Doctrine on its head, he implemented the Roosevelt Corollary; instead of preventing foreign intervention in the Americas in order to protect each nation's sovereignty, Roosevelt advocated interference in the domestic affairs of Central American nations in order to maintain the peace—and U.S. business profits.

Although later North American presidents, from William Taft through Calvin Coolidge, would try to soften the "big stick" nature of Roosevelt's Corollary, they also used military force when their preferred method, "Dollar Diplomacy," failed. Even President Woodrow Wilson meddled in the affairs of Costa Rica in order to protect U.S. oil interests (1918–20), despite his claim that the Monroe Doctrine meant unhindered self-determination for all nations of the world.

Honduras: The Big Stick

You are the United States,
you are the future invader . . .

■

Rubén Darío, "Ode to Roosevelt," 1905

In 1907 the United States had not thought Honduras important enough to have a diplomat in residence there. Yet in that same year, U.S. Marines landed on Honduran soil in keeping with Teddy Roosevelt's interpretation of the Monroe Doctrine. In that year, President Zelaya, with the assistance of El Salvador, attempted to overthrow the Honduran president, General Manuel Bonilla (1903–07), a great friend of the banana companies.

During the armed turbulence that followed, U.S. troops landed at Puerto Cortés to protect business interests, and other troops protected Bonilla from Nicaraguan attack at the Pacific port of Amapala. In the end, the United States negotiated a truce and selected an interim Honduran president. But the peace was short-lived, and military intervention did not bring about greater stability. From 1911 to 1925, U.S. warships frequently anchored in the Bay of Honduras, and the U.S. intervened six times in Honduran political affairs. In one three-year period, there were 17 coups and revolutions.

Honduran instability did not result simply from Central American factionalism. Rival banana companies instigated many of the conflicts, including the overthrow of the U.S.-selected interim president in 1907. Each corporation bribed Central American governments for favors, and if that method failed, they paid for coups and conflicts that would give them the desired result—even if, at times, such actions were in direct conflict with the policies of the United States government.

The banana companies even hired U.S. mercenaries to achieve their goals. "General" Lee Christmas and his sidekick "Machine Gun" Molony were the most famous soldiers of fortune courted by the largest corporations. The Cuyamel Fruit Company, for example, attempted to build a railroad from its plantations in Honduras into Guatemala, but Guatemalan forces defended their territory—with substantial support from the United Fruit Company. Not until United Fruit merged with Cuyamel Fruit in 1929 did some semblance of political stability come to Honduras.

A Peaceful Alternative

In 1904, a group of progressive Central Americans created an educational movement designed to communicate the benefits of Central American unification. The Partido Unionista advocated the democratic reforms and centralized government of the formerly disgraced federalist, Morazán. They gained adherents in each of the five republics, and their peaceful way of approaching problems common to Central Americans had considerable influence. Although they never achieved a federation, they created an atmosphere in which less ambitious joint efforts were undertaken.

Tribunals for resolving conflicts were established and, in 1906, Nicaragua and Honduras submitted to arbitration in order to settle their boundary in the Mosquitía (although they continued to disagree on the findings until 1960). In 1907 the United States and Mexico sponsored an expansion of the regional tribunal into a Central American Court of Justice. Although Zelaya protested U.S. involvement in what should have been isthmian business, all five Central American nations supported the court and hammered out the terms by which it would operate. The court established peaceful procedures for settling disputes as well as rules for avoiding them, such as restrictions on activities of exiles and the nonrecognition of governments established by force. The court was an excellent idea and did reduce conflicts between Central American nations. The court failed, however, because the United States refused to follow its rulings and, instead, militarily intervened in Nicaragua in 1912 and made it a protectorate in 1916.

Nicaragua: U.S. Occupation

I spent thirty-three years [in the Marine Corps] . . . I was a racketeer for capitalism. I helped purify Nicaragua . . .

■

General Darlington Smedley Butler, 1931 (Schmidt 1931, 231)

Central American and U.S. leaders at the 1907 peace conference in Washington, D.C., that led to the creation of the Central American Court of Justice. (Photo from U.S. National Archives)

The United States had decided on an interoceanic canal in Nicaragua. With the future of such a canal in mind, the U.S. government carefully negotiated its way through the 19th century conflict between U.S. companies in the Mosquitia and President Zelaya's attempt to assert Nicaragua's rightful control over that territory. It maintained positive relations in order to keep the option of a canal agreement alive, yet still resented the many protective restrictions that Zelaya insisted upon in order to maintain Nicaraguan sovereignty. Trouble between the two nations began in 1903, when the United States opted instead for a canal in Panama, where it could dictate its own terms. (SEE page 199.)

Zelaya wanted the prosperity such a canal would bring to his country with or without the United States. He invited the other world powers, among them England, Germany, and Japan, to discuss a canal agreement. The United States balked. It saw Zelaya's action as one of defiance and interpreted his nationalism as anti-American. The United States, of course, did not want competition for its Panamanian canal, and believed a European-owned canal would threaten its political dominance of the isthmus.

The United States began a major campaign against Zelaya, arguing that he posed a threat to democracy on the isthmus and undermined

196

the well-being of his own people. President Roosevelt attempted to garner North American sympathy for an action against Zelaya, and also supported revolts within Nicaragua and tried to persuade other Central American nations to join the conflict. Costa Rica did not support the intervention of the northern colossus in the sovereignty of a neighboring nation; Guatemala, under President Estrada Cabrera, was not so farsighted.

Estrada Cabrera was as tyrannical as Zelaya, but he catered more easily to U.S. interests. As a result, he managed to stay in power until 1920. Zelaya was forced to resign in 1909 after foreign businesses in the Mosquitía sponsored a conservative party revolt that was aided by the presence of U.S. officers. The revolt began in Bluefields, grew with support from U.S. President Taft, and led to the installation of a conservative government very much dependent on the Taft administration. The U.S. action brought about financial and political instability in Nicaragua.

In 1912, not liking the protests by both liberals and conservatives against its puppet government, Taft sent in the U.S. Marine Corps. The marines kept the "peace" and protected the puppet president, Adolfo Díaz; U.S. agents took over the customs office, national bank,

North American colony in Bluefields, Nicaragua, 1893. Bluefields was a center for U.S. companies and an example of the increasing U.S. presence in regions where Britain had formerly ruled. The approximately 100 North American residents were employees of the Bluefield Steamship Company and the 19 banana plantations in the region (all of which would be controlled by the United Fruit Company within a few years). To make Bluefields as much like home as possible, they built in the style of "Small Town, U.S.A.," and even imported the lumber to do so. (Photo Popular Science Monthly, June 1904)

and railroad. In 1916, the Bryan-Chamorro Treaty made it official: Nicaragua was a U.S. protectorate and General Emiliano Chamorro was "elected" president—and the United States had perpetual rights to a canal along the San Juan River. The protestations of the Central American Court of Justice and the hesitation of the U.S. Congress changed little: The U.S. Marines occupied Nicaragua almost continuously until 1933. By then, Yankee imperialism was a well-recognized fact on the isthmus, and those who opposed it would become Central American heroes.

Unrest

> ... the United States has aroused strong antagonism in Central America.
>
> ■
>
> *Dana G. Munro, 1918 (1967, 306)*

With both the U.S. Marines and local dictators to back up their interests, North American businesses doubled their investments in Central America in the decade from 1919 to 1929. But both the investments and gunboat-enforced "stability" undermined the development of more democratic institutions and failed to distribute any of the benefits of economic growth to the working class. Central Americans felt increasingly betrayed by the liberals, and anti-Yankee sentiments grew.

Dictators stayed in power only as long as they pleased the United States—as Estrada Cabrera learned when President Woodrow Wilson did not prevent his overthrow in 1920. The dictators responded to foreign power, not to their own people; a coup, not an election, was the only way to change a regime. When the Mexican Revolution (1910–17) succeeded in ridding that country of its dictator and instituting progressive social policies, Central Americans became restless with their own situation.

The first strikes started in Honduras on the banana plantations in 1917. The strikes were isolated and were easily put down by the military in collusion with foreign companies. Strikes spread throughout Central America, and national police forces were created to keep the domestic peace. In the cities, the working class and intellectuals were more easily influenced by international labor movements. From the cities, ideas spread across nations and reenergized the Partido Unionista, which had long advocated a new political order in Central America. The ideas were carried into the rural areas where 90 percent of the workforce resided, and the labor unrest became more organized.

PANAMA CANAL

Panama, separated from Colombia by the Darién wilderness, had been subject to Colombia, but never integrated into that nation; it had tried to secede several times during the 19th century. In 1902, encouraged by the bankrupted French canal company's desire to sell its concessions and property, the United States landed troops in Panama without Colombian or Panamanian permission. It tried to force a canal agreement on Colombia, but that outraged nation refused to surrender control over the proposed canal zone. The United States and France then arranged an insurrection with some Panamanian politicians and immediately recognized the newly "independent" republic. Within two weeks, a canal agreement was finalized that granted the United States 10 percent of Panamanian territory as a protectorate. The eradication of yellow fever and malaria as well as engineering ingenuity and a $353 million investment permitted the construction of the canal. Nonetheless, more than 5,600 workers lost their lives building it. Completed in 1914, the Panama Canal was (and remains) the largest human-constructed project in the world, and required the removal of 400 million cubic feet of earth. Its sheer physical size divided Panama in half and hindered development of a Panamanian national identity until late in the 20th century. Its linking of the Atlantic and Pacific Oceans changed the ecosystems of the two vast seas that had been separated since the isthmus was formed. Its completion left a heavy social burden on Panama: an enormous newly unemployed workforce of Chinese and West Indian immigrants.

Construction of Miraflores Locks, Panama Canal, 1913. (Photo [detail] Library of Congress, Prints and Photographs Division)

THE NATIONAL GUARD

Sandino's struggle against U.S. imperialism captured the sentiment of Central America. He had vowed to lay down his arms as soon as the U.S. forces withdrew. In order to withdraw, the United States had created, trained, and armed a "politically neutral" Nicaraguan force, called the National Guard, to replace the marines. Anastasio Somoza, educated in the United States and fluent in English, was made its commander. In 1934, Sandino entered Managua under a negotiated truce to dine with President Sacasa. At this critical moment in the peace negotiations, U.S. minister Arthur Bliss Lane reported to Washington that Somoza had guaranteed Sandino's safety. Sandino, however, was treacherously assassinated by the National Guard upon leaving the president's house. Somoza had his own political agenda, and it quickly led to control of Nicaragua—and the unflagging support of the United States. Chamorro and Sacasa, who as presidents had cooperated in the development of the "neutral" National Guard, now begged the United States to put an end to the Guards' control of Nicaraguan politics—but to no avail. Sandino became a legendary hero and, in the future struggle against the Somoza dictatorship, the rebels would call themselves "Sandinistas."

General Anastasio Somoza Garcia (1896–1956) and César Augusto Sandino (1895–1934). (Photo Nicaraguan National Archives)

A general strike on the banana plantations forced the companies to respond with a pay increase.

The unrest—and the watchful eyes of organizations like the newly formed League of Nations—transformed Central America's leadership. In Guatemala, Estrada Cabrera was overthrown and replaced by a new reform government that recognized opposition parties, including the Communist Party. In El Salvador, the conservative dictator Pío Romero Bosque (1927–31) legalized labor rights and freedom of the press. In Costa Rica, the government acknowledged the legitimacy of labor unions without even trying to repress them. The new leaders initiated plans for a Central American federation in time for the 1921 centennial celebration of independence; such unionist dreams once again went unrealized, however, much to the liking of the United States.

At the Havana Conference of 1928, the reform leaders joined Caribbean leaders in resolving, over U.S. objections, that "No State has a right to interfere in the internal affairs of another." Such sentiments were embodied in the popular Nicaraguan revolt led by César Augusto Sandino, an officer in the liberal opposition army. From 1926 until 1933, Sandino and his band of a few hundred guerrillas successfully harassed the U.S.-supported government. Sandino had a single purpose: to rid Nicaragua of the U.S. Marines. His defiance of the United States became a symbol of anti-imperialism in Central America and a source of embarrassment to the U.S. When Nicaragua's new liberal president, Juan Bautista Sacasa, urged the withdrawal of the marines in 1933, the United States eagerly agreed.

The 1930s and Depression

The few reforms won during the 1920s were soon lost. The crash of the U.S. economy in 1929 was disastrous for Central America as well. Coffee exports were cut in half. In El Salvador, wages, too, were halved. Honduran banana exports declined for the first time. Thousands of workers became unemployed; those lucky enough to keep their jobs had their wages reduced.

More than anything, the depression revealed the failure of liberal policies. Central America had grown heavily dependent not just on its two export crops, but also on a single market: the United States. There were no alternative sources of revenue; there was no domestic commerce. With trade revenues plummeting, money was too scarce to import an adequate food supply—again, one made necessary by the devotion of land to export crops. Many republics were forced to default on their foreign loans; most increased their debt by refinancing, usually through U.S. banks—but the United States, the largest investor in the region, was in no position to be very helpful. Already dismayingly dependent, Central America was put even more at the mercy of the United States.

The destroyed economy and leftist political agitation created considerable fear among many in Central America, especially the oligarchies and foreign investors. In the 1930s, any demand for social change was deemed a communist threat. Even Costa Rica temporarily suspended constitutional protections in 1932. In the other four

PRUDENCIA AYALA, PRESIDENTIAL CANDIDATE

Prudencia Ayala, crusader for women's rights in El Salvador. (Photo courtesy Museo de la Palabra y Imagen ["Museum of Word and Image"], San Salvador)

Central Americans were inspired by many international political movements, including that of the suffragists. The Salvadoran Prudencia Ayala (1890–1946) struggled for women's rights and was often imprisoned for her views as well as her participation in public demonstrations. A member of the Partido Unionista, she was imprisoned in Guatemala for plotting the overthrow of Estrada Cabrera. Born in an Indian village in the Sonsonate region, she grew up in the more sophisticated city of Santa Ana, where she became a journalist, activist, and author of two literary works. In 1930, Ayala became the first woman to declare herself a candidate for the Salvadoran presidency—or for any Latin American presidency, for that matter—as a way of protesting the laws that barred women from politics. Women's suffrage, however, would not be recognized anywhere in Central America for almost two more decades.

nations, new military dictators came into office, and these were more reassuring to the United States and ruling elite. They brought into office with them an increasingly powerful military.

General Tiburcio Carías Andino (1932–48) provided stability in Honduras; indeed he ruled longer than anyone in Honduran history. Just as important, he effectively put down labor strikes and, at a time when increasing numbers of Hondurans were unemployed and destitute, he devoted the budget to military expenditures and U.S. debt payments. In Guatemala, General Jorge Ubico (1931–44), although something of an embarrassment to the United States for his admiration of the fascist dictatorship of Generalissimo Franco in Spain, remained in office by giving new concessions to foreign investors and terrorizing his own country with a newly organized secret police. In 1934, General Somoza began the ruthless domination of Nicaragua, which would continue for 22 years.

The most violent reaction, however, occurred in El Salvador, under General Maximiliano Hernández Martínez (1931–44). Hunger had caused numerous uprisings on the coffee *fincas*, and many Indian and mestizo workers had joined the Communist Party, led by Agustín Farabundo Martí. The military, dissatisfied with the governmental response, overthrew the president and tried to wipe out the Marxists. In 1932, a peasant revolt swept El Salvador. Within three days and after 30 civilian deaths, the military regained control. Then, in what is known in Salvadoran history as *la matanza* ("the slaughter"), the government killed Martí, other rebel leaders, and as many as 30,000 peasants, most of them Indians. The military then ruled, uncontested, for the next 50 years. When trouble broke out again, the name of the martyred Farabundo Martí would be its rallying cry.

Good Neighbor Policy

As early as the 1920s, the United States had wanted to end its armed intervention in Central America. For the Republican presidents, it was too costly; for the U.S. Congress, it was an international embarrassment. Given U.S. economic and political influence on the isthmus, military intervention also was simply unnecessary—the Central American dictators of the 1930s looked after U.S. interests better than the U.S. Marines could.

Franklin D. Roosevelt (1933–45), however, was the first U.S. president to convince the Central American republics that nonintervention was truly part of U.S. policy. He ended all U.S. protectorates and developed military agreements with each nation to supply them with armaments and to train officers. Just as important, FDR overcame some of the disillusionment caused by the depression. He created a system of trade preferences whereby Central American exports enjoyed privileged access to the North American markets. And to reciprocate, of course, tariffs were lowered on U.S. imports. In 1940 a timely agreement guaranteed the import to the United States of Central American coffee, just as the war with Europe was blocking exports to that continent.

Roosevelt's Good Neighbor policy created a period of unusual cooperation and collaboration throughout the 1930s. Even in Nicaragua, where anti-Yankee sentiments were strongest, President Somoza had the U.S. embassy built on the grounds of the presidential palace. With the onset of World War II, the cooperative relationships continued. All the Central American nations declared war on Germany when the United States did in 1941, even those nations, such as Guatemala, that depended heavily on German trade.

Legacy

... and it would be difficult to persuade them that the [U.S.] interference ... in their affairs will ultimately be for their own good.

■

Dana G. Munro 1918, 306

In the first half of the 20th century, Central America became economically and militarily dominated by the United States in a manner unequaled in the rest of Latin America. Even British Honduras was absorbed into the banana trade and Panama gained its independence at the cost of the Panama Canal. U.S. military intervention intensified political instability, especially when judged by events in Honduras and Nicaragua, and it increased the power of already tyrannical dictators. The Good Neighbor policy smoothed over some of the anti-Yankee sentiments that resulted, but did nothing to correct the political and economic backwardness of the isthmus. Sandino's nationalism and Farabundo Martí's cry for greater economic equity had not been forgotten. As world peace was negotiated, Central Americans looked for change at home.

11

CHALLENGE TO
THE OLD ORDER
(1944–1975)

. . . we live in an antiquated society, which is disappearing. A
society divided between "the governing class" and "the people . . ."

■

José Figueres Ferrer, president of Costa Rica, 1955
(Edelman and Kenan 1989, 120)

World War II ended in 1945, but the struggle against fascism continued. New international organizations, such as the United
Nations, were founded to promote social development and democratic
values as well as world peace. For once, global events supported movements for reform within Central America, and one by one, the repressive dictators were thrown out. Nicaragua's Somoza was the only
exception. Progress, however, was stopped short of complete success by
the cold war. Under the guise of anticommunism, the oligarchies and
U.S. businesses protested reforms of the new governments, and the
United States supported the overthrow of elected officials whom they
suspected of leftist sympathies. The brief period of reform in Central
American politics created a sense of nationalism and brought many new
social groups into the political process. The economy benefited from
reform, too; exports were diversified and industrialization was initiated
through the Central American Common Market. In the 1960s, the U.S.
Alliance for Progress resulted in direct governmental aid in order to
correct some of the social ills plaguing the region. These efforts, like the
unfinished political reforms, failed to improve the lives of most Central
Americans.

Demands for Change

The country is a victim of foreign capital . . .

■

Surco, a Costa Rican magazine, 1940
(Edelman and Kenan 1989, 107)

Central America did not shake off the economic effects of the depression of 1929 until after World War II. Price controls on exports, established by the United States during the war, had contributed to the delayed recovery. And imported goods needed for development were unavailable from a war-driven United States. U.S. investments declined as well, by as much as 50 percent between 1929 and 1944. Under such conditions, state revenues did not reach their predepression levels until 1944 in Guatemala and El Salvador, and not until the 1950s in Honduras and Nicaragua. Yet the dictators' very conservative fiscal policies, which pleased foreign investors, actually generated a surplus by the end of World War II.

The protracted economic stagnation was devastating to the vast majority of Central Americans. El Salvador, almost totally dependent on coffee revenues, temporarily abandoned the harvest of beans as unprofitable. Conditions on the *fincas* were so bad that many workers fled; peasant migrations persisted until Salvadorans eventually constituted 10 percent of the workforce in Honduras, a situation that would erupt in violence in the 1960s. Unemployment plagued the countryside and city alike. Everyone suffered, not just peasants but also middle-class bureaucrats, 40 percent of whom were laid off in the budget cutbacks in Nicaragua, Honduras, and Guatemala. Even in Costa Rica, the family farm and self-employed workers were disappearing. The oligarchies suffered the least, and for them, the national governments created coffee institutes to protect investments and develop the crop for future exports.

By the 1940s Central Americans were agitating for a restructured economy. They wanted economic growth that benefited them, not just foreigners and the elite. World organizations supported them, encouraging the peasant use of fallow lands and the development of factories and export diversification, not just the improvement of the elite's coffee crop. New agreements with foreign concessionaires, such as the United Fruit Company, were demanded that would pay better wages to workers and send more taxes into the treasury.

Central Americans had little doubt that it was time to challenge the political order. Human rights and social justice had been too long omitted from the liberal agenda. The middle class, including young, professionally educated military officers, argued for constitutionally protected elections instead of tyrannical dictators; workers demanded laws providing social security, an eight-hour workday and the right to strike. The poor required land. Intellectuals demanded nothing less than a restructuring of social and political life.

Sweeping Reforms

We are left with the only path: Resistance. And their only path is dictatorship. There is no middle ground. No shades of gray. The die has been cast.

■

Eugenio Rodríguez Vegas, Costa Rican journalist, 1948
(Edelman and Kenan 1989, 114)

Frustrated Central Americans from a diversity of classes and backgrounds supported these reforms. Shoe cobblers and students, small landowners and shopkeepers, bureaucrats and novelists, young military officers, peasants, and intellectuals—all were desperate for new opportunities. New political parties were organized: local ones, such as the National Renovation Party (PRN) in Guatemala, and isthmian ones, such as the Unión Patriótica de Centro-America that advocated a democratic federation of states. They provided alternatives to the tired exchange between liberals and conservatives. Yet the dictators and the elite class saw any demand for reform equivalent to a revolution. Failing to respond to any needs but their own, they provoked popular uprisings and national strikes led by the urban middle class and executed by discontented army officers. The United States, believing its political role was more global, was initially preoccupied with matters in Europe and Asia. In fact, during the postwar years, Latin America received less U.S. aid than any other region of the world.

In 1944 Ubico in Guatemala and Hernández Martínez of El Salvador were overthrown. Change soon followed elsewhere—everywhere, in fact, but Nicaragua. It was in Guatemala and Costa Rica, however, that the greatest challenges to the old order occurred.

207

Guatemala 1944–1954

*We are going to add justice to humanity and order, because
order based on injustice and humiliation is good for nothing.*

■

Juan José Arévalo, inauguration speech, 1945 (Hardy 1984, 103)

In the first free and honest elections in Guatemalan history, Juan José
Arévalo was elected president in 1944. A middle-class revolution, its
agenda articulated by university students and its seriousness backed by
young military officers, had forced the resignation of General Ubico and
ushered in one of the most optimistic periods in the nation's history.
For 10 years, Guatemala's government, led first by Arévalo and then by
General Jacobo Arbenz (1950–54), passed social legislation to lift
Guatemalans out of their abject poverty. In 1945, a new constitution
was promulgated that created an open government with democratic
institutions such as a free press and opposition political parties. In
keeping with the idealism of the times, the constitution also proposed
a union with other Central American nations.

The 40-year-old Arévalo, a former philosophy professor who had
been living in political exile in Argentina, described himself as neither
communist nor capitalist, but rather as a "spiritual socialist." A political moderate, he was nonetheless convinced Guatemalan society needed restructuring before it could become a viable, modern nation. He
forced large landholders to rent their fallow land to peasants at low
prices and passed laws that protected workers' rights. Both policies, of
course, threatened the oligarchy and foreign business interests, such as
the United Fruit Company, even though business profits had been
unusually good throughout the reforms. But to implement his program,
Arévalo had to rely on the support of the Guatemalan communists who
controlled the Central Labor Federation; he attempted to assuage U.S.
concerns about Soviet influence by outlawing all parties with international affiliations.

As the next election neared, conservatives hoped to undo Arévalo's
social reforms by voting in the popular candidate General Francisco
Arana, who had participated in the coalition that overthrew Ubico. His
assassination in 1949 precipitated a serious conservative revolt—the
22nd coup attempt that Arévalo had to defeat. Despite troubling political undercurrents, Arévalo made significant progress. Free elections
had been instituted for the first time. Urban wages increased 80 percent

from 1945 to 1950. Hospitals, schools to reduce the nation's 75 percent illiteracy rate, electrification, and other public works programs began to improve the quality of life for Guatemalans.

Yet more reform was needed, especially in rural areas, where the health and well-being of peasants, most of them Mayans, had long been neglected. In 1950, there was an average of only one doctor per 6,300 inhabitants, the worst ratio in all of Central America. Even impoverished Honduras had one per 4,800 inhabitants, and Nicaragua and Costa Rica each had ratios under 3,000. The average annual income from a small peasant farm in Guatemala was U.S. $220, half that of Nicaraguan and Salvadoran peasants. Yet income from large Guatemalan estates were the highest in Central America. Agrarian reform was desperately needed.

In 1949 Arévalo's minister of defense, the 37-year-old Arbenz, was able to garner 65 percent of the vote. Arbenz was not a communist, nor was his government, but he was more sympathetic to Communist Party members than Arévalo had been and less cautious about permitting them to hold government positions. Guatemala would soon suffer for his progressive politics. Arbenz's agrarian reforms were criticized by U.S. investors as communistic, even though they had been recommended by the International Bank for Reconstruction and Development.

The Agrarian Reform Act of 1952 authorized the redistribution of unused lands to peasants from large estates of more than 223 acres, and the government was eager to implement this program in the western part of the country where subsistence crops were desperately needed. In return for the expropriated land, owners would be compensated at the recorded assessed value. Large landowners, such as the United Fruit Company, had long undervalued their land in order

Average Income from Farming (in U.S. Dollars)				
	Guatemala	El Salvador	Nicaragua	Costa Rica
Small Plots	220	420	445	908
Medium-sized	8,000	7,106	2,247	2,117
Large Estates	40,000	25,748	18,226	20,473

Source: After Torres Rivas (1993, 75)

CULTURAL RESURGENCE

The sun that beats down on the sugar plantations burned him inside: it burned his head till his hair no longer felt like hair, but like a pelt of ashes, and it burned the flittermouse of his tongue in the roof of his mouth, so he could not let the words of his dreams escape as he slept . . .

■

Miguel Ángel Asturias, Men of Maize *(1949) (Martin 1993, 9)*

Political optimism and growing nationalism gave birth to a new wave of Central American literature and art—and Central American pride. Salvador Salazar Arrúe ("Salarrúe") of El Salvador started contributing to the national culture as early as 1934 with his classic short stories, *Cuentos de Barro* ("Tales of Mud"); Carlos Luis Fallas ("Calufa") of Costa Rica wrote literary classics about life on the United Fruit plantations after he organized a strike of 10,000 United Fruit workers in 1934. María de Baratta (1890–1978), musician and ethnographer, was the first Salvadoran to study local folklore and recreate traditional songs and dances. The great Guatemalan novelist Miguel Ángel Asturias (1899–1974) was the first Latin American writer to receive the Nobel Prize in literature (1967) and his life and work, much like that of other writers and artists of the time, epitomize the contribution of intellectuals to the formation of a national consciousness. As a middle-class student at the University of San Carlos, Asturias was a political activist and demonstrator; upon graduation, he cofounded the Populist University of Guatemala for those who could not afford tuition at his alma mater. His Nobel-winning novel, *El Señor Presidente,* was about political dictatorship and was based on the repressive conditions under President Manuel Estrada Cabrera; the novel didn't see print until 1946 because another tyrant, Ubico, prevented its publication. Although Asturias lived in Europe for almost a decade, he was an ardent Americanist. He collaborated on the first translation of the *Popol Vuh* into Spanish and incorporated themes from this Mayan creation myth into his novel *Men of Maize* (1949). He served President Arévalo, a novelist himself (*The Shark and the Sardines,* 1961), as cultural attaché in Mexico and Argentina, and continued to write novels about conditions in Guatemala, such as his "Banana Trilogy," about the role of United Fruit in Guatemala. Despite the harsh social realities exposed in his novels, Asturias was not only a political writer, but also a founder of the Latin American school of magical realism.

210

Monument to the Revolution in San Salvador, 1948. The mural mosaic captures the spirit of change in the mid-century Salvadoran movement toward democracy. Guatemala, under President Arévalo, undertook the construction of an entire complex of buildings, called the Civic Center, as a symbol of the new Guatemala. Guatemalan artists, including Carlos Mérida, one of the most famous modern Latin American artists, painted and sculpted the complex with themes inspired by Mayan temples and a new "mestizo" culture. (Photo courtesy Ministry of Education, El Salvador)

to keep tax payments down; the new law meant the Arbenz government offered to pay United Fruit less than $1 million for land they then claimed was worth almost $16 million. United Fruit asked the U.S. State Department to intervene and, unfortunately for Guatemala, it did. As U.S.-trained Guatemalan forces gathered on the border with Honduras, Arbenz took repressive measures at home. Although he retained enough popular support to remain in office, the military abandoned him.

Red Menace

During most of the years of Guatemala's social revolution, the United States had not issued a single official criticism of its policies. The Good Neighbor policy of nonintervention remained intact. But in the late 1940s and in the 1950s, anticommunism replaced antifascism as the guiding principle in U.S. foreign policy. Anticommunist "witch hunts," led by U.S. Senator Joseph McCarthy, saw subversive activity everywhere. When the United Fruit Company complained to its good friend John Foster Dulles, secretary of state under President Dwight D. Eisenhower (1953–61), that communism was taking root in Guatemala and threatening its business, the United States officially expressed its concern to Guatemala. When Guatemalans supported the Soviet Union over the U.S. in a United Nations vote on Korea, Dulles saw U.S. policies openly flouted. When Czechoslovakia (then under Soviet control) shipped arms to Guatemala, he saw U.S. hegemony in the Western Hemisphere threatened by communism.

The United States once again intervened. A group of Guatemalan exiles in Honduras were trained for Operation El Diablo ("Operation Devil") by the U.S. Marines and the Central Intelligence Agency (CIA). U.S. arms were airlifted from Somoza's Nicaragua. In 1954, the military deserted Arbenz and the invasion of Guatemala quickly resulted in the overthrow of the constitutionally elected government. The United Nations and the Organization of American States (OAS), founded in 1948, could not act quickly enough to prevent Arbenz's forced resignation and exile. The new government, headed by the reactionary leader of the invasion, quickly purged Guatemala of its elements they believed to be communist. Once again the coffee oligarchy was in power under the protection of a military dictatorship. And other Central American nations had been instructed in the limits of U.S. tolerance for political independence.

Cover of an anticommunist pamphlet issued by the U.S. State Department in 1957. An aggressive public relations program, led by the United Fruit Company, convinced many North Americans that President Arbenz was a communist. Government pamphlets as well as private endeavors, such as United Fruit's film Why the Kremlin Hates Bananas, *were typical of the late 1950s.* (Photo U.S. National Archives)

213

Costa Rica: Figuerismo

I will win more battles against Yankee imperialism than they [the communists] have in twenty years, simply because it is a question of tactics.

■

José Figueres Ferrar, 1948 (Edelman and Kenan 1989, 107)

As usual, the situation in Costa Rica was unique. The revolt was not against conservative oligarchs, but rather against the populist government of Dr. Rafael Calderón Guardia (1940–44), who had enacted progressive legislation that provided social security benefits and a minimum wage—the very reforms desired in other Central American nations. Calderón's alliance with both the Catholic Church and the Communist Party, however, became the target of middle-class professionals, small business owners, and intellectuals. Operating under the socialist banner of José Figueres's Social Democratic Party, these groups wanted greater industrialization and domestic development, not just worker protections. When the coffee elite threw its backing to this faction in order to defeat Calderón, it facilitated the successful revolt of 1948.

The Social Democrats claimed electoral fraud against the popular *calderonistas* in the presidential election of 1948, and, on this pretense, plunged the nation into the Civil War of 1948. National divisions reflected isthmian ones as well: Guatemala aided Figueres, and Nicaragua backed the government of Calderón. And on the international front, the United States was concerned to end any government with a communist affiliation; it prevented Somoza from supplying arms to Calderón. Nonetheless, more than 2,000 Costa Ricans were killed before negotiations ended the fighting after 40 days. The political settlement placed Figueres at the head of an autocratic junta. Figueres outlawed the Communist Party and clamped down on the unions that supported it, defying the many constitutional guarantees that Costa Ricans had enjoyed. At the same time, Figueres's anticommunist leanings deflected U.S. criticism of his socialism—although Nicaragua, with U.S. support, continued to support the more conservative exiles living in Nicaragua.

Fortunately for Costa Rica, the junta resigned after 18 months under conditions that would assure the survival of the nation's democratic institutions and domestic development in the decades to come. A new constitution was ratified in 1949, legalizing many reforms, including many of the social welfare programs already enacted by Calderón for the working class. It also nationalized the banks and created credit unions to assist in the development of the domestic economy in ways that would protect owners of small- or medium-sized landholdings. And it assured a more democratic nation by granting voting rights to women and full citizenship to African-Americans—the first Central American country to do so. The constitution also eliminated the standing army—another Central American first—and created a civil service as well as an elections tribunal to guarantee honest elections.

The Civil War of 1948 laid the foundation for the modern Costa Rican social welfare state. It would be the only Central American nation where the reforms of the post–World War II years would endure. And José Figueres Ferrer (1906–90), engineer, philosopher, coffee farmer, and economist, would twice become Costa Rica's president (1953–57, 1970–74) and would be affectionately known by Costa Ricans as "Don Pepe."

Widespread Reforms

Reform movements swept through other Central American nations, not just Guatemala and Costa Rica, but were not as far-reaching. Honduras experienced a wave of modernization beginning in 1948 that resulted in its first paved roads in 1950, and a massive strike of 30,000 banana workers gave labor better wages and improved medical coverage. Its popularly elected civilian president, the pediatrician Ramón Villeda Morales (1957–63), implemented social welfare programs as well as limited agrarian reforms recommended by the U.S. Alliance for Progress. El Salvador's reform period (1948–56) lasted only briefly before a coup returned another oppressive military government to power, but for those few years a coffee boom permitted Colonel Oscar Osorio and his Revolutionary Party of Democratic Union to provide improvements in housing and health care for the working class. A new constitution was instituted in 1950 that provided voting rights to women.

Change became the rallying cry even along the borders of the traditional five states. In British Honduras, unemployment and poverty sped the unionization of the workforce and in 1949, George Price organized a movement for independence. Nationalism inspired Panamanian politics, too, and mob demonstrations, led by students, forced the United States to relinquish its military bases outside the Canal Zone in 1948. Although an increasingly powerful National Guard under Commander

Colonel Oscar Osorio assumes the presidency of El Salvador, 1950. President Osorio gave his nation a constitution that included provisions for the respect and rights of all citizens. (Photo courtesy Ministry of Education, El Salvador)

José Antonio Remón (1948–55) militarized Panamanian politics, Remón instituted social and agrarian reforms, if not democratic ones, and negotiated better terms for his nation in a new Canal Zone treaty in 1955.

Nicaragua was the only Central American country not to participate in the political and social reforms that mobilized the rest of the isthmus. In fact, it actively opposed progressive movements in other nations, such as Costa Rica and Guatemala. Anastasio Somoza, firmly in control of the National Guard, and receptive to every U.S. wish, was the only dictator to survive the post–World War II period. Yet even he could not control all the forces for change: He was shot in 1956 and died eight days later, despite the attentions of President Eisenhower's personal physician. Unfortunately for Nicaragua, Somoza's sons would take over and rule with the same iron-fisted control for almost two more decades.

Although the brief challenge to the power structure ended, the reforms did not completely disappear. Central Americans had become too politically mobilized for dictators to ignore them as in times past, and world organizations were more watchful for violations of human

216

rights. Minimum wages and some redistribution of farmland gave the appearance of reform, just as rigged elections lent a thin veneer of democracy to the new military dictatorships. Occasionally, pressure from the middle class and foreign interests would force a free election. Despite such small changes, the military became increasingly powerful—and brutal.

Counterreform

> *The U.S. can win wars, but the question is whether we can win revolutions.*
>
> ■
>
> *Henry Cabot Lodge, U.S. ambassador to the United Nations, 1959 (LeFeber 1991, 15)*

The purge of the communist threat from Central America by the United States was not limited to Guatemala. Whispering the promise of more development aid, the United States persuaded the Organization of American States in 1954 to declare its solidarity against the intervention of international communism in the Western Hemisphere. But just a few years later, in 1959, communist revolutionaries led by Fidel Castro were victorious in Cuba. The United States, through its embassies and CIA representatives, became increasingly active in the region. In 1960, a leftist threat to a U.S.-supported dictator in El Salvador resulted in a swift right-wing coup and the end of diplomatic ties with Cuba; that same year, the popular Honduran president Villeda was overthrown by U.S.-trained troops.

U.S. support of dictatorships over democratically elected governments did little to alleviate anti-American sentiments, and protection of U.S. business interests blocked the necessary restructuring of the Central American economy, a matter commented on by a conference of Latin American Catholic bishops. Strongly identified with the dictators, the United States saw every attack on local governments as attacks on itself, and there were many. Groups like the MR-13 Revolutionary Movement disrupted the U.S.-supported Guatemalan government with guerrilla tactics throughout the 1960s. The urban-based Revolutionary Coordinator of the Masses (CRM) organized rallies of tens of thousands of Salvadoran teachers, students, and workers in the 1960s and 1970s, and guerrilla raids disturbed the countryside even in Somoza's Nicaragua. Riots broke out through the 1950s and 1960s in Panama, forcing the United States to erect an eight-foot-high fence around the Canal Zone. In 1958, Venezuelan demonstrators stoned and spat on U.S. Vice President Richard Nixon during a goodwill tour of Latin America; demonstrations, in fact, broke out in each of the eight countries he visited—except Nicaragua.

> I had been passing through the Canal Zone when the worst riots were taking place. Several students had tried to plant the Panamanian flag on the banks of the canal, and a number of them died in the shooting that followed. The shooting came from the Panamanian Army, which was protecting the country's treaty with America.
>
> ■
>
> Thomas P. McCann, United Fruit Company representative, 1957
> (1976, 137)

Voter Participation in Guatemalan Elections			
Year	Eligible Voters	Votes for Winner	Eligible Voters for Winner
1944 (Arévalo)	310,000	296,200	82.5%
1950 (Arbenz)	583,000	266,800	45.7%
1958 (Ydígoras)	736,400	191,000	25.9%
1978 (Lucas)	1,785,876	269,979	15.1%

Source: Based on Julio Castellanos Cambranes (Ropp and Morris 1984, 136)

Alliance for Progress

The 1958 demonstrations convinced many in the United States that new policies, not CIA-sponsored coups, were needed. Nixon himself thought there should be less support for dictatorships, and more for raising the standard of living of the masses. When John F. Kennedy became president in 1960, he decided new tactics were indeed necessary to defeat communism in the region. Under his Alliance for Progress, he promised a 10-year program of governmental aid—not just private investments—to raise the standard of living in Central American nations and promote democracy. Adult literacy projects reached rural areas, and peasant cooperatives were formed, often with the assistance of U.S. Peace Corps volunteers, so that goods could be more efficiently marketed.

The Alliance for Progress planned to prevent communism in the region with military as well as social and economic aid. The Nicaraguan National Guard had worked so well, from the U.S. perspective, that U.S. military advisers were sent to train and assist the local military and police in counterinsurgency tactics in other nations. In 1969, once Nixon became president, the military support became an even more important component of the alliance. Young officers from all over Central America were sent to the Panama Canal Zone for training in the School of the Americas. The school would later be known in the U.S. press as the "School of Assassins" for the terrorist tactics and brutality of many of its graduates, such as Major Roberto D'Aubuisson, head of El Salvador's death squads. (SEE page 244 ff.)

The U.S. Congress prohibited the use of funds for land purchases that would have permitted agrarian reform. It did, however, appropriate millions of dollars in direct military assistance and permit easy loans for the purchase of military equipment—in one year, Guatemala added $6.5 million to its national debt simply for the purchase of arms. Costa Rica, having disbanded its standing army, complained about the growing militarization of the isthmus; the United States responded with enormous pressure for the reformation of a Costa Rican army. When the Central American Defense Council was established in 1965, with strong U.S. support, Costa Rica was, once again, the only nation to protest.

The Alliance for Progress succeeded insofar as the guerrillas were assassinated or forced underground and economic growth was adequate to avoid a total insurrection—for a while. It failed to achieve political stability, however. During the decade-long alliance, there were 17 coups in Central America, more than in any other region of the Americas.

Economic Diversification

Although efforts to transform the political structure had failed everywhere but in Costa Rica, efforts to diversify and modernize the Central American economy persisted. Loans and new foreign investments encouraged the use of chemical pesticides and fertilizers as well as new varieties of crops, such as bananas that were more disease resistant. The introduction of industrial agriculture made the costs of developing new export crops feasible. Despite the introduction of new crops, coffee remained the most valuable for the region, and thanks to agro-industrial techniques, its production actually doubled from 1950 to 1980.

Cotton became a major export, as did beef, and both were especially important in Nicaragua and Guatemala. Sugarcane became an important tropical export crop everywhere in Central America, but particularly in Honduras and Guatemala. Costa Rica reinvested in cacao production. When coffee prices fell in 1959, the new exports made up for the difference. When the United Fruit Company started divesting its interests in Honduras and Costa Rica (by 1964, Ecuador, not Honduras, was the world's largest banana producer) because of diseases, so it said, other agricultural investments helped the rural sector. Honduras, for example, became a successful exporter of coffee, despite its lack of the rich volcanic soils that are favorable to coffee cultivation.

In 1960 the value of coffee, bananas, and cotton crops accounted for almost 76 percent of all exports, but not all exports were agricultural. In the 1950s, Costa Rica and Guatemala both granted foreign concessions for the exploration and refining of petroleum. And diversification continued. In the 1960s and 1970s, shrimp and lobster became exports from the Pacific shores of most Central American nations, except Guatemala and Costa Rica. For Panama, shrimp exports almost matched those of bananas; on the Caribbean side, spiny lobster became important. By the late 1970s, coffee, bananas, and cotton constituted less than 50 percent of the value of all exports.

Economic Unification

In the 1950s, the new middle class argued for a restructuring of the economy, not just diversification. They felt that industrialization and domestic trade were imperative for regional development. Instead of

Central American Export Diversification *as percentage of total export value*				
	Coffee	Bananas	Cotton	Silver/Gold	Other
1938	52.2	24.7	—	9.1	14.0
1960	53.2	14.1	8.5	—	24.1
1972	26.4	14.0	10.9	—	48.7

Source: Woodward (1985, 277)

importing many popular items—cars, tires, processed food, toys, textiles, and clothing, for example—they wanted to manufacture them on the isthmus. During the reform governments, new taxes were placed on agricultural exports to finance industrialization; even the coffee oligarchy of El Salvador found itself paying taxes on coffee to aid other economic sectors.

Individual nations could not industrialize by themselves. The domestic markets were simply too small to warrant the necessary investments. Also, the five nations, having similar geography, tended to produce the same products. In order to expand the size of the local market and the variety of goods to be traded, it was argued that a coordinated approach to such development was imperative. Even if Central America could not form a political federation, it needed greater economic integration.

Throughout the 1950s, Central American governments discussed ways of cooperating economically. In 1960, the Central American Common Market was founded to coordinate industrialization among the five nations. The hope was to create commerce among the nations by developing different industries matched to each nation's need and resources. The common market provided fiscal incentives for new industries; and private investors provided the funds. The Central American Bank for Economic Integration, a cornerstone of the U.S. Alliance for Progress, added public funds for the modernization of infrastructure. The United States loaned $200 million to start both projects.

A free trade zone was created and, at last, geographical isolation no longer prevented isthmian integration. The Pan-American Highway, running 1,600 miles along the isthmus from the Mexican border to the Darién wilderness in Panama, was upgraded and completed, with most of the financing provided by the United States. By 1964, the highway linked the Americas from Canada to Chile, except for the Darién gap. Until then, the only international highway, an unpaved road, and the only international railroad line on the isthmus linked Guatemala and El Salvador. Railroads were so inadequate, except around tropical fruit plantations, and paved roads so rare, except around cities, that air travel was easier than ground travel. Honduras alone had 75 small airfields. The Pan-American Highway changed isthmian commerce.

During the 1960s, interregional commerce grew tenfold and manufacturing accounted for 17 percent of Central America's gross domestic product (GDP). The common market, however, was marginalized by the interests of foreign investors on several fronts. First, U.S. corporations succeeded in convincing President Lyndon Johnson, who was increasingly preoccupied with the war in Vietnam, that the common market should rely on foreign investments rather than public monies— which deprived Central America of funds to direct development. Second, businesses had little interest in creating balanced growth throughout the isthmus and developing an industry where it would be most useful for Central Americans. Foreign investors, that is, U.S. corporations, not only bought out Central American firms, but they insisted on developing their factories wherever they wanted to; that is, in the cities with a readily available workforce and cheap labor supply. Industrialization in Guatemala and El Salvador grew rapidly, according to the preferences of such foreign interests. Costa Rica and Nicaragua developed more slowly. Honduras, still rural and without densely populated cities, received little benefit.

Central Americans became disillusioned with the common market. Although Central America had the highest annual economic growth rate in the Americas from 1960 to 1971, from an average of 7.1 percent in Nicaragua to 5.1 percent in Honduras, the growth rate per capita was not equally satisfying to each nation. In Honduras, for example, the growth in GDP per capita was less than 1 percent. By contrast, in Costa Rica, where social and political development accompanied industrialization, the growth rate was 33 percent per capita. Economic cooperation had increased the size of the market for locally manufactured products, but the common market alone could not increase domestic consumption in each country. Purchasing power for the vast majority of people remained abominably low.

Disputes between nations tore at the union, just as they had since independence. In 1969, Honduras went to war against El Salvador, as unemployed Salvadoran immigrants continued to pour into its territory (SEE page 230). The so-called "Soccer War" disrupted commerce among all Central American nations for two weeks in 1969, and in 1971, led Honduras to withdraw from the common market and reestablish tariffs. Within a few years, civil wars made commerce impossible along the length of the isthmus.

Legacy

Reform movements breached the oligarchy's monopoly on power, but could not replace it for long. Desperately needed changes in land resource distribution began in Guatemala and Costa Rica, but only Costa Rica experienced the structural changes that permitted such reforms to endure. The economy did diversify, and modernization and

Top: Cerrón Grande hydroelectric project in El Salvador. (Photo Inter-American Development Bank, U.S. Library of Congress.)
Bottom: Garbage collection in Guatemala City, 1978. Modernization existed side by side with technology left from the colonial period. (Photo courtesy Roger J. Cooper)

industrialization were sped along by a combination of private invest-ments and U.S. aid through the Alliance for Progress. But poverty remained too widespread for sustained economic growth.

Despite the exile of leftists and the weakening of communist parties in all five nations, other political parties and social organizations continued to provide an outlet for the grievances of those left out of government. Students and workers still went on strike and demonstrated in the streets, but not as often; the middle class remained politically mobilized. Their voices challenged the status quo and eventually would undermine it. But that moment was delayed by the United States. For the second time, the United States intervened and reinforced governments tarnished by profound social inequities and political tyranny. Police and military training resulted in growing political repression. These problems would foment revolutions that the U.S. could not control.

12

CIVIL WARS
(1975–1996)

These people will not accept this kind of existence for the next generation. We would not; they will not. There will be changes. So a revolution is coming—We can affect its character, we cannot alter its inevitability.

■

U.S. Senator Robert Kennedy (New York Times, May 10, 1966)

To fight, you've got to give up your tranquility, your liberty, your way of life, and sometimes your life itself.

■

Edén Pastora, Sandinista militia commander, 1976
(Edelman and Kenan, 1989, 252)

I am part of a generation that lived the best years of its life believing in revolution . . .

■

Norma Vásquez, Salvadoran intellectual, 1996

n the 1970s, the world economy took a downturn, and the failure of development policies in Central America would once again be made painfully apparent. Inadequate reforms had left most people living in harsh poverty with no legitimate political recourse. With new export crops and grazing cattle occupying land once on the frontier, an expanding population could no longer find unclaimed land from which to eke an existence. With no democracy, the populace—intellectuals, the displaced, the middle class, rural peasants, and even some members of the aristocracy and Catholic clergy—increasingly saw revolution as the only path to a better future.

Economic policies throughout the 1970s and 1980s further impoverished the population; dictators backed by a strong military prevented every attempt at democratization and upward mobility desired by the middle class. At a point in history when massive numbers of Nicaraguans, Salvadorans, and Guatemalans were so disillusioned as to resort to violence, the United States saw its interests in the preservation of the oligarchies. When U.S. Secretary of State Henry Kissinger visited the region in 1976, riots broke out against the reactionary policies of the United States. Demonstrations and sit-ins escalated into what U.S. Senator Robert Kennedy saw as inevitable revolutions. The U.S. response under President Ronald Reagan (1981–1989) would be militaristic, justified by anticommunist Cold War rhetoric. As war enveloped Guatemala, Nicaragua, and El Salvador, the U.S. made Honduras into its military headquarters and challenged the neutrality of Costa Rica. All of Central America would be caught up in a devastating vortex of war that persisted until the 1990s.

Policy Failure

The Alliance for Progress gave the middle class false hopes. The increased aid that had built new dams and the Pan-American Highway never redressed the social and economic inequities that plagued the isthmus. Although development did improve the average per capita income, income levels, except in Costa Rica, remained considerably below that of Latin America as a whole. In 1980, Guatemala had the highest income figures after Costa Rica, but its per capita income was 40 percent below that for Latin America; compared to their neighbors, Nicaragua and Honduras were far worse, with per capita income only a third of that for Latin America. The skewed distribution of wealth rendered income growth illusory for most Central Americans: No more than 2 percent of the growth trickled down to the poorest 20 percent in Guatemala, for example. In fact, the dictators and the highest echelon of the military had used much of the aid to enrich themselves and create their own family dynasties, even organizing their own banks. By mid-1970, the Somozas owned one-fourth of the total assets of Nicaragua and the president of Guatemala was said to have a salary of $650,000, not to mention income from his business "opportunities." A Mayan Indian living in Guatemala in 1972, however, earned U.S. $82 annually.

Income Per Capita in Constant U.S. Dollars				
	1950	1960	1970	1980
Guatemala	293	322	417	521
El Salvador	265	319	397	399
Honduras	232	250	289	317
Nicaragua	215	271	354	309
Costa Rica	347	474	656	858

Source: Pérez-Brignoli (1989, 31); *Statistical Abstract of Latin America*, vol. 21 (1981).

While the economy grew, middle-class Central Americans remained hopeful. Limited improvements in the quality of life occurred through electrification, educational opportunities, and public health programs. But in 1973, the Central American economic boom was halted by the world oil crisis. The cost of oil imports rose from $189 million to $1.5 billion by 1980, a heavy burden for nations already heavily in debt from military expenditures. When high interest rates, caused by a recession in the U.S. from 1979 to 1981, were added to these problems, the Central American economy crashed. Very quickly, social problems were no longer addressed; funds for importing food and industrial parts were increasingly scarce. As inflation gripped many nations, wage controls, but not price controls, were instituted; in El Salvador, the real wages of an already poor worker declined by one-third in the early 1980s, and the 1980 average per capita income in Nicaragua fell below 1970 levels. Unemployment, already high as the result of mechanized agriculture, worsened as the world economy stalled and coffee prices plummeted in 1978. In 1981 even Costa Rica was forced to default on its debt payments. In 1982 the gross domestic product declined in all five countries. The long-unresolved problems of Central American politics and society were thrown into tragic relief.

Land and Food

As early as 1960, 86 percent of the agricultural workforce owned little or no land. The vast majority of the land was held by the oligarchies. In Honduras, which had the weakest elite class, 50 percent of the land was owned by a mere 5 percent of the population; more than 50 percent of all Honduran farms occupied only 9 percent of the land. Yet the large

Modern San Salvador. The capital cities grew fast in comparison to other cities. Manufacturers preferred operating where there was a large labor supply, and the largest cities were targeted for development. The governments, flush with aid funds, also added to the growth and wealth of the capitals, as new government centers were constructed. Provincial cities, such as Cartago in Costa Rica and Granada and León in Nicaragua, were eclipsed by San José and Managua. Guatemala City and San Salvador, the largest cities in Central America, had populations over 1 million in 1985. Rural areas were neglected; in Guatemala, after 10 years of direct U.S. aid, there were no schools for 80 percent of the children living outside cities. (Photo courtesy of Hon. Patricia Maza-Pittsford)

estates cultivated less than 10 percent of their land and they cultivated export crops. Since the Alliance for Progress did little to redistribute fallow lands, most of the land in Central America remained in the possession of large estates and few domestic crops were cultivated. In Nicaragua only 11 percent of the harvested land was devoted to domestic crops; in Costa Rica, 9 percent. More and more subsistence crops had to be imported for Central Americans to survive, but many could not afford the cost of imported goods.

The diversification of exports and modernization projects had created an even greater shortage of land for domestic crops. The export of beef required new grazing lands for cattle, and pasture often replaced farms for subsistence crops, such as maize and beans. Nearly one-third of the land of Costa Rica, El Salvador, and Nicaragua was devoted to cattle by 1980. Yet domestic consumption of beef dropped, because of rising prices, while exports increased. Cattle grazing and the addition of new export crops, such as cotton, exacerbated the problem of landless peasants. Modernization made its own contributions. The construction of hydroelectric dams in El Salvador, for example, displaced thousands of peasants and eroded the surrounding countryside.

Population and Urbanization

Central America's population grew at one of the fastest rates in the world—a striking 3.5 percent in 1966—which contributed to land and food shortages, as well as decreasing wages and increasing unemployment. Despite economic growth in Central America, the number of jobs created did not keep up with the growth in population. In Guatemala new workers outnumbered new jobs by more than 30 to one. Costa Rica suffered severe unemployment even though it experienced rapid industrial development. Nowhere was the problem worse than in El Salvador, where 40 percent of the population was unemployed or underemployed in 1965.

The Central American population doubled between 1950 and 1980, and by 1985 it reached almost 27 million. The resultant population density per square mile put enormous pressure on the land of these small nations. In the central Quiché Mayan area of Guatemala, for example, the population grew beyond the carrying capacity of the land to 100,000 per square mile in 1974, double the size of the population

Population Estimates in 1985		
	Total *in millions*	Density *per square mile*	Largest City
Guatemala	8.4	201	1,500,000 (Guatemala)
El Salvador	5.7	701	1,117,850 (San Salvador)
Honduras	4.4	102	890,420 (Tegucigalpa)
Nicaragua	5.7	53	792,000 (Managua)
Costa Rica	2.5	128	660,000 (San José)
Source: Woodward (1985, 363)		

A DIFFERENT BELIZE

While overpopulation and social inequality fueled rebellions in most of Central America, that was not the case in British Honduras. Unlike the rest of Central America, British Honduras was underpopulated. The country, 2,000 square miles larger than El Salvador, had developed from the single British settlement at St. George's Caye, but remained the least populous nation on the American continents. There was no industry and little in the way of natural resources to attract new settlers—only tropical commodities, such as bananas and other fruits, mahogany, and chicle for making chewing gum. The population grew, but gradually, just as the colony moved slowly from British rule to British-style representative self-government and, in 1981, to independence as a democratic nation. Diverse peoples joined the creole (descendants of the British loggers and their black slaves) and Mayan populations. In the mid-19th century, Mayans from Mexico and Guatemala moved into the Petén forest, and Garífuna peoples resettled from turbulent Honduras to coastal areas, such as Dangriga (Stann Creek). Indians and other Asians from the British Empire settled as merchants in Belize City. American Mennonite farmers, with encouragement from the government, became the providers of foodstuffs to the nation. In the 1980s, thousands of refugees from war-torn Central America arrived. By 1985 these diverse groups and the majority creole population added up to a total of 165,000 Belizeans: a density of only 16.3 per square mile. The land, primarily rain forest, became a national resource when ecotourism was promoted in the 1990s. In addition to the blessing of ample land, Britain's ongoing military presence in Belize protected it from

at the time of the conquest. The population of El Salvador, the smallest nation in terms of acreage, grew from 400 per square mile in the 1960s to almost 700 in 1985. Since the 1930s, Salvadorans had found refuge to the north in rural Honduras; by 1969, 300,000 had followed the same path. The Salvadoran emigration to Honduras, which at that time had a population averaging only 55 per square mile, precipitated the "Soccer War" that killed several thousand people before the OAS was able to forge a cease fire between the two nations. The negotiated settlement sealed the border in a territorial dispute that would not be completely resolved for almost 40 years.

Even Costa Rica no longer had public lands to distribute to peasants; squatters had settled on 10 percent of the agricultural land by 1973.

Belize City in 1914. Belize City has changed little in size and scale since this photograph was taken almost a century ago. It is, however, considerably less picturesque and much seedier. Hurricane Hattie ravaged the Belizean coast in 1961. After the hurricane, the seat of government was moved inland to the modern city of Belmopan, but Belize City, with a population of 56,000 in 1985, remained the largest settlement in the country. (Photo [detail] Frank E. Read, U.S. Library of Congress, Prints and Photographs Division)

Guatemalan ambitions (which had almost resulted in an invasion in 1975) and U.S. military maneuvers. Such blessings contributed to the political tranquillity and democratically secure institutions of the new nation, but did not resolve the lack of economic opportunities. As Central American refugees poured into Belize, Belizeans immigrated to North America, looking for work, despite the local presence of international corporations such as United Fruit and Wrigley.

With borders closed and new export crops and increased cattle grazing taking over virgin lands, Central America lost the frontier that had provided a safety valve during the liberal land "reforms" of the 19th century.

Landless peasants went in search of work, and many became migratory workers within their own countries; the cotton industry alone employed 1 million seasonal workers. Others ended in the cities as day laborers, where they joined better-organized manufacturing workers. The landless created an uprooted, underemployed, and hungry class in societies that had once been primarily rural and traditional. The percentage of people living in the cities doubled in Nicaragua (32 percent) and Honduras (20 percent) during the 1960s. By 1980, only half of Central Americans lived in rural areas.

The 1970s transformed Central America into an overpopulated, impoverished and increasingly urbanized region. The new landless and urban classes proved a volatile combination with the disillusioned middle class.

The Church: Liberation Theology

I gave bread to the poor and they called me a saint. I asked why they are poor and they called me a communist.

■

Archbishop Helder Pessoa Camara of Recif, Brazil
(The London Times, August 28, 1999)

In the 1960s the Catholic Church undertook an evangelizing effort unparalleled since the 16th century. Under the encyclicals of Pope John XXIII, the church declared the importance of human rights and a decent quality of life for everyone. It was only through the accomplishment of these goals, the pope said, that the social unrest and violence around the world would end. In 1968, the new pope, Paul VI, addressed the Latin American bishops at Medellín on these themes; many priests, nuns, and lay persons were inspired to commit themselves to these religious goals by living and teaching in rural communities.

The social realities these religious individuals encountered mobilized them politically, and they advocated more direct church involvement in social issues. In Latin America, this movement has been called liberation theology. At a conference in 1979, bishops—vowing they were siding with neither communists nor capitalists—argued that democratic rights were inadequate to address the basic Christian needs of Indians, peasants, and the urban dispossessed. As guerrillas gained the support of these very groups, the liberationist priests often were sympathetic, believing that a restructuring of society was necessary to eliminate institutionalized violence against the poor. Although the bishops insisted social justice should be accomplished peacefully, some priests believed such deep societal changes could never be achieved without revolution. In Nicaragua and in El Salvador in particular, some priests, such as the poet Ernesto Cardenal, became guerrillas themselves. Pope John Paul II, installed in office in 1978, eschewed liberation theology, but his more conservative stance in world affairs could not stop the revolutionary events happening in Central America.

The liberation theologians had an enormous impact on the church, on the nations where they preached, and on the world. With parishes in every region from the largest cities to the most rural areas, the priests touched people in all walks of life and awakened in many the desire to better their circumstances. As the moral conscience of nations, bishops stirred many to political reform and protest—and even violence. The liberationist theologians angered others, such as many of the Salvadoran oligarchy, who converted to Evangelical Protestant sects; in the late 1970s, bumper stickers encouraged Salvadorans to "Be a Patriot, Kill a Priest." In the 1970s alone, 850 Latin American clergy were tortured, expelled, or assassinated.

The voices of the liberationist clergy stirred human rights and religious organizations throughout the world to join in the demand for greater justice and peace in Central America. The nongovernmental political forces became so strong that U.S. president Jimmy Carter (1977–81) attempted to cut off military aid to countries with demonstrated records of human rights abuses. The policy did decrease the torture and violence somewhat in Somoza's Nicaragua, but the dictatorships in El Salvador and Guatemala temporarily refused U.S. military aid rather than comply.

When U.S. president Reagan, Carter's successor, replaced human rights policies in favor of a military victory, world concern remained a potent political force and that concern spread throughout the United States as well when U.S. citizens were assassinated in El Salvador or disappeared in Guatemala. And when U.S.-funded bombing missions attacked Nicaragua, North Americans and other concerned citizens of the world traveled to the affected regions to prevent the bombings as "witnesses for peace." The liberation theologians of the Catholic Church and other religious and human rights organizations were essential parties to the governmental strategies developed during the civil wars of the 1980s. Their support permitted Central American and other Latin American nations finally to negotiate a peace.

Nicaragua

This is the face of the liberated land . . .
so beautiful, not only the land
but the people in it, . . .

■

Ernesto Cardenal, 1985 from "Vision from the Blue Plane-Window"
(after Cohen 1986, 15)

PANAMA:
THE NEW NATIONALISM

Having finished with the oligarchy, the Panamanian has his own worth with no importance to his origin, his cradle, or where he was born.

∎

President Omar Torrijos, 1970 (Evans-Smith 1981: 44)

Omar Torrijos, commander of the National Guard and a graduate of the School of the Americas, became dictator of Panama in 1969 after a series of coups. Although he began his regime with the usual appearance of conservative support, he soon shifted power away from the oligarchy. He eventually was criticized for nepotism and corruption, yet he brought Panama onto the world stage and gave it an independent voice in Central American affairs for the first time in its history. His domestic policies concentrated on populist and rural programs, which were less a threat to the Panamanian oligarchy than elsewhere in Central America because elite power there was based on revenues from commerce, not landholdings. In 1972, he authorized the redistribution of land and the expansion of rural schools and health programs. But he also encouraged private enterprise and established policies that would make Panama City a center of international banking. Nationalistic sentiments had long protested the U.S.-controlled Canal Zone on Panamanian territory, but Torrijos, with the support of his new Latin American allies and the United Nations, was able to succeed where his predecessors could not. In 1977 he signed a new canal treaty with U.S. President Jimmy Carter that recognized Panama's sovereignty over its territory and eliminated the Canal Zone by 1979. In addition, the entire canal, and the 5 percent of world trade that passed through its locks, would revert to Panama by 2000. In 1981, Torrijos

On July 17, 1979, Anastasio Somoza Debayle, the younger and sole surviving son of General Anastasio Somoza García, fled for his life with all he could take: $100 million from the Nicaraguan treasury, his mistress, and the bodies of his father and brother. It was said that he would have taken the land, too, if possible. Within a matter of months, he was assassinated by two Argentinians while driving his armored Mercedes-Benz in Paraguay.

died in an unexplained air crash, and Panama underwent a series of presidents, all from the National Guard and each more repressive and corrupt than the one before. By 1984, General Manuel Noriega, another graduate of the School of the Americas but a less illustrious one than Torrijos, was clearly in control, much to the dismay of many Panamanians. He embarked on a rocky relationship with the United States. Although the Organization of American States attempted to mediate between the two governments, tensions mounted. On December 20, 1989, U.S. forces invaded Panama, took over the National Palace, and installed a temporary president until a democratic election could be held. "Operation Just Cause," as U.S. president George Bush called the invasion, was over in a week but the damage done to Panamanian national pride was not. General Noriega was imprisoned in the United States on charges of drug trafficking and sentenced to a 40-year prison term, despite his years of service as a paid CIA informant. His party, the Democratic Revolutionary Party (PRD), founded by Torrijos, took control of the country again in 1994, but this time it was elected democratically and the new government transformed the National Guard into the civilian-controlled police force and coast guard, and then passed a constitutional amendment abolishing the military.

General Omar Torrijos Herrera, President of Panama (1969–81). (Photo U.S. National Archives)

The events leading up to this ignominious end of the 43-year-old Somoza family dynasty began in 1961 with the formation of the Frente Sandinista de Liberación Nacional (FSLN), better known as the Sandinistas. In the intervening years, the Sandinistas organized small guerrilla attacks and strikes and sabotaged power plants. Occasionally, they committed daring acts in the capital, as in one episode when they demanded, and received, $5 million in exchange for some well-connected hostages. As the commandos departed, cheering crowds lined the road. The National Guard retaliated with rural campaigns that included atrocities against the populace, and at various times pronounced the Sandinistas dead. But the Sandinistas persisted: they cached arms and plotted Somoza's overthrow from the safety of neighboring Costa Rica, which had longstanding disagreements with the Somozans. Within Nicaragua, the FSLN provided a rallying point for other discontented factions. By the 1970s, there were many.

The Somozas

The Somozas had maintained their power through the National Guard and such unstinting loyalty to the United States that their government had been called a subsidiary of it (La Feber 1991, 238). At the age of 22, Anastasio, or "Tacho" as he was known, had taken over command of the National Guard after his father's assassination. By the time he assumed the presidency upon the death of his brother Luis in 1967, the National Guard was thoroughly corrupt and despised, a mobster organization profiting from its control of prostitution and gambling—and a violent one that thought little about murdering and torturing innocent citizens.

Somoza also corrupted the economy. Every development project, from cotton to sugarcane, lined the family coffers. Even natural disasters provided opportunities for them to make more money. When an earthquake destroyed 80 percent of Managua in 1972, the medical supplies received from international relief organizations were sold for profit. The National Guard was so busy sacking stores that 600 U.S. troops had to be flown in from the Canal Zone to maintain security. What had once been downtown Managua was left a pile of rubble while Tacho and his friends constructed shopping malls and offices outside the capital on Somoza-owned property. Damaged roads were repaved with bricks from the family factory.

After 43 years in power, the net impact of the Somoza family dictatorship was Somozan wealth—to the disadvantage of everyone else. By the 1970s, it was not just the poor peasant and urban unemployed worker who was angry. Members of the coffee elite and the old ranching elite were angry, too; the finest families from Granada and León resented the importance of Managua at the expense of their once noble cities. The answer to all criticism was increased repression and violence. The Catholic bishops, too, criticized the dictator, and refused to attend what would turn out to be his last inauguration. In 1978, soon after the first major Sandinista offensive, Pedro Joaquín Chamorro, editor of the opposition newspaper *La Prensa,* was assassinated and, in some regions, the National Guard systematically killed all males over the age of 14, an event documented at the time by a fact-finding tour of the Organization of American States.

Sandinista Victory

The Sandinistas reorganized under the umbrella of a moderate political faction that had the support not only of conservative business owners but also of Mexico, Costa Rica, Venezuela, and Panama. Everyone except the United States, it seemed, wanted Somoza removed. In 1978 the Sandinistas led the groundswell against Somoza; mass uprisings broke out in city slums for the first time and Commandante Zero (Edén Pastora) temporarily held the legislature hostage in Managua. The National Guard, despite its $14 million in arms from the United States, seemed to disintegrate against the revolutionary forces. They rocket-bombed the slums, where mostly women and children remained, and murdered a U.S. television reporter—on camera.

The United States finally realized that some change was necessary. It tried first to get the OAS to send in a peacekeeping force, but that organization refused. It tried negotiating with the Sandinistas to let Somoza serve out his term. They refused. And once it was clear that Somoza had to resign, the United States scandalized everyone by making a plea for the National Guard to remain. The Sandinistas did, however, appease the North Americans by appointing an 18-member cabinet composed of business leaders, professionals, church members, and only one Sandinista.

Revolutionary Government

The five-member Junta of National Reconstruction, installed by the Sandinistas in 1979, was representative of the various interests that had propelled them to victory. It included Violeta Chamorro, representative of the landholding elite, and Alfonso Robelo, an agro-industrialist in cotton-seed oil; it also included Commander Daniel Ortega Saavedra, a former anti-Somoza street fighter and self-declared socialist who was soon to emerge as the leader among leaders. Leftist political labels alarmed the United States, and the revolutionary government set out to reassure them that they welcomed private business and good relations with the United States. When some labor leaders tried to organize strikes against Coca-Cola and United Fruit (by then known as United Brands), the government

237

REVOLUTIONARY WRITERS

. . . only songs make us great, not war.

■

Ernesto Cardenal, 1960s (Bierhorst 1990, 198)

In revolution, Central Americans found their voices. Despite their centuries of poverty and underdevelopment, they expressed themselves most eloquently in poetry. Inspired by their great poet Rubén Darío, an astonishing number of Nicaraguans described their struggles and hopes in poetry and song, so many that their poems seemed an essential part of the revolution. As the poet Giaconda Bella said, "There was never time for novels." (Rushdie 1987, 159) The Sandinista minister of culture was the master of Nicaraguan poetry, Ernesto Cardenal (1925–). Although the son of a conservative family of Granada, Cardenal became a liberationist priest and wrote the Misa Campesina ("Peasant Mass") to the accompaniment of music by Carlos Mejía Goday. For his refusal to quit politics, he was barred by the anti-liberationist Pope John Paul II from officiating at mass. He continued his religious work, however, with the "People's Church," even if he no longer could say mass, and his poetry continued to combine the spiritual with the political. Among the other Nicaraguan writers was the intellectual Sergio Ramírez, who was vice president; even the Sandinista president, Daniel Ortega, occasionally penned a poem. The political opposition wrote poems, too, and Pablo Antonio Cuadra had his published by the new press, run by the revolutionary government. The Salvadoran revolution also inspired many poets. The most famous was Roque Dalton (1935–75), who many believe was the finest Salvadoran poet who ever lived. Dalton, the estranged, illegitimate son of a member of the landowning elite, wrote about traditional themes of love and death, but he also captured the painful reality of his country. A prolific writer, he wrote hundreds of poems, several novels, essays, a history of his country, and a play, all by the time he was 40 years old. A revolutionary himself, he was imprisoned twice by the right-wing government, and was often forced underground, but it would be his fellow leftist guerrillas who executed him in 1975 over ideological differences. For years, Dalton's work was banned by the government, but in 1998, the Salvadoran legislature unanimously added him to the pantheon of national heroes and proclaimed him "a poet of great merit."

expelled them. On the other hand, the junta was committed to creating a more equitable society, and it was definitely leftist: one of its first acts was to nationalize Somoza's property for distribution to the poor.

In the first years of the Sandinista government, Nicaragua had to overcome the economic destruction caused by the revolution. The United Nations estimated that it would take a decade to rebuild the economy. As it turned out, the Sandinistas had far less time to implement their social and economic agenda. International loans, however, enabled them to begin reconstructing the infrastructure of the country. Gains were made in educational and health services and even in the arts, as poet Ernesto Cardenal organized cultural centers so that workshops on writing, painting, and music reached into every level of society. Production improved on exports and domestic crops as well. A new constitution recognized civil and social rights, and local organizing efforts attempted to realize those rights; by 1986 more than half the workforce had been unionized, for example, and the Nicaraguan Women's Association organized to give women a voice in politics.

Nicaraguans were also desperate to shed Somoza-style dependency on the United States. The junta declared itself among the nonaligned nations and accepted technical assistance from Cuba for the development of rural schools and health clinics, and it accepted loans from everywhere, including the Soviet Union. Such policies contributed to U.S. suspicions that it was dealing with communists. But the United States and its corporations maintained good relations with the new government until U.S. president Ronald Reagan assumed office in 1981.

The Contras

the chapel was set on fire
and the little schoolhouse. The health center.
And the buzzards circling, circling. . . .

■

Ernesto Cardenal, 1986 from "U.S. Congress Approves Aid to the Contras"
(after Cohen 1986, 22)

The Sandinistas had vowed there would be no bloodbath when they assumed power, and there was not. They permitted many National Guard members to relocate to the United States and Honduras. Within two days of Somoza's resignation, the CIA began reorganizing and transforming the guardsmen on Honduran territory into a counterrevolutionary army

U.S. PRESIDENT RONALD REAGAN (1981–89)

Central America is the most important place in the world for the United States today.

■

Jeane Kirkpatrick, U.S. ambassador to the United Nations, 1981 (LaFeber 1993, 5)

U.S. President Ronald Reagan introduced a bellicose resolve that had not been seen in United States foreign policy since Theodore Roosevelt. His military response to the socially complex problems of

Honduran army (Photo U.S. National Archives)

called the *contras*. In 1981, Reagan intensified U.S. commitment to policies to destabilize the Sandinista government. A campaign to label the Sandinistas "communists" was undertaken, and $19 million in secret money was given to the CIA to do the rest. The next year, $24 million was authorized. The amounts, which kept escalating, did not even include direct military support to Honduras, which was $77.5 million in 1984, for example, and $140 million in 1987 and 1989.

U.S. bases were established in Honduras in order to train and "advise" the contras and keep them well supplied, in even such sophisticated weaponry as Red-Eye missiles. In 1982, limited democratic reforms had ushered in a new Honduran government, but the elected

240

Central America failed to achieve the desired peace and political stability just as it had failed Theodore Roosevelt. Reagan, like Roosevelt, believed Central America was strategically the most important place in the world for the United States, and that the isthmus had to be kept free of communism and any other foreign presence. Reagan's policies not only created a war in Nicaragua and sustained one in El Salvador, they also spread instability into Costa Rica and Honduras as well. Not until 1990, when cold war rhetoric subsided with the political fragmentation of the Soviet Union, was peace brought to Central America.

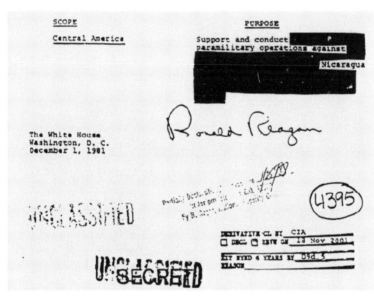

A declassified document authorizing contra attacks on Nicaragua.

officials often were not consulted on their country's involvement in a war on Nicaragua. Nor were 12,000 Hondurans consulted when they were removed from their land so that U.S. military base could be constructed. Instead, the United States relied on military strongman General Gustavo Álvarez Martinez, who gave his full cooperation to the contra effort. Throughout the 1980s, Honduras conducted massive joint maneuvers with the United States, sending a clear message to the revolutionaries in Central America that the U.S. Marines were back. In 1985, the largest maneuver, 7,000 U.S. and 5,000 Honduran troops simulated an invasion of Nicaragua with a landing on the Caribbean coast supported by 39 U.S. warships; these exercises disturbed not just the

Sandinista government but also Hondurans who, fearing they were losing their national autonomy, protested their government's continued support of the contras. But the discontent in Honduras, basically an occupied country, could not grow into revolt.

By the end of 1982 the contras were launching major offensives, forcing Nicaragua to mobilize its population once again for war and, eventually, to declare martial law. The contras had few battle victories and failed to win any Nicaraguan territory. The only support they found within Nicaragua was on the still remote Caribbean coast, where the English-speaking Miskito Indians resisted the Sandinista efforts to incorporate them into the larger Nicaraguan society. Failing to make any headway in most of Nicaragua, the U.S. policy shifted to guerrilla-style attacks on rural communities and the disruption of economic production.

The war continued, fueled by U.S. cash and U.S. policies. Nicaraguan harbors were mined with the help of the Pentagon and CIA, and acts of military aggression continued even after orders to desist from the International Court of Justice in 1984 were blocked. A U.S. trade embargo further cut off the nation. Even when Nicaragua undertook the freest election in its history—and elected the Sandinista, Daniel Ortega, with 67 percent of the vote—Reagan refused to recognize the results, calling them rigged. He was aided in this by conflicts within Nicaragua. Members of the junta had resigned in protest: Violeta Chamorro devoted herself to the more conservative politics voiced in her family's opposition newspaper, *La Prensa,* and Alfonso Robelo became the political leader of a contra force based in Costa Rica. And the divisiveness between the traditional hierarchy and the liberation movement within the Catholic Church also undermined Sandinista credibility internationally.

As the blockades disrupted trade and Reagan's politics prevented international loans, Nicaragua became increasingly disarrayed. Its economy had never recovered from the Sandinista revolt and was now deteriorating even more. The promised social improvements stalled, and droughts and other natural disasters added to the demoralization and devastation. Moreover, President Ortega's suspension of civil liberties during wartime angered many Nicaraguans. The contras, however, were flush with funds, even after the U.S. Congress cut off their military aid. The contras received a steady stream of "humanitarian" aid—$100 million in 1986 alone—and the Reagan Administration found devious ways of sending funds for arms, which resulted in what became known as the Iran-contra scandal in the United States. Internal dissension over policy began to weaken the Sandinistas, and more and more citizens came to believe that Ortega could never achieve peace—or a better life for Nicaraguans.

Peace Negotiations

A major diplomatic effort for regional peace was undertaken by the Contadora Group, composed of Mexico, Venezuela, Colombia, and Panama and supported by many other Latin American countries. The Nicaraguan government agreed to the plan, but others did not, especially El Salvador and the United States. The peace process, involving so many governments in addition to those directly involved, was too cumbersome and lost its momentum by 1986. The Contadora Group had created an atmosphere for negotiations, however, and the Central American nations started discussing peace among themselves. By 1987 the Central American negotiators had come up with a new peace plan known as the Arias Plan (SEE page 248). Nicaragua signed the plan, but there were delays in its implementation. When the Sandinista government agreed to a temporary truce in 1988, the contras broke off the negotiations. Finally, in 1989, the Central American presidents, led by Oscar Arias Sanchez of Costa Rica, intervened again, and negotiated the Costa del Sol peace accords, which called for the contras to disband. Instead, the U.S. Congress authorized another $50 million to keep them intact, justifying their action by saying it was for "non-lethal" aid.

But peace was near. Reagan's term in office was ending and Nicaragua agreed to a new election, one monitored by international organizations to convince the United States of its fairness. Violeta Chamorro ran for president under the newly formed Nicaraguan Opposition Union (UNO), and received aid for her campaign from the United States. Nonetheless, the world was considerably surprised when she defeated Ortega in February of 1990 with 60 percent of the vote. Nicaraguans could not bear more poverty and more war, and they were convinced the United States would not permit the war to end as long as the Sandinistas were in power. The Sandinistas peacefully turned the government over to the opposition. By then, 30,000 Nicaraguans had died in the contra wars.

El Salvador

... the sad ones, saddest in the world,
my compatriots,
my brothers.

■

Roque Dalton, Salvadoran poet from "Cara de Patria,"
(Face of the Homeland), 1968

243

El Salvador was cited by the United States as the great success story of the Alliance for Progress. Salvadoran workers were industrious, and the oligarchy was quick to respond to new economic opportunities. El Salvador had resisted the kind of indebtedness that made other nations dependent on foreign powers, but under the Alliance for Progress, it had taken on increasing debt in order to modernize and industrialize—and build up its military. It had benefited from the aid and, under the Central American Common Market, sustained considerable industrial growth. Despite being the smallest country in Central America by geographical area, its GDP was second only to that of Guatemala.

Nowhere, however, do the problems of the 1970s and 1980s dovetail more dramatically than in El Salvador. The "14 families" of the oligarchy (estimated by this time to actually form an extended dynastic network of 254 families) had long concentrated the most valuable lands in its hands and owned 95 percent of the land, none of it used to grow subsistence crops. At the same time, El Savador had the densest population in Central America. The economic morass of the 1970s eventually harmed El Salvador, because of its crippling foreign debt, which was due mostly to military expansion. The excess in military expenditures was well illustrated when a Salvadoran general was convicted in New York City for attempting to sell 10,000 machine guns to an organized crime ring.

The political situation in El Salvador became increasingly unsettled in the 1970s as the middle class struggled against repressive military dictatorships. In 1972 José Napoleón Duarte ran for president for the Christian Democrats, a new, somewhat progressive party that spoke to the growing concerns of the middle class while its anticommunism satisfied the United States. When the popular candidate "lost" the election to the military dictatorship, unrest spread through the country and was met with increasing government violence. Duarte himself was imprisoned, beaten, and exiled.

Death Squads and Guerrillas

Murder, torture, and mutilation are alright if our side is doing it and the victims are Communists.

■

Declassified Memorandum, U.S. Department of State, 1968

The pattern of repression and violence toward civilians escalated, as the despotic government attempted to eliminate all voices of opposition. Political leftists and liberals formed the United Popular Action Front (FAPU) as a forum for public dialogue. Others abandoned electoral politics as hopeless, and the first guerrilla movement appeared along the Honduran border in 1977. The guerrillas were countered by terrorist squads with names such as "White Warriors Union" and "Revolutionary Anti-Communist Extermination Action," but whatever they called themselves, these death squads were part of the military and supported by the oligarchy. They attacked armed guerrillas and civilians alike. The groups proliferated in the next few years until Major Roberto D'Aubuisson, a 1972 graduate of the School of the Americas, formed the Secret Anti-Communist Army to better coordinate their terrorist activities.

In an attempt by the Catholic Church to appease the elite, Monsignor Oscar Arnulfo Romero, a moderate liberation theologian, was installed as archbishop of El Salvador in 1977. Romero did little to reconcile the oligarchy, however, as he broadcast statistics on the death squads in his weekly radio program and appealed to U.S. President Jimmy Carter to end military aid to his country. Amid the condemnation of international human rights groups and the increasingly successful guerrilla attacks, a group of junior officers led a coup in 1979. With the cooperation of the Catholic Church, some members of the new agricultural industry, and centrist political parties, they installed a junta that included civilians, such as Duarte and the more progressive politician, Guillermo Unga.

The civilians in the junta learned they had little control over their military counterparts, and some of them became targets of the death squads. Salvadoran priests, students, and union members "disappeared"—or were killed outright and left dismembered in the street as a public lesson. Many civilians resigned in protest and the junta government changed hands three times.

Archbishop Oscar Arnulfo Romero of El Salvador. (Photo courtesy Ministry of Education, El Salvador)

In 1980 the junta became more centrist; Duarte and some conservative Christian Democrats joined the original military officers to form a new government. Although many Christian Democrats and leftists had attacked the government as hopeless, Duarte believed he could effectively influence events from within government. With support from the United States, he attempted to implement agrarian and economic reforms, but the economy was stalled as investors pulled out of the country and the oligarchy and death squads made progress impossible. In March 1980 Bishop Romero protested the resumption of U.S. military aid. Shortly thereafter he was assassinated while saying mass. Roberto D'Aubuisson was implicated, but the judiciary, controlled by the oligarchy, refused to investigate.

Just as the Sandinistas were installing their government in Nicaragua, the violence intensified in El Salvador. In 1980 right-wing death squads killed an estimated 500 people every month; in 1981 their attacks escalated, killing 1,000 people each month. More Salvadorans gave up on the government and its rigged elections and death squads. The Revolutionary Democratic Front (FDR) was formed as the political arm of opposition and guerrilla groups; its leaders included Christian Democrats of the stature of Guillermo Unga and Rubén Zamora. In October, the various guerrilla groups united as the Farabundo Martí Front for National Liberation (FMLN), named for the socialist martyr killed in 1932.

Civil War

El Salvador was at war. All opposition groups were repressed and many FDR leaders were kidnapped or assassinated; some, such as Unga and Zamora, made their way safely into exile. On December 10, 1981, the army tortured and killed more than 200 unarmed men, women and children in the village of El Mozote. The killings were not limited to Salvadorans, however. In the capital, two U.S. agrarian advisers were murdered, and four U.S. churchwomen were raped and killed. As centrists and leftists looked for alternatives, electoral politics were left primarily to the right wing. Roberto D'Aubuisson's newly formed National Republican Alliance (ARENA) took control of a constituent assembly in 1982, much to the embarrassment of the United States, and ratified a new constitution to legitimize the ARENA government.

U.S. president Reagan was undeterred by the violence of the reactionary Salvadoran government. He resumed U.S. military aid to prove his determination to eliminate what he saw as communism in the Americas. Over the objections of the U.S. Congress, he poured funds into El Salvador—$4 billion by the end of the decade. Using the contra military bases already established in Honduras against the Sandinista government, he trained Salvadoran ground forces and attempted to block the flow of arms from revolutionary Nicaragua to the guerrillas. As it turned out, U.S. weapons stolen from the Salvadoran army were adequate to keep the conflict going.

In 1984 Duarte—with strong support from the United States—was installed as president. Although he was in no position to control the military, he did attempt peace negotiations with the FMLN and initiated a process that would eventually succeed, but not until the military was convinced it could not win—and Reagan was out of office. The war, with assassinations and kidnappings committed by both sides, continued, punctuated only by a deadly earthquake in the capital in 1986 that left thousands more Salvadorans homeless. Pressures for peace increased. The Contadora Group brought pressure from concerned Latin American nations and, when that effort failed, the Central American presidents committed themselves to the Arias Plan (SEE page 248) in 1987. But even that effort stalled until new pressures mounted in 1988, led by the National Debate for Peace sponsored by the Catholic Church.

The year 1989 was a critical time in El Salvador. Nicaragua was preparing for the internationally monitored election that would end its civil war, and pressure was mounting for a settlement in El Salvador, where there was a military stalemate. The army, despite having received $1 billion in direct military aid from the United States, could not defeat the poorly armed FMLN forces. There was a flurry of negotiations as international and Central American organizations attempted to broker a peace agreement. Direct negotiations began between FMLN and the new ARENA government, led by President Alfredo Cristiani (1989–94). President Cristiani represented a more moderate wing of ARENA that was interested in peace. His family was the 10th-largest Salvadoran coffee processor as well as the sixth-largest cotton producer. Although the Cristianis were members of the coffee oligarchy—his brother-in-law, also a member of his administration, was the fifth-largest coffee processor—they belonged to the emerging agro-industrial elite that saw its interests in less militaristic political institutions. These agriculturists would become an important moderating force in Central American in the 1990s.

But the war was not yet over as the FMLN instituted a unilateral cease-fire as a sign of its good intentions. The government took advantage, and tried for victory one last time. Bombings and assassinations escalated. Negotiations ended. The FMLN responded with a major offensive that included attacks on army personnel in the capital; the

THE ARIAS PEACE PLAN

The [Central American] governments commit themselves to promote an authentic democratic, pluralist, and participatory process that includes the promotion of social justice; respect for human rights, [state] sovereignty, the territorial integrity of states, and the rights of all nations to freely determine, without outside interference of any kind, its economic, political, and social model . . .

■

The Arias peace plan, 1987 (Edelman and Kenan 1989, 364)

In 1986, President Arias of Costa Rica was elected to office on a platform that supported regional peace efforts and Costa Rican neutrality. At the time, Costa Rica had become a staging ground for the contras and U.S. policies, and the plentiful supply of arms had found their way into the hands of emerging right-wing Costa Rican paramilitary groups, much to the alarm of that nation. The regional wars also were attracting foreign mercenaries, some in the employ of the CIA, and waves of Nicaraguan refugees were flooding the country. Costa Ricans wanted an end to the civil wars, and Arias began openly criticizing the policies of U.S. president Reagan. And despite the determination of the United States to defeat the Sandinista government

only response the military could think of was to bomb poor neighborhoods in the city. Widespread arrests and assassinations of citizens culminated in the army killing of six Jesuit priests from the University of Central America, their housekeeper, and her daughter—and once again, the world was disgusted. The United Nations censured El Salvador. Against President Reagan's wishes, the U.S. Congress voted to suspend military aid. Peace negotiations finally began in earnest in April 1990.

Cease-fire

In April of 1991, President Cristiani of El Salvador and the FMLN signed a peace agreement mediated by the United Nations in Mexico City, but the agreement was not finalized until 1992. The peace treaty promised that the police would be placed under civilian control and the military reduced by almost half its size. The FMLN agreed to disarm and trans-

militarily, Arias initiated steps for a negotiated peace and drafted a preliminary peace plan in 1987 that became the foundation for negotiations among the five Central American nations. Arias was a reasonable
voice in the din of anticommunist rhetoric. He had earned a doctor-
ate in political science from the University of Essex in England and, as
a member of one of the preeminent coffee-producing families and the
new agro-industrial elite, his aristocratic credentials were impeccable.
His plan provided something attractive to all the Central American
parties, except the contras and their U.S. supporters—and in
response, U.S. economic aid to Costa Rica was reduced. The plan provided for simultaneous amnesties and cease-fires, direct negotiations
between opposition forces in Guatemala, Nicaragua, and El Salvador,
and democratization. A crucial element of the plan permitted governments, but not insurgent groups, to receive international military aid.
After a heated exchange among the five Central American presidents
on August 2, 1987 in Esquipulas, Guatemala, they signed the plan with
a timetable for implementation. The negotiations were successful, in
part because Reagan's policies had been undermined in the United
States by the Iran-contra scandal. The timetable could not be met,
however, and the presidents had to ask the United Nations to continue the negotiations for El Salvador and Guatemala. The "Arias Plan,"
also known as the "Esquipulas II Plan," initiated the process that led to
peace in Nicaragua in 1990, in El Salvador in 1992, and in Guatemala
in 1996.

form itself into a political party. Judicial, electoral, agrarian, and labor
reforms, too, were promised. And it guaranteed a "truth commission" to
investigate the disappearances and assassinations. On December 15,
1992, the civil war officially ended. In 1993 the United Nations fact-finding commission, mandated by the treaty, found that 85 percent of all
human rights violations had been committed by the government and its
death squads. Nonetheless, peace continued, and in 1994 an election pitted the FMLN's Rubén Zamora against ARENA's Armando Calderón Sol
in a run-off presidential election: Calderon won 68 percent of the vote,
and the FMLN won the second largest bloc of seats in the legislature.

El Salvador was tired: 80,000 of its citizens had been killed and
more than 500,000 had fled the country seeking safety; the once-flour-
ishing economy had been reduced to its 1967 size. The civil war had
lasted 12 years.

Guatemala

The last days . . . resembled a sick burro reluctant to move a step. More corpses kept appearing in the outskirts of town, and machine gun volleys shattered the silence every night.

■

Victor Montejo, Jacaltec Mayan writer and witness to a 1982 massacre
(Perera 1987, 470)

Guatemala's civil war lasted 36 years. In the 10 years from 1966 to 1976, death squads and army counterinsurgency attacks killed 50,000 Guatemalans—and it was just the beginning of the civil war. The devastation of the country continued with an earthquake in 1976, which destroyed villages surrounding the highland capital and left 25,000 dead and a quarter of the population homeless. The impact of terrorism and displacement was to increase the numbers of Guatemalans involved in guerrilla activities. By the time peace would be achieved in the 1996 cease-fire there would be 150,000 dead and 50,000 "disappearances," not to mention the tens of thousands of refugees.

The political situation evolved in a way similar to that in El Salvador. Military dictatorships prevented electoral politics and refused to negotiate any democratic reforms. The opposition took to the streets, the guerrillas to the countryside and the remote Petén, and the government devoted itself to the elimination of what it saw as a communist threat. Any and all criticism was met with government brutality that united the middle class, the landless, and the long-reclusive Mayans. Those who were noncombatants, not even guerrilla sympathizers, were treated by the army as if they were, especially if they were Mayan peasants.

Terrorism Escalates

During the presidency of General Romeo Lucas García and his hand-picked successor (1978–82), army terrorism became the norm. A scorched-earth policy destroyed the countryside. In one village, Mayans who requested government assistance in protecting their lands from cattle were slaughtered; within two months, 1,500 Mayan civilians were killed in Chimaltenango province. In the cities, labor leaders, students, and intellectuals were assassinated or "disappeared"; soldiers attacked the Spanish embassy and machine-gunned 38 people to death when Mayan peasants took refuge there. The atrocities convinced Lucas's vice president to resign in protest. The guerrillas responded as well; in 1982 the various guerrilla factions united their forces into the Guatemalan National Revolutionary Unity (URNG). At the same time, the United States was forced to suspend arms sales to General Lucas when he refused to improve his human rights record.

The military leaders started fighting each other over the spoils. A military "reform" junta, led by retired General Efraín Ríos Montt, attempted to provide some appearance of legitimacy to the government by implementing limited economic and social programs. He also pursued the guerrillas with special vigor, and slaughtered thousands of Mayan villagers on the suspicion that they might become guerrilla supporters. Those Mayans not killed, 900,000 by some estimates, were forced into special patrols to help the army—or else. Mayans who made their way into refugee camps in Mexico were fired upon from helicopters.

An Evangelical Protestant, Ríos Montt also alienated those who could strike back, not because of *La Violencia* ("the violence"), but rather because of his minority religion. The major power groups, including the Catholic Church and other army factions, arranged to overthrow him. He did, however, convince the United States, through the lobbying of U.S. groups such as the Moral Majority, to renew aid to Guatemala.

International opinion escalated against the Guatemalan government. In 1982 the World Council of Churches reported that the army and paramilitary forces had killed 9,000 Guatemalans in just the five preceding months; in that same year the United States sent $15.5 million in economic aid. In 1984 the World Council of Indigenous Peoples accused the military of systematically exterminating the Indian population; a few months later the United States resumed military aid. In 1985 international sympathy was once again stirred by the killing of the founder of the Mutual Support Group (GAM), an organization concerned for Guatemalans who had "disappeared." In total, more than 75,000 civilians were killed in the early 1980s and 20 percent of the population was displaced. Half a million Mayans became internal refugees after their land was burned and stolen from them; almost 400,000 Mayans fled to other countries.

Civilian Presidents

Although the government blamed independent paramilitary groups for the kidnappings, assassinations, and terror (a 1999 United Nations study would implicate the government in the atrocities, however) the

QUICHÉ MAYANS

Many Quiché Mayan villages were located in the mountains of Verapaz, El Quiché, and other districts. Remoteness had long protected Mayan culture from outside influences. But during the civil wars, it also provided safe refuge for many guerrillas. To ensure that Mayans did not assist the guerrillas, the government began a massive extermination of defenseless Mayan communities; 83 percent of those killed during the civil war were Mayans. Many of those who survived were radicalized by the violence against them. Rigoberta Menchú Tum, a Quiché Mayan born in 1959, lived through La Violencia and witnessed her family and people tortured and killed. She joined the Committee of Peasant Unity in 1979, and after her persecution she joined a guerrilla group before fleeing to Mexican refugee camps in 1981. She continued to organize opposition to the Guatemalan government, and her autobiography, *I, Rigoberta Menchú*, brought world attention to the Mayans' plight. After she won the Nobel Peace Prize in 1992, she continued to work for Guatemalan peace, leading a tense but peaceful hunger strike in Guatemala City's main plaza during a critical juncture. After the peace accords, her autobiography was criticized for including details presented as autobiographical that in fact were less true of her own life than the war experiences of the Mayan people. Not all Mayans suffered to the same extent during the civil war: Momostenango was removed from the centers of violence and was never the target of an army attack, although some individual Quichés were killed by paramilitary squads, including a Mayan worker for a U.S. aid program. The Quiché Mayans of Momostenango had almost always supported conservative governments, as had many of Guatemala's indigenous population. It helped them very little during the civil war.

Rigoberta Menchú Tum, Quiché Mayan activist and Nobel Peace Prize winner, 1992. (Photo © The Nobel Foundation)

military realized it had to offset international opinion in order to continue receiving U.S. aid. In 1985, Vincio Cerezo Arévalo was elected the first civilian president under a new constitution supported by the military. Not only was the election free of fraud, but Cerezo belonged to the moderate Christian Democratic Party (DCG) and was supported by 70 percent of those who voted. Cerezo signed the Arias peace plan, but he could not control the military or the oligarchy. Nor did he resign or protest, but rather, while the peace agreement was dismantled and popular economic reforms undermined, he enriched members of his party with appointments and contracts.

The army responded to the Arias peace plan with new massacres and the announcement of a major offensive, even though the URNG had shifted its policy from direct conflict to political dialogue and negotiations. Then, although the army clearly had suffered major defeats, it declared the rebels defeated and the war over. Cerezo withstood two coup attempts by the military, but by the time he left office, he had lost the support of the populace. It was left to the next civilian president, the conservative Jorge Serrano (1991–93), to restart the peace process with direct negotiations with the URNG. It was clear that no one could win the civil war, and the stalemate permitted other organizations, such as the National Dialogue for Peace sponsored by the Catholic Church, to develop a national consensus for peace—despite the opposition of the military and oligarchy.

Peace was further delayed by attempts to overthrow the constitutional government (one by Serrano himself, in what was dubbed an "auto-coup"). But in 1993, Guatemala's human rights ombudsman, Ramiro De León Carpio, became president and renewed the peace effort, permitting the United Nations to broker an agreement. During the next few years, various agreements were hammered out and signed: One downsized the military and disarmed the UNRG; others concerned agrarian reforms and human rights—including indigenous rights. On December 29, 1996, the democratically elected president, Álvaro Arzú Irigoyen, signed the final peace agreement.

The Toll

Approximately 300,000 Central Americans died in the wars. Two million Central Americans became refugees, landing in Mexico, Belize, Costa Rica, Panama, and the United States. Economies were wrecked; in El Salvador, just during 1989, the civil war resulted in $30 million in damages to the infrastructure and $90 million in economic losses.

Nicaragua, which had suffered through a civil war against Somoza and another against the contras, as well as a series of natural disasters, was even more devastated. Honduras and Costa Rica suffered as well. Honduras's fragile electoral system was severely undermined by the U.S. military presence, and the national debate concerning the contra presence resulted in death squads and violence in that nation as well. Costa Rica's economy suffered; its independence and political neutrality were threatened.

The regional peace, then, was welcomed. Democratic elections, with opposition political parties participating, installed new civilian governments. The question remained as to what lessons had been learned and for how long.

13

THE CHALLENGE OF PEACE
AND DEMOCRACY

Democracy became the primary legacy of the revolution . . .

■

Sergio Ramírez, former Sandinista vice president of Nicaragua
(1999, 17)

Salvador is reinventing itself after the war, but it's still like
running a Ferrari on a dirt road.

■

Francisco Flores, President of El Salvador, 1999
(Geyer 1999, 13)

I n 1997, President Álvaro Arzú of Guatemala could quite rightly proclaim the good news of peace and democracy in Central America
when only a decade before the region had been consumed by war.
Factions that once had fought one another in terrible civil wars now sat
together in legislatures to debate national policy. The remarkable gains
in democracy and civil rights politically empowered many groups that
were formerly repressed. Elections and demonstrations, newspapers
and political rallies, not battlefields, had become the forums for change.
The political changes permitted a cultural resurgence of the many ethnic groups on the isthmus, from Garífuna artists and Mayan writers to
Kuna artisans.

By 2006, the difficulty of further advancing these remarkable gains
had become apparent. The democratization of the isthmus had not yet
eliminated corruption or political abuses—or, in Guatemala especially,
violence. Peace had permitted impressive demilitarization, but it had

255

not secured citizen safety as gangs and international drug trafficking threatened the public order. Nor had poverty or social inequalities been reduced, much less eliminated: In these first years of peace, half of Central Americans were living in abject poverty. New economic undertakings and new efforts to correct the abuses of the past may eventually bring about a more prosperous and stronger Central America, but in 2006 much remained to be accomplished.

Democracy

For nations that had lived under authoritarian rule for centuries, their rapid transformation into democratic republics after the peace accords was impressive. Universal suffrage had been included in constitutional clauses since the middle of the 20th century, but the opportunity to exercise that right meaningfully was limited to very few Central

THE PAN-MAYAN MOVEMENT

I recognize the voices of my ancestors . . .

■

Humberto Ak'abal Ajyuq', contemporary Quiché Mayan poet

Many Mayans survived the genocide of the civil war continuing the rituals that had always united them as a people. Ancestor altars marked the sacred corners and mountains of the community, and the sacred divination calendar from preconquest time marked ritual celebrations. These traditions continue despite inroads made by Protestant missionaries and Catholic priests. At the same time, a more secular Pan-Mayan movement was awakened by the violence and displacement of the civil wars—as well as by increasing archaeological knowledge about the pre-Columbian Mayan civilization. Mayan identity now can transcend the Mayan's birthplace or language, such as Mam, Cakchiquel, or Quiché, which, with 1 million speakers, is the most prevalent single Mayan language. Young Mayans learn to write their names in the now-deciphered hieroglyphs of their predecessors. Guatemalan Mayans, during their years in a refugee camp, helped Mexican Mayans reconstruct the ruined ancient city of Edzna. Mayan shaman-priests from all over Guatemala make pilgrimages to Momostenango to learn the 260-day sacred calendar maintained there for the past 500 years. This Pan-Mayan

Americans, except in Belize and Costa Rica. Not only did the various peace accords require elections (and their monitoring by international organizations), but the agro-industrial elite that had been created during the 1970s, supported them as well. Seeing democracy as the only way to achieve the political stability and progress necessary to sustain the economy, the new elite distanced itself from the military dictatorships supported by the old landholding oligarchies. The agro-industrialists helped pave the way for democracy, except in Guatemala, where as of this writing such modernizing forces have not yet swept the elite.

Many other Central American interests have played an important role in creating more open societies. During the civil wars, self-governance had been a necessity. Peasant groups and refugee organizations, women's groups, labor unions, and lay church groups matured and clarified their political needs. These grassroots organizations that formed

8 Batz' Festival with masked Quiché Mayans performing in Momostenango, 1997.
(Photo courtesy Naomi Smith)

movement also produced contemporary voices that reached beyond Mayan communities. Among them were writers such as Victor Montejo; political activists such as the Nobel laureate Rigoberta Menchú; and poets such as Humberto Ak'abal Ajyuq', whose Quiché poetry won the Swiss Premio Internacional de Poesía Blaise Cendrars in 1997.

during the 1980s became the basis for more democratic and pluralistic societies once peace was achieved. In Nicaragua, the Miskito Indians won greater political autonomy; in Guatemala, the Pan-Mayan Movement fought for multicultural and multilingual education for the Garífuna and other ethnic groups as well as for the 24 different Mayan linguistic groups. In Honduras, grassroots organizations gained considerable political power after proving themselves capable of reconstruction efforts in 1998, when relief efforts in the wake of Hurricane Mitch overwhelmed government agencies.

Needed Reforms

Despite this progress in democratization, the transition has encountered serious obstacles. Violence has been employed sporadically against those deemed to be political threats. For example, as recently as 2006, Lenca Indian leaders in Honduras were falsely accused of murder, and some labor and human-rights leaders have been killed under mysterious circumstances in El Salvador and Guatemala. Yet community groups continue to organize and pressure the fledgling democracies for judicial reforms and greater transparency in government decisions, both of which could help end the violence.

Electoral reforms are also needed to create broader based, representative democracies, but such reforms have not been completely implemented. Traditional ethnic groups and rural communities still have little access to the electoral process. Community radio operators, broadcasting in rural areas in a number of countries and providing the only news available in native languages, help integrate traditional groups into national politics, but these stations have lost government support or have been shut down on legal technicalities. Expanded registration and decentralized polling drives are necessary to include the poor in the electoral process. As Nicaragua and Honduras have proven, such reforms can be implemented without much difficulty. Guatemala and El Salvador, however, persist in forcing many citizens to travel a full day or more in order to exercise their vote. The 1999 Guatemalan referendum on constitutional amendments demonstrates how this lack of electoral inclusion undermines the democratic process. Only one-third of the eligible population voted in that historic referendum resulting from the peace accords. One of the amendments extended new rights to the Mayans and other ethnic groups, yet the amendments were defeated, despite the fact that Mayans constitute about half of the population.

National Politics

The new democracies began with a wealth of political parties represented in the legislatures, most of them new to Central American politics and with little recognition among the populace. There were 35 parties in Nicaragua alone. By 2004 the number of parties declined significantly (only five sponsored candidates in the 2006 presidential elections in Nicaragua), permitting greater voter identification of the significant parties and their political positions. Only Guatemala has failed to develop strong political parties, and only there has the revolutionary opposition failed to become important in electoral politics. However, former revolutionary groups are among the most important political parties in both El Salvador (the FMLN) and Nicaragua (the FSLN, or Sandinista Party); they have won significant victories in municipal and legislative elections, but as of 2005 none had won a presidential election. They have been defeated by parties representing the same alliances of wealthy conservatives who fought against them in the civil wars and defeated them in the first democratically held elections, although the Salvadoran ARENA party subsequently tried to shake off the death-squad image of its founder, Roberto D'Aubuisson, by selecting Francisco Flores Pérez, an acolyte of an Indian guru who preached nonviolence, as its new leader, in 1999.

Central American elections continue to be monitored by international organizations, such as the Organization of American States (OAS). Even when the elections are clean, the political debate often seems mired in the past and focused on old animosities. The candidates are often from the past as well: Oscar Arias, the president during the civil wars and a Nobel laureate, became president of Costa Rica for the second time in 2006; Schafik Handal, defeated in his bid for the Salvadoran presidency in 2004, was a former revolutionary in El Salvador and longtime leader of the opposition party until his death in 2006. The Nicaraguan presidential election in 2006, however, was almost a replay of that in 1990, with the same factions competing. Daniel Ortega ran for the Sandinistas (FSLN)—for the fourth time. His principal opponent, Eduardo Montealegre of the Nicaraguan Liberal Alliance (ALN), was the choice of the former contras and agro-industrialists, as well as of the United States, whose ambassador, Paul Trivelli, publicly offered financing for a scheme to guarantee a conservative victory. There were some variations, however. A former Sandinista challenged Ortega by running on the Sandinista Renewal Party (MRS) slate, while a former contra accepted the nomination as Ortega's running mate, saying "I prefer the strange to the unknown." (*Miami Herald*, May 29, 2006.)

Venezuelan President Hugo Chávez (left) and Sandinista Daniel Ortega in 2006. In support of Ortega's presidential campaign, Chávez shipped low-cost oil to Sandinista-controlled cities during an energy crisis. (AP Photo/Miraflores Press Office)

Polls suggest that many voters do not believe any party can bring about needed social and political changes: After a scandal in Guatemala in 2000, the most popular party was *ninguno* (or "none"). Nonetheless, until 2006 the conservative parties consistently won the presidencies in the newly democratic nations. The reasons vary somewhat with each nation. In Honduras two dominant parties are both right of center, providing little choice of candidates, although an unusually populist-sounding candidate, Manuel Zelaya, won in 2006 with a slogan of "citizen's power." In Nicaragua and El Salvador the revolutionary parties have suffered from factionalism, unlike the conservative ones that have less to argue about because they dominate presidential politics. Not all the conservative successes have been due to local politics: The role of the United States in these elections cannot be overlooked. It has consistently supported the conservative candidates, just as it did during the civil wars, and with development monies on the line, its support has often been decisive. In the Nicaraguan election of 2006, however, the former revolutionary party won despite intensive U.S. lobbying against it. Perhaps promises of financial assistance by Hugo Chávez, president of Venezuela, offset U.S. threats to suspend its own aid. More important, El Pacto (SEE sidebar) had divided the conservatives into two parties for the first time, providing a unique opportunity for the FSLN. The two conservative

EL PACTO: THE CREEPING COUP

There is only one Sandinismo, the Sandinismo that has remained honest and revolutionary. The other is of corrupt millionaires and thieves who have betrayed the revolution, betrayed themselves, and betrayed the people of Nicaragua.

■

Ernesto Cardenal (Rogers 1006, 7)

No corruption has quite equaled that of former Nicaraguan president Arnoldo Alemán (1998–2002), who was convicted of embezzling nearly $100 million from his impoverished nation. Further scandals unfurled when Daniel Ortega, in what is known as El Pacto in Nicaragua, initiated in 1999 a power-sharing deal with President Alemán and his conservative ruling Liberal Constitutional Party, the PLC, to trade off Ortega's congressional and judicial influence with that of the executive. In 2003 Ortega arranged for Alemán's release from prison (through his influential appointments on the judiciary). In what was called a creeping coup by the press, these leaders of the two major parties combined their votes in congress (90 percent of the total) and attempted to take over the executive branch as well. They tried to impeach President Enrique Bolaños (2002–06), who, although a member of the PLC, had been responsible for Alemán's conviction, and passed laws stripping away the powers of the presidency. Alemán's conservative party was scandalized by the alliance with Ortega and formed the new ALN to contest the 2006 presidential election. Many in Ortega's party had tired of his authoritarian ways long before, including the poet Ernesto Cardenal and the writer and former vice president Sergio Ramírez, and had created the alternative MRS party in 1999. A ruling by the Central American Court of Justice found the "lawmaking" of El Pacto unconstitutional, and pressure from the OAS in 2006 averted this assault on Nicaraguan democracy. Ironically the restrictions on presidential power enacted through El Pacto will encumber Daniel Ortega during his own presidency.

candidates as well as the candidate for the Sandinista Renewal Party split the anti-Ortega vote among themselves, leaving Daniel Ortega the winner, with only 38 percent of the votes.

Corruption

The old rhetoric and lingering animosities have little appeal to an entire generation of new voters who did not live during the civil wars and who see the need for fresh approaches to old problems. Government corruption has also been a major issue in every country, rotting government institutions and eroding the public trust. Corruption has had an impact even on the mature democracy of Costa Rica, where the abstention rates reached historic highs (more than 30 percent) in the last two presidential elections, after three former presidents were implicated in schemes to enrich themselves at public expense. Yet as these nations have started to prosecute former leaders and, in the case of Nicaragua, recover embezzled funds from foreign banks, public confidence has improved. A 2005 opinion poll by the *New York Times* (July 30, 2005) suggested that most Central Americans believe progress is being made in reducing corruption.

Guatemalan Democracy

> We're a people who have been terrorized for many years, beaten down by the forces of corruption.
>
> ■
>
> Roberto Ramírez, Guatemalan businessman
> (Weiner 2003, A9)

Guatemala, the last country to achieve peace, has had just a decade to develop democratic institutions. But time is not the only factor that has made it the most vulnerable democracy in Central America. One of the leaders of the leftist opposition was assassinated in the months leading up to the first presidential election under the peace accords in 1999, and such echoes of death-squad tactics have marred all subsequent elections. The 1999 election subsequently installed as president Alfonso Portillo, a confessed murderer (in self-defense, he said) and a member of General Ríos Montt's party, the right-wing Guatemalan Republican Front (FRG); the general himself took control of the legislative assembly. Given the atrocities associated with the general's presidency in the 1980s—he could be tried for crimes against human-ity on the basis of the UN Commission of Historical Clarification report, and many Guatemalan human rights groups have agitated for just that—this was an inauspicious beginning. Portillo ended his term in scandal, fleeing the country to avoid arrest, and the party was rumored to be involved in drug trafficking. In the next election, Ríos Montt campaigned for the presidency even though he was not eligi-ble, having previously taken power by military coup. But after Guatemala City was subjected to an intimidating day of rioting by his supporters, now called Black Thursday, the highest court ruled he could, on second thought, legally be president. In a country where voter apathy has too often prevailed, 80 percent of registered voters turned out for the 2003 presidential election, defeating General Ríos Montt and electing Oscar Berger, who promised a sweeping reaffirma-tion of the democratic principles of the peace accords. Ríos Montt was placed under temporary house arrest for his presumed role in Black Thursday, and although he was later released, the once all-powerful FRG was reduced to a minority party.

Despite the victory for democracy represented by the 2003 elec-tion, Guatemala is plagued by weak political and legal systems that are vulnerable to threats and unilateral actions taken by the powerful military and economic elite. From land evictions of the poor by the rich to violence against political opponents, these forces are immune from prosecution and operate clandestinely within the country, desta-bilizing representative and lawful government. The most notorious example of the impunity of these shadowy forces is the 1998 murder of Bishop Juan Gerardi Conedera, head of the archdiocese office of human rights in Guatemala, who was bludgeoned to death in his home two days after announcing the results of his report implicating the military for 80 percent of the deaths and disappearances of 200,000 Guatemalans during the civil war. During the investigation of his death, several prosecutors resigned, one fleeing the country after receiving death threats. Although international pressure resulted in the prosecution of three army officers, their convictions were over-turned on appeal and no charges were ever brought against their superiors. The murder was still unresolved in 2006. In recognition that Guatemalan democracy needed international assistance to suc-ceed, the UN High Commissioner for Human Rights was charged with reopening an office in Guatemala in 2005, just a year after closing one that monitored implementation of the peace accords.

Demilitarization

The findings of the UN Commission for Historical Clarification, issued in 1999, found that the Guatemalan military had committed acts of genocide against the Mayans. The report also blamed the United States for direct and indirect support of such human-rights abuses through its policies and CIA-supported military programs. These findings made demilitarization one of the most important objectives of the peace agreements.

Fortunately the new civilian governments have done much to take control from the military. The formerly militarized Honduras, although not under a peace accord, has made remarkable progress towards this goal. During President Carlos Roberto Reina's term (1993–97), Honduras actively prosecuted military officers for human-rights abuses from the 1980s (it was the only Central American country to do so) and appointed its first civilian minister of defense in 1999. While not all Central American countries have so definitively brought their military under civilian review, the military is no longer a political factor in El Salvador or Nicaragua, and even in Guatemala, where it remains an ominous presence in domestic affairs, it no longer controls the government.

All nations have reduced the size of their armies and military spending significantly: Nicaragua went from spending the most on its military ($177 million in 1990) to spending the least ($32.8 million in 2004), except for much smaller Belize. Not one Central American nation spent more than 2 percent of GDP on the military in 2004, but the military in Nicaragua, Guatemala and El Salvador supplement their

Military Expenditures in 2003/2004		
	In dollars	% of GDP
Guatemala	201.9 million	0.8
El Salvador	157.0 million	1.1
Honduras	100.6 million	1.4
Nicaragua	32.8 million	0.7
Costa Rica	64.2 million	0.4
Panama	147.0 million	1.1
Belize	18.0 million	2.0

Source: *The World Factbook 2005*, U.S. Central Intelligence Agency.

governmental budgets through various military-run businesses, such as banks and agricultural holdings, that are not open to public scrutiny. The constitutions of Costa Rica and Panama ban standing armies

Crime

A critical aim of the demilitarization process was to develop police forces to control domestic crime so that the military could be properly restricted to border security and national defense. The police forces were developed, but their number could not keep up with the skyrocketing crime rates that immediately followed the end of the civil wars. The initial crime wave was due, in part, to displaced but armed soldiers. Subsequent crime waves became harder to control, as organized criminals increasingly used the isthmus to run cocaine and heroin to the United States, hiding fast boats in unpopulated Caribbean coves, landing planes in remote jungle clearings, exploiting undeveloped financial systems to launder money. Even the security forces of Panama and Costa Rica have been taxed by this rise in organized crime.

By 2006 the U.S. State Department was reporting that 90 percent of the cocaine reaching the United States was coming through Central America, especially through Guatemala's unguarded borders and along the less developed Miskito coast of Nicaragua. Not only is the law enforcement inadequate (more than 200 Honduran municipalities have no police), but low pay makes the police an easy target of bribery. A Nicaraguan police officer earns $200 a month; a judge earns $500. Guatemalan military elites have also been implicated in drug smuggling, as has the anti-drug czar, who was arrested while visiting the United States. Citing Guatemala's limited resources, President Berger requested in 2006 that U.S. troops patrol the remote borders of the Petén jungle.

Street gangs have added to the violence in Guatemala, El Salvador, and Honduras. The gangs mushroomed from 1998 to 2004, when 34,000 Hispanic gang members were deported from the United States, overwhelming the already insufficient law-enforcement capability of these three nations. According to conservative estimates, there are now 60,000 to 80,000 gang members. Notorious for their brutality, gangs like Mara Salvatrucha and Mara 18, have given the three small nations some of the highest homicide rates in the world. El Salvador, for example, with a population about the size of New York City, had almost seven times as many violent deaths in 2005 as New York City. Guatemala City, with a population of 2 million and 5,000 homicides during 2004, is the most dangerous city in Latin America. The horrific crime rate has increased despite tough police policies towards the gangs, such as arresting any youth with a tattoo. Arrests for murder are rare, however: Only 15 murders out of the 5,000 committed in Guatemala City resulted in convictions. Frustrated with the violence, vigilantes and paramilitary groups have taken matters into their own hands, raising the specter of death squads and social cleansing. The Honduran government has reported assassinations of youth by their own police.

A U.S. MILITARY BASE

The United States maintains a military presence in Central America at the Soto Cano Air Base in Honduras. During the civil wars, the base had the most sophisticated small fighter aircraft fleet on the isthmus and one of the most technologically advanced airports. These supersonic aircraft could be armed with 20 mm cannon, two Sidewinder air-to-air missles, and up to 3,000 kilograms of bombs, rockets, and air-to-ground missles. With the closing of other U.S. bases associated with the Panama Canal in 1999, the Soto Cano Air Base became critical to U.S. regional defense, yet the focus of U.S. activities at the base has changed. Black Hawk and Chinook helicopters, better suited to fighting the war on drugs and providing disaster relief, have replaced the jets. In 1998 the base was first used to stage relief efforts after Hurricane Mitch killed an estimated 9,000 Hondurans and Nicaraguans. The military relief effort was the largest since the Berlin Airlift in 1949 and involved 5,600 U.S. troops. Since then, the number of U.S. troops permanently assigned to the base has been reduced to 560, and the training of Central American forces for combined operations, such as drug interdiction, has been emphasized.

F-5 fighter ground attack aircraft at Honduras's Enrique Soto Cano Air Base, 1993.
(Photo U.S. Department of Defense)

Renewed Militarization

The lawlessness is daunting. Many international agencies argue that it can end only with a more adequate and more professional law enforcement that actually can solve crimes and convict both criminals and corrupt officials. Many church and civil society groups cite the need for social outreach programs and more jobs for impoverished youths. Honduran gangs themselves had a more direct solution when they offered to negotiate a truce with President Manuel Zelaya in 2006, but with no success. Instead, the response has been the deployment of military troops to work with the police. Unfortunately, the joint patrols have used violence against political protestors, not only suspected criminals. The United States has encouraged the trend towards military solutions by relying on its Southern Command to respond to these problems by dispensing increasing amounts of military aid and training—and for the first time since 1990, even to Guatemala.

Economic Growth

These countries have undertaken in the last five years big reforms—reducing inflation, trying to put their house in order. It'd do a lot of good if they had more investments and more exports, and that's why cooperation with the United States is extremely important.

■

Enrique Iglesias, President of Inter-American Development Bank
(New York Times, March 7, 1999)

The Central American nations have had to overcome war debts and war-damaged infrastructure from the 1980s, a period during which Nicaragua had negative economic growth and Guatemala and El Salvador's growth was less than 1 percent. Honduras, which was not officially at war, nonetheless accumulated $4.1 billion in debt, the highest in Central America after Nicaragua, which had a $6 billion debt. As the civil wars ended, foreign aid decreased. For the decade after the peace accords, however, the average annual growth rate was about 4 percent in every country except Honduras. In addition, a new form of foreign aid emerged from the emigrants and war refugees who sought a better life in the United States and, for Nicaraguans, in Costa Rica: remittances. In 2005 Salvadorans received more than $2.83 billion, Guatemalans $2.99 billion, Hondurans $1.76 billion, and Nicaraguans

$850 million in remittances sent from family members who had emi-grated, amounts far in excess of the foreign investments and aid com-bined for those nations and a considerable percentage of their GDP: 21 percent for Honduras, the highest in the region. The remittances fueled private consumption.

Natural disasters have had a considerable impact on the region's econ-omy, especially in those countries just overcoming the effects of civil war. In 1998 Hurricane Mitch destroyed 80 percent of the banana plantations in Honduras and damaged other crops and irrigation networks, bridges, roads, hospitals and schools in Nicaragua as well. Raging forest fires in the late 1990s and volcanic eruptions repeatedly displaced Salvadorans. In 2005 hurricanes once again ravaged the western part of the isthmus and displaced over one-half million Central Americans, most of them Guatemalan victims of Hurricane Stan, which caused landslides that swept away whole villages and rendered one, the Guatemala village of Panabaj, a mass grave. Although these disasters attracted relief assistance for reconstruction, the isthmus has yet not fully recovered. Almost a decade after Hurricane Mitch, Honduras still lags in food production and infrastructure; in the first year after Hurricane Stan, Guatemala reported that 80 percent of the reconstruction projects were unfinished or never begun because of scarce resources.

Central American nations have relied heavily on free-market princi-ples to revive their economies. El Salvador and a few other countries

Economic Overview: 2005					
	GDP (PPP) in dollars	Growth Rate	Industry % of GDP	Agriculture % of GDP	Services % of GDP
Guatemala	56.9 billion	3.2	19	23	58
El Salvador	31.2 billion	2.8	30	10	60
Honduras	20.6 billion	4.2	13	13	56
Nicaragua	16.0 billion	4.0	27	18	55
Costa Rica	44.7 billion	4.0	28	9	63
Panama	22.8 billion	6.4	18	8	74
Belize	1.8 billion	3.8	23	22.5	54.5

Source: *The World Factbook 2006*, U.S. Central Intelligence Agency.

attracted more investment through the privatization of public services, such as telecommunications and health care. The influx of foreign investments enabled the region to diversify its exports more rapidly—and its economy. No nation is dependent on only one or two crops, and each has developed manufacturing and service sectors. (SEE chart on page 268.) El Salvador now manufactures chemical products and textiles; Guatemala, machinery and construction materials. Costa Rica exports avocados and figs as well as electronic parts in addition to coffee and bananas. Honduras trades zinc and lead concentrates in addition to its agricultural products; bananas and coffee account for less than one-third of all export revenues in contrast to a century ago. In 2006 Belize struck oil, adding the small reserve to its exports of timber and sugar.

The tax-free for-export-only *maquila* ("assembly line") industries have enabled Central American nations to export a great variety of manufactured products, especially textiles and apparel. Certainly in overpopulated nations, these businesses provide an alternative to the former reliance on farming. Many economists worry, however, that such industries, attracted by the lowest wages possible to make products for export, do little to develop national markets. And as China demonstrated in the last five years, to the dismay of Central America, competition can suddenly end the maquiladora boom.

Not all industrialization has occurred on the maquila model, however. Costa Rica, with its educated task force, has become a thriving Latin American center for high-tech corporations such as Hewlett-Packard and Intel. Its workforce includes not only minimum wage workers but also professional software designers; its products are not only exported but consumed: Costa Rica has the highest per capita personal computer penetration, almost 24 percent, in Latin America. Across Central America, small businesses are developing, encouraged by microloans from international development agencies.

Tourism has been an enormously successful new industry for Central America. Tourism brings in more foreign currency to Nicaragua and Costa Rica than any traditional export product, and in Honduras, it is second only to coffee. Ecotourism has made formerly ignored Belize into a world destination, and a number of international initiatives hope to do the same for other Central American nations. El Salvador has less appeal as a tourist destination than other nations, but it has been able to benefit from the increased demand for regional airline service by promoting TACA, the national airline. The airline, which has expanded its flights to North America and the Caribbean as well, has taken over competing airlines in many other Central

ENVIRONMENTAL PROBLEMS AND ECOTOURISM

They stripped the land and damned the rivers.
Few iguanas sunning themselves, few armadillos.

■

Ernesto Cardenal, "New Ecology" (after Cohen 1986, 17)

entral America has suffered considerable environmental degradation from fertilizers, pesticides, and soil depletion. More than 35
percent of the land has been degraded or eroded. Commercial shrimp-
ing and fishing have destroyed at least 40 percent of Central America's
mangrove forests. Cattle grazing and commercial crops have required
forest clearing, and overpopulation has forced people to attempt farm-

Corti Village, San Blas Islands, Panama. The Kuna Indians of the San Blas Islands
have taken advantage of their pristine beaches and forests by welcoming tourists.
When the Panamanian government authorized the construction of a large chain
hotel on one of the islands, it learned the limits of national authority. The Kunas,
granted semiautonomous status since 1925, successfully fought the large-scale pro-
ject, which they believed would destroy the environment as well as their own control
of local tourism. (Photo courtesy Mary Alice Raymond, 1999)

ing in the rain forests, where the soil is too thin to sustain such efforts. An average of 1.3 percent of Central American primary forest is lost each year—El Salvador has little more to lose as the agricultural industry has left forest and woodlands on only 6 percent of the land. As formerly dense forests are cleared, drought and fires have increased; in the summer of 1998, wildfires destroyed 2 million acres of forest in Nicaragua alone. Ironically, the settlement of the Petén by landless Mayan peasants has exposed the ruins of their pre-Columbian ancestors to wind and rain erosion, not to mention the cutting of forest for farmland and cooking fuel. Drug traffickers have added to the destruction, clearing airfields and roads in the wilderness.

Understanding that much environmental destruction is driven by economic necessity, Central America and world organizations have developed ecotourism projects to make the preservation of forests, reefs, and beaches, and the flora and fauna they sustain, financially rewarding. Much of the land designated for preservation under such programs is occupied by the most traditional ethnic groups of Central America—the Mayans, the Garífuna and the Miskito Indians, Guaymi and other Indians of the Talamanca Massif, and the Kuna of Panama. Belize and Costa Rica were the first to aggressively pursue such projects, and they have found ecotourism a great boon to their economies. In Belize, for example, the Sierra Club and other environmental advocacy groups advise the nation on the preservation of howler monkey and jaguar habitats, and archaeological excavations have added restored Mayan ruins to rain forest preserves. Belizeans have found new employment as tour guides and hotel and restaurant managers and workers, and the salaries they earn have become incentives to preserve the nature around them. Mayans and Garífunas, for example, took legal action in 2006 to prevent a U.S. oil company from carrying out seismic testing in the Sarstoon Temash National Park that they now manage. Honduras, Guatemala, and El Salvador have joined Mexico and Belize in an ecotourism project called the *Mundo Maya* ("Mayan World"); these countries have done everything to realize the project from setting aside vast acreage of rain forest as nature preserves to coordinating their airline schedules. Another new multination project is the Mesoamerican Biological Corridor which hopes to preserve a continuous wildlife corridor through Central America. Such projects have won the support not only of the participating governments, but also of a diverse number of organizations, among them the U.S. Agency for International Development (USAID) and the European Union to the National Geographic Society and the Wildlife Conservation Society.

American countries. Copa Airlines in Panama has also seen rapid growth by emphasizing regional service.

Central American nations have also diversified their trading partners and investors. Through regional coordinating councils, they have increased trade with other Latin American nations and with Europe; through a revived Central American common market, they have become significant trading partners with each other as well. Panama and Belize frequently establish separate accords because of their distinctive traditional interests: Belize with the Caribbean and Panama with transshipment industry. The resultant diversity of trading partners in the region—Venezuela and Mexico but also South Korea, France, and Japan—if not in each nation, is remarkable. Panamanian imports from Asian nations are almost twice those from the United States. Central American nations are among the few that have diplomatic and economic ties with both China and Taiwan; these two adversarial nations often compete with each other in the region, much to the advantage of the tiny isthmian republics. Honduras recently received offers from both to develop several hydroelectric dams.

The new economic initiatives have had some encouraging results. Despite natural disasters, persistently high public debt, and the costs of corruption and crime, the Central American economies have grown quite rapidly in the first years of peace, since the civil wars, achieving diversity as well as growth. Much of the buoyancy in the economy, however, has

U.S. and Central American Trade 2005			
	% of Imports from U.S.	% of Exports to U.S.	% of Exports to Other*
Guatemala	34.3	58.6	8.6 (El Salvador)
El Salvador	50.0	67.8	11.5 (Guatemala)
Honduras	54.0	66.1	2.6 (El Salvador)
Nicaragua	24.8	35.9	17.3 (El Salvador)
Costa Rica	23.2	14.2	4.7 (Guatemala)
Panama	11.3	13.2	33.0 (Japan)
Belize	41.4	38.9	24.9 (United Kingdom)

* Next most active importing country

Sources: Heritage Foundation, *2006 Index of Economic Freedom.*

been fueled by remittance money, money that may one day disappear. Although population growth (about 2 percent) no longer outpaces economic growth, renewed pressures will develop if immigration to the United States no longer provides a safety valve. It is estimated that more than 15 percent of Salvadorans, for example, live in the United States.

CAFTA–DR

The United States remains the foremost trading partner in Central America, and once CAFTA–DR (the Central American–Dominican Republic Free Trade Agreement) is implemented, it could dominate the region even more. CAFTA–DR was negotiated between the United States and five Central American nations and the Dominican Republic, but not Panama and Belize. The agreement, inspired by the NAFTA accords between Canada, the United States, and Mexico, but without many of the safeguards of that agreement for environmental protection and the rights of labor, has generated massive protests in every Central American country and squeaked through the U.S. Congress by one vote.

After the negative impact of NAFTA on Mexico's small farmers and modest-size businesses, CAFTA–DR has produced worries of job losses and increased poverty. Forced deregulation of public utilities, as a result of the privatization of electricity, could raise rates without subsidies for the poor, as has already occurred in El Salvador, where 14 percent hikes occurred in 2006. These concerns were aggravated by sidebars to the agreement added by the United States as "clarifications" after the signing; the sidebars basically replaced local laws with those of the United States regarding issues such as copyright, telecommunications, and customs inspection standards. The requirements came not only as a surprise but were also seen by Central Americans as a violation of national sovereignty. At the socioeconomic level, the impact of the sidebars could be devastating to many sectors. The new intellectual property laws, for example, could force generic drugs out of the market in favor of more costly brand names. For health-care systems that often lack sufficient funds for even generic medications, the impact on health standards could be tragic.

The agreement was signed in 2004 but not completely ratified and implemented even two years later. Only El Salvador ratified the treaty quickly. The deadlines for ratification lapsed before Guatemala, Honduras, and Nicaragua complied, and even then, those three nations did so under pressure from the United States. Costa Rica, divided over concerns that CAFTA–DR demands for privatization would destroy the

273

PANAMA

At this moment, when we are to end the century and our nation ends a historic era with the departure of a foreign presence, when we are ready . . . to usher in the new millennium with our sovereignty fully rescued . . .

■

President Mireya Moscoso, inauguration speech, September 1, 1999

The Panama Canal under the United States attracted world banking, commerce and, of course, shipping to Central America in an unprecedented manner. As a result, Panama today has an economy of service industries and commerce rather than export crops—although bananas are part of the mix, too. More than half the population lives near the canal area that runs between Balboa and Colón; Panama City, with its sleek office towers, is among the most modern on the isthmus., and Colón, as a free-trade zone, is second only to Hong Kong. Yet most of the country remains undeveloped, including much of the canal area itself. From the moment the canal gave birth to an independent Panama, it has been the most important element in national life—yet it did not

Modern Panama City from the ruins of old Panama. (Photo courtesy Mary Alice Raymond, 1999)

274

belong to the nation until recently. On December 31, 1999, the United States relinquished all control of the Panama Canal to Panama. In that same year, two other "firsts" occurred: Mireya Moscoso was the first woman elected as Panama's president, and Enrique Quiqui Garrido, a Kuna Indian, became the first indigenous leader of the legislative assembly. President Moscoso promised an efficient and safe canal transfer, and she was the popular choice over Martín Torrijos, the son of General Omar Torrijos, whom many suspected would use the canal to the

President Mireya Moscoso, elected in 1999. (Photo courtesy Lic. Antonio Roberto Morgan, 1999)

advantage of political cronies rather than the nation. Ironically, Torrijos was elected in 2004 after Moscoso was disgraced by charges of graft. The canal under both presidents has functioned without a hitch and contributed to the economy. Most of the $1.4 billion in tolls raised annually is required for canal maintenance, but approximately $500 million in tolls contributed to government revenue in 2004. Ecotourism projects developed in the 232,278-acre canal zone—such as replacing the former School of the Americas with a hotel and a military radar tower with an eco-lodge, added almost another $800 million in 2005. The former airfield now serves the region for business and leisure travel. Canal business is booming, yet there is concern that the canal may soon become obsolete. New, larger cargo ships do not fit through the locks. Panama worries that other nations might try to divert some of its traffic by creating new routes across the isthmus—by high speed rail in Nicaragua or super-highways in Mexico. To prevent this, Torrijos proposed widening the canal in order to accommodate the giant ships, an enormous under-taking that would cost over $5 billion. Voters endorsed the proposal resoundingly in 2006.

social programs that have distinguished the country, is the only country that has not.

Poverty Persists

... we're not going to alleviate poverty by accident.

■

Luis Humberto Guzmán, Nicaraguan politician, 1998
(Baxter 1998, 21)

Despite important economic changes, most Central Americans are still entrenched in poverty, and the free market initiatives and privatization of state holdings have done nothing to correct persistent inequalities. Remittances may have averted increases in poverty or, in the case of El Salvador, even reduced it somewhat (to 36.1 percent), yet half the population of Nicaragua (50 percent) and Honduras (53 percent) lived below the poverty line in 2004. Although official statistics from Guatemala are not available, all other social indicators point to similar pervasive impoverishment of that population and, for the indigenous populations, poverty rates of almost 75 percent.

Honduras and Nicaragua vie for the ignoble claim of being the poorest nation in the Americas after Haiti, a situation that is not easily remedied. Nicaragua, no longer a revolutionary country, suffers poverty that has sunk to the level present during the Somoza regime. Its combined unemployment and underemployment rate is 52 percent, and some advocacy groups have estimated that 80 percent survive on less than two dollars a day. A half-million more Hondurans have joined the ranks of the poor in the last three years.

Guatemala has been criticized for its failure to raise taxes adequately to pay for social programs, a requirement of the peace accords. Social conditions have been aggravated by the repatriation of refugees under the auspices of the United Nations and the return of soldiers to their homes after demilitarization. Individuals returning home have found their land taken over by agriculture and new mining companies—2% of the population now owns 70% of the arable land. Many who tried to resettle their land were evicted by the new corporate owners, sometimes with violence—at least three police and seven squatters were killed during a forced eviction at Nueva Linda in 2004. This displacement was exacerbated in 2005 by Hurricane Stan, which left thousands more of the rural poor homeless. The lack of sufficient land for farming has been devastating to a nation in which 60 percent of its people subsist from farming. Violent evictions continue, yet President Berger, a large landowner himself, has failed to implement a process for distributing land and adjudicating disputes. He pledged to enforce tax collections, however, to increase social spending.

Costa Rica, although decades ahead of its neighbors, now has 21.7 percent of its population living below the poverty line, the highest rate in a decade. The country initially suffered from the burdens of absorbing a million Nicaraguan war refugees while at the same time struggling with political initiatives to reform the welfare state. In 1999 Costa Rica started deporting the refugees, creating tensions with its neighbor. By 2006, however, the number of Nicaraguan residents remained high, with an estimated .5 million immigrants looking for work—more than 10 percent of the population. Yet Costa Rica remains the only nation truly committed, ideologically and financially, to correcting economic hardships through social welfare programs. The impact of these programs is seen in both social and economic indicators. And Costa Rica's long-standing commitment to education has given the nation a workforce that attracts high-tech investments.

Social Indicators 2005			
	GDP (PPP) Per Capita in U.S. dollars	Life Expectancy at Birth in years	Infant Mortality Rate per 1,000 live births
Guatemala	5,200	69.38	30.94
El Salvador	5,100	71.49	24.39
Honduras	2,800	69.33	25.82
Nicaragua	2,400	70.63	28.11
Costa Rica	10,100	77.0	9.7
Panama	7,100	75.22	16.37
Belize	6,800	68.3	24.89
Latin America	8,105	71.0	33.0
European Union	26,900	78.3	5.1

Sources: *The World Factbook 2006*, U.S. Central Intelligence Agency; *World Development Indicators*, World Bank 2005, Latin America, Wikipedia.org

Central American nations have undertaken school and health clinic construction projects, and there is little doubt that great improvements have been made in health and education throughout the isthmus. Throughout Latin America, in fact, life expectancy rates have increased and infant mortality rates have decreased since the 1980s because of vaccination and prenatal care programs. Although progress has been made in education, literacy rates leave room for considerable improvement, and primary as well as secondary education remains elusive to many Central Americans. In Guatemala, for example, only 41 percent of eligible students attend primary school, and in El Salvador and Nicaragua close to 30 percent of adults aged 15 and over have had no schooling at all. In fact, most Central American adults have never attended secondary schools, a postsecondary education is even further outside their reach. Although the percentage of adults aged 25 and over who have attended postsecondary institutions in Costa Rica (19 percent) and Panama (19 percent) is encouraging, such education remains the preserve of the select few in Guatemala (6 percent), Belize and Honduras (7 percent), and Nicaragua (9 percent).

Central American Education 2005				
	Literacy Rate	Compulsory Education	Attending School	Public Investment*
Guatemala	71.0	Grades 1-6	41%	4.7
El Salvador	80.2	Grades 1-9	85%	9.4
Honduras	76.2	Grades 1-6	88%	N/A
Nicaragua	67.5	none	80%	9.1
Costa Rica	96.0	Grades 1-9	99%	17.1
Panama	92.6	Grades 1-6	95%	9.9
Belize	94.1	Grades 1-9	60%	15.7
Caribbean & Latin America	90.2	N/A	N/A	N/A
European Union	90.7	N/A	N/A	N/A

Sources: U.S. Department of State, Background Notes, 2005; *The World Factbook 2006*, U.S. Central Intelligence Agency; World Development Indicators, World Bank, 2006.
* As percentage of GDP
** 2000 estimate

Populism

The fact is that trade liberalization has not reduced poverty nor inequality.

■

Inter-American Development Bank (2006, 1)

Democracy with extreme poverty is not the solution we were seeking.

■

Carlos Roberto Reina, president of Honduras
(Honduras This Week, September 29, 1997)

Encouraged by the United States, Central American nations have embraced free-market capitalism, implementing tight fiscal policies and the privatization of state services in the belief that they were on the fastest track to prosperity. Free-trade agreements and IMF budget restraints on governments have been implemented despite the risks to social programs and even to national sovereignty. El Salvador and Panama gave up their currency and replaced it with the U.S. dollar; CAFTA nations changed their laws; and Nicaragua and Honduras, their budgets micromanaged by IMF, could not find the funds for education and health.

Central America has, in fact, become wealthier in terms of GDP and even GDP per capita. Unfortunately, that wealth has primarily benefited the elite few. In El Salvador the income disparity between the wealthy and poor is the same it was a century ago, only now the landowning oligarchy is the business elite that also makes money from privatized banks and utilities. In Costa Rica pressures for a fiscally austere government have reduced funds for public services and created greater income disparities: From 1988 to 2004, the income of the richest doubled while that of the poorest increased by only 7 percent. In Central America the inequalities in income distribution are among the worst in the world. The trickle-down theory has not worked.

Central Americans have grown increasingly impatient and frustrated. Seeing no benefit in giving concessions to foreign corporations, angry citizens in both Guatemala and El Salvador attempted to close down mining operations that polluted their rivers. Physicians in Nicaragua went on strike, disrupting the public health system for months in order

279

to demand wage increases that were denied them by budgetary agreements with the IMF. Quiché Mayans prevented the privatization of water on their lands by persistent demonstrations, and, similarly, the Garífuna may prevent the resort development of their traditional Caribbean lands. Union protesters in Costa Rica have stalled the ratification of CAFTA–DR. Such protests against the open market system have become commonplace throughout Latin America. Some have ended in violent police retaliation, while others have forced multinational corporations to withdraw or renegotiate their government contracts for greater benefit to the host country. A Latinobarómetro poll of Central Americans in 2005 found that 40 percent were dissatisfied with open-market economies; almost 70 percent were dissatisfied with privatization.

Politicians have tapped into the disgust—and despair—by promoting populist agendas and, at times, a certain amount of anti-U.S. sentiment. President Hugo Chávez of Venezuela has been foremost among them. And Chávez has joined forces with Cuba to gain popularity in

Distribution of Income			
Percentage Share of Income			
Lowest 10%	Lowest 20%	Highest 20%	Highest 10%
Central America			
Costa Rica 1.3	3.9	54.8	38.4
El Salvador .7	2.7	55.9	38.8
Guatemala .9	2.9	59.5	43.4
Honduras 1.2	3.4	58.3	42.2
Nicaragua 2.2	5.6	49.3	33.8
Panama .8	2.5	60.3	43.6
Other Countries			
USA 1.9	5.4	45.8	29.9
Germany 2.2	8.5	36.9	22.1
Bangladesh 3.9	9.0	41.3	26.7

Sources: World Development Indicators, World Bank, 2006

Central America, offering discounted oil and subsidizing literacy and health programs. Populist politicians have had some success in Central America but without the high-octane rhetoric of Chávez. President Martín Torrijos of Panama has balanced free-market reforms with the demand for social programs. The anti-CAFTA yet somewhat conservative candidate Ottón Solís almost defeated Oscar Arias, a national hero and free-market advocate, in the 2006 Costa Rican election. In Nicaragua the popularity of the leftist Daniel Ortega seemed to increase with each U.S. attempt to undermine his presidential candidacy.

The United States and Populism

The United States has responded to the new currents in Central America, populism and the expanding presence of China and the European Union, as a threat to its security and hegemony in the region. Judging by the political attacks on President Chávez, populism is seen as something akin to the communist threat of the 1950s. General Brantz Craddock, the U.S. military commander for the region, reported to Congress that "anti-free trade demagogues" (Craddock 2005, 7) are a threat to security, and War College strategists suggested that populism must be preempted by the military. Furthermore, the U.S. ambassador to Nicaragua has not been the only U.S. official to argue that democratic principles are not violated by interfering in the elections of governments who do not support U.S. concerns. Such threats have weakened U.S. credibility in the region, however, leading the United States to shift to a gentler approach. In 2006 career diplomats, not politicians, were assigned to implement a U.S. policy that recognizes the concerns of the Central Americans themselves. And when Daniel Ortega was elected president of Nicaragua, the United States adopted a policy of wait and see rather than immediately suspending aid.

The Question of Unification

During the initial optimism following peace and democracy in the region, Central American nations undertook steps to unify the isthmus, both politically and economically, with the encouragement of the United Nations. The end result has been little unification but more coordination through a proliferation of formal organizations, such as the Central American Parliament and the Central American Court of Justice, with little authority and with individual nations—especially Costa Rica—opting out as they see fit.

SICA Summit on regional integration, March 2006. From left to right: Panamanian president Martín Torrijos, Costa Rican president Abel Pacheco, Honduran president Manuel Zelaya, Nicaraguan president Enrique Bolaños, Guatemalan president Oscar Berger, and El Salvador's vice president Ana Vilma de Escobar. (AP Photo/Panamanian Presidency)

The agency with the greatest potential to realize the integrated development of the isthmus is the Central American Integration System (SICA), which coordinates isthmian issues from health and energy to disaster relief and security with the participation of all seven member nations. It also has been the major forum for trade agreements and the development of regional infrastructure. In regard to trade, it has revived the common market and successfully created more open borders as well as a common tariff among four members (Guatemala, Honduras, El Salvador, and Nicaragua), if not all. Although individual countries continue to pursue bilateral, not coordinated, trade agreements, CAFTA–DR and the proposed agreement with the European Union are the important exceptions.

SICA's greatest impact may be in the energy sector. An interconnected electric power system is scheduled for completion in 2008, but an even more impressive undertaking was initiated in 2006 under the Declaration of Cancun, a joint project of SICA, Mexico, and Colombia to develop low-cost oil and gas for the region. The project, also known as the Plan Puebla–Panama, envisions a gas pipeline from southern Mexico to Colombia and an oil refinery, in either Guatemala or Panama, to produce Mexican and Colombian oil at low cost to the region. If implemented, the project would be the most significant undertaking since the construction of the Panama Canal.

While there are pressures to integrate the isthmus, there is much that also prevents it. Panama and Costa Rica fear their own prosperity might be harmed by joining with the weaker economies of their neighbors. Belize's cultural traditions are with the Caribbean and not its Spanish-speaking neighbors; it participates in many Central American efforts as an observer, but its major focus is with the Caribbean Community and Common Market (CARICOM). Border conflicts persist, emphasizing nationalism over unification. While El Salvador and Honduras totally opened their shared border in 2006, finally ending their dispute dating from the Soccer War of 1969, Belize and Guatemala continue to require OAS mediation over Guatemalan communities spilling into Belize territory. Also, a disagreement over navigation on the San Juan River has pitted Costa Rica against Nicaragua, and brought the intervention of regional groups to maintain the peace.

The Future

If we look back over the last 25 years, we see a great leap forward; if we look ahead, we see uncertainty. Can a backward country that implements democracy consolidate or break the cycle of poverty? That is the question for the future . . .

■

Roberto Turcios, Salvadoran journalist (1999, 118)

The peace in Central America has proven to be durable, its electoral democracy surprisingly resilient. The new democracies may be imperfect but voters have poured into the polls when they see the system threatened, and human rights commissioners and social organizations have dared to confront death squads and corrupt politicians and military officers. Indigenous and other ethnic groups that have been oppressed and exploited now exercise their rights; Mayans formerly fearful of the Guatemalan government now join it, and Nobel Peace laureate Rigoberta Menchú has presidential aspirations. For nations that have been dominated by family oligarchies and military dictatorships for centuries, these are genuine achievements.

Central America's economy continues to leave most of its people in some of the worst poverty in the Americas, and poverty underlies other problems currently plaguing the region, gangs and drug trafficking among them. Recent economic initiatives have done little to correct social inequalities and poverty, but they may have provided a healthier foundation for corrective social and educational policies. Central America's improvements in infant mortality and other social indicators in the last decade place the region high in comparison with other developing regions. The extreme inequities in wealth, however, will be difficult to eradicate. The energy initiatives of SICA and the expansion of the Panama Canal may bring not only infrastructure development and cheaper energy but also much-needed jobs. International programs such as the UN Millennium Poverty Reduction will help, but compensatory programs are necessary to protect subsistence farmers from free trade agreements, and more micro loans are needed for small businesses.

In summer 2006 a Spanish judge issued international warrants for the arrest of two of Guatemala's military dictators, General Efraín Ríos Montt and General Óscar Humberto Medía, for the international crimes of genocide, torture, and terrorism during the civil war. Although the principles of international law will surely be appealed and debated, such judicial actions could do much to change the belief that violence to human rights can be committed with impunity. There is already evidence that a new generation of military officers would like to move beyond the shame of the war era. And, in this, there is considerable hope.

. . .groups and movements nourish the belief that changes are possible, that we have rights, and that we can live with dignity . . .

■

Equipo Maíz (2001, 14)

APPENDIX 1

GUATEMALA: BASIC FACTS

Official Name
Republica de Guatemala (Republic of Guatemala)

Geography
Area	42,000 sq. miles (108,780 sq. km.) About the size of Tennessee
Borders	Mexico, Belize, Honduras, and El Salvador
Elevations	Highest: Tajumulco Volcano, 13,896 feet (4,211 m)
Terrain	Mountainous with narrow, but fertile coastal plains, and limestone plateau of the Petén. Forests and woodlands cover 36% of the land.

Government
Under the Constitution of 1985, as amended in 1993, Guatemala is a democratic republic with three branches of government. The executive branch is led by a president, who is also the commander in chief, and elected for a four-year term. The legislative branch is composed of the unicameral 158-member Congress; each member is elected for a four-year term. The Constitutional Court, composed of five judges elected for five-year terms, is the country's highest court. The judiciary also includes a 13-member Supreme Court of Justice; each judge is elected by Congress for a five-year term. There is universal suffrage for adults 18 and over.

Political Divisions
Capital	Guatemala City (population in metropolitan area in 2005: 2.5 million)
Major Cities	Guatemala City, Quetzaltenango, and Escuintla
Subdivisions	22 departments administered by governors, each appointed by the president

People

Population	12,293,545 (July 2006, estimate)
Growth Rate	2.27% (2006 estimate)
Ethnic Groups	Indian (primarily Mayan) 51%*; mestizo and European 49%
Languages	Spanish 60%, Mayan languages 40%
Religions	Roman Catholic, Protestant, traditional Mayan
Literacy	71%

Economy

GDP**	$56.9 billion (2005 estimate)
Natural Resources	Oil, nickel, fish, rare woods, hydropower
Economic Sectors:	
Agriculture	23% of GDP
Industry	19% of GDP
Services	58% of GDP
Agricultural Exports	Coffee, sugar, and bananas
Industries	Sugar refining, textiles and clothing, furniture, chemicals, oil, metals, rubber
Services	Government, transportation, and tourism
Major Exports	Coffee, sugar, cardamom, bananas, fruits, oil and vegetables
Labor Force	
Agriculture	50%
Services	35%
Industry	15%

Sources: *The World Factbook 2006* (U.S. Central Intelligence Agency); *Background Notes* (U.S. Department of State, 2005)

* Estimates vary from 41% to 60%.
** Purchasing power parity

Appendix 2

EL SALVADOR: BASIC FACTS

Official Name
Republica de El Salvador (Republic of El Salvador)

Geography

Area	8,260 sq. miles (21,476 sq. km) The smallest nation in Central America, El Salvador is about the size of Massachusetts
Borders	Between Guatemala and Honduras on the Pacific ocean
Elevations	Highest: Cerro El Pital, 9,009 feet (2,730 m)
Terrain	Mountainous with narrow and fertile Pacific coastal plain and highland plateau. Forest and woodlands cover 14% of the land. El Salvador is the only Central American nation without a Caribbean coastline.

Government

Under the Constitution of 1983, the democratic republic of El Salvador is administered by three branches of government. The executive branch is dominated by a president elected for a term of five years; the legislative branch is composed of the unicameral Legislative Assembly with 84 members, each elected for a term of three years. Judges on the Supreme Court of the judicial branch are selected by the Legislative Assembly. There is universal suffrage for adults 18 and over.

Political Divisions

Capital	San Salvador (population 2.2 million in 2005)
Other Cities	Ahuachapan, San Miguel, Santa Ana, Sonsonate
Subdivisions	14 departments

People

Population	6,822,378 (July 2006 estimate); most densely populated nation in Central America
Growth Rate	1.7% (2006 estimate)
Ethnic Groups	Mestizo 90%, Indian 1%, white 9%
Languages	Spanish; some Nahua spoken among Pibil Indians
Religions	Roman Catholic 83%; Protestant and other, 17%
Literacy	80%

Economy

GDP*	$31.2 billion (2005 estimate)
Natural Resources	Hydropower, geothermal power, oil
Economic Sectors:	
Agriculture	10% of GDP
Industry	30% of GDP
Services	60% of GDP
Agricultural Products	Coffee, sugar, corn, poultry, sorghum.
Industries	Food processing, beverages, petroleum products, chemicals, fertilizer, textiles, furniture, light metals
Major Exports	Coffee, sugar, shrimp, textiles
Labor Force	
Agriculture	17%
Industry	17%
Services	66%

Sources: *The World Factbook 2006* (U.S. Central Intelligence Agency); *Background Notes* (U.S. Department of State, 2005).

* Purchasing power parity

Appendix 3
HONDURAS: BASIC FACTS

Official Name
Republica de Honduras (Republic of Honduras)

Geography

Area   43,270 sq. miles (112,100 sq. km) About the size of Louisiana

Borders   Guatemala, El Salvador, and Nicaragua

Elevations   Highest: Cerro Las Minas, 9,471 feet (2,870 m)

Terrain   Mountainous interior with narrow coastal plains. Long Caribbean coastline with significant Central America port of Puerto Cortés. Forests and wood-lands cover 42% of the land.

Government
Under the Constitution of 1982, Honduras is a democratic republic with three branches of government. The executive branch includes a president elected for a four-year term; the legislative branch is composed of the uni-cameral Congress and each of its 128 members elected to a four-year term; and the judicial branch includes a Supreme Court of Justice with each judge appointed by Congress and confirmed by the president. There is universal and compulsory suffrage for adults 18 years and older.

Political Divisions

Capital   Tegucigalpa (population of metropolitan area in 2006 estimate: about 1.2 million)

Major Cities   Tegucigalpa, San Pedro Sula

Subdivisions   18 departments

People

Population	7,326,496 (2006 estimate)
Growth Rate	2.1% (2006 estimate)
Ethnic Groups	Mestizo 90%, Indian 7%, black 2%, white 1%
Languages	Spanish, with some English and Garífuna spoken along Caribbean coast as well as Indian languages such as Chortí Mayan, Paya, and Lenca
Religions	Roman Catholic 97%; Protestant and other, 3%
Literacy	76%

Economy

GDP*	$20.6 billion (2005 estimate)
Natural Resources	Timber, gold, silver, copper, lead, zinc, iron ore, antimony, coal, fish
Economic Sectors	
Agriculture	13% of GDP
Industry	31% of GDP
Services	56% of GDP
Agriculture	Coffee, bananas, shrimp, beef, timber, lobster, sugar, fruits
Industry	Sugar refineries, textiles and clothing, cement, wood products, cigars
Services	Government, tourism
Major Exports	Coffee, bananas, shrimp, lobster, citrus fruits, lead/zinc concentrates, meat, lumber, gold
Labor Force	
Agriculture	34%
Services	45%
Industry	21%

Sources: *The World Factbook 2006* (U.S. Central Intelligence Agency); *Background Notes* (U.S. State Department, 2005).

* Purchasing power parity

APPENDIX 4

NICARAGUA: BASIC FACTS

Official Name
Republica de Nicaragua (Republic of Nicaragua)

Geography

Area — 50,446 sq. miles (103,688 sq. km) The largest Central American country and about the size of New York state.

Borders — Wedged between the two seas by Honduras and Costa Rica

Elevations — Highest: Mogoton, 8,045 feet (2,438 m)

Terrain — Mountainous interior with extensive coastal plain along the Caribbean and a narrow one on the Pacific coastal punctuated by volcanoes. Lake Nicaragua is the largest freshwater lake between the Great Lakes and Lake Titicaca. Forests and woodlands cover 43% of the land.

Government
Under the Constitution of 1987, as amended in 1995, Nicaragua is a democratic republic with four branches of government. The executive branch includes a president elected for a five-year term and the legislative branch is composed of a unicameral National Assembly with 92 seats: 90 members are elected but, as a result of El Pacto, one member is the previous president and one is the runner-up in the previous presidential election; all members have immunity from prosecution during their five-year terms. The judicial branch includes the Supreme Court with 16 judges elected by the National Assembly for 5-year terms. The electoral branch includes the Supreme Electoral Council, responsible for organizing elections. There is universal suffrage for adults 16 years and older.

Political Divisions

Capital   Managua (population in 2005 estimate: 1.4 million)
Other Cities   León, Granada, Jinotega, Matagalpa, Chinandega, Masaya
Subdivisions   15 departments

People

Population   5,570,129 (2006 estimate)
Growth Rate   1.9% (2006 estimate)
Ethnic Groups   Mestizo 69%, white 17%, black 9%, Indian 5%
Languages   Spanish, with some English as well as Sumu and Rama Indian languages spoken on Caribbean coast
Religions   Roman Catholic 73%, Evangelical 15%, other 3.5%, none 8.5%
Literacy   68%

Economy

GDP* $13.2 billion (2005 estimate)
Natural Resources   gold, silver, copper, tungsten, lead, zinc, timber, fish
Economic Sectors:
     Agriculture   18% of GDP
     Industry   27% of GDP
     Services   55% of GDP
Agriculture   Coffee, bananas, sugarcane, cotton, rice, corn, beans, beef, veal, pork, poultry, dairy products, shrimp, lobster
Industries   Food processing, chemicals, metal products, textiles and clothing, petroleum refining, beverages, footwear, wood
Services   Commerce, construction, government, banking, transportation, and energy.
Major Exports   Coffee, seafood, meat, sugar, gold, bananas, peanuts
Labor Force
     Agriculture   31%
     Services   52%
     Industry   17%

Sources: *The World Factbook 2006* (U.S. Central Intelligence Agency); *Background Notes* (U.S. State Department, 2005).

* Purchasing power parity

APPENDIX 5

COSTA RICA: BASIC FACTS

Official Name
Republica de Costa Rica (Republic of Costa Rica)

Geography

Area	19,652 sq. miles (51,032 sq. km). About the size of West Virginia
Borders	Wedged between Nicaragua and Panama on the Pacific and Caribbean
Elevations	Highest: Cerro Chirripo 12,573 feet (3,810 m)
Terrain	A rugged central plateau separates the Caribbean and Pacific coastal plains. Forests and woodlands cover 47% of the land.

Government
Under the Constitution of 1949, Costa Rica is a democratic republic with three branches of government. The executive branch includes a president elected for one four-year term and the legislative branch is a unicameral Legislative Assembly with 57 members elected for four-year terms. The judicial branch includes the Supreme Judicial Court, its 22 justices elected by the Legislative Assembly for renewable eight-year terms. Costa Rica has democratic traditions dating from the 19th century and is one of two Central American nations to have abolished the army (Panama is the other). Suffrage is universal and compulsory for adults 18 years and older.

Political Divisions

Capital	San José (population in metropolitan area in 2004 estimate: 1.5 million)
Major Cities	San José, Alajuela, Puntarenas, Limón, Cartago
Subdivisions	7 provinces

People

Population	4,075,261 (2006 estimate)
Growth Rate	1.5% (2006 estimate)
Ethnic Groups	White (including mestizo) 94%, black 3%, Indian (mostly Bribri and other Talamanca groups) 1%, Chinese 1%, other 1%.
Languages	Spanish; English spoken around Caribbean port of Limón.
Religions	Roman Catholic 76%, Evangelical 14%, Jehovah's Witness 1%, other Protestant 1%, other 5%, none 3%
Literacy	96%

Economy

GDP*	$44.7 billion (2005 estimate)
Natural Resources	Hydropower
Economic Sectors:	
Agriculture	9% of GDP
Industry	28% of GDP
Services	63% of GDP
Agriculture	Coffee, bananas, sugar, corn, rice, beans, potatoes, beef, timber, dairy products, ornamental plants, and other fruits
Industries	Food processing, textiles and clothing, construction materials, fertilizer, plastic products, electronics
Commerce	Tourism: restaurants and hotels; banks, insurance.
Major exports	Bananas, coffee, textiles and apparel, fruits, sugar
Labor Force	
Agriculture	20%
Government and services	58%
Industry and commerce	22%

Sources: *The World Factbook 2006* (U.S. Central Intelligence Agency); *Background Notes* (U.S. State Department, 2005)

* Purchasing power parity

APPENDIX 6

PANAMA: BASIC FACTS

Official Name
Republica de Panamá (Republic of Panama)

Geography

Area	29,762 sq. miles (77,381 sq. km). About the size of South Carolina
Borders	Pacific Ocean, Caribbean Sea, Costa Rica, and Colombia. Strategic location at southeastern end of the isthmus, where North and South America are joined
Elevations	Highest: Chiriqui Volcano, 11,468 feet (3,475 m).
Terrain	Extensive coastal plains (coastline 1,786 miles or 2,857 km) with some rolling hills and rugged interior dissected by steep mountains and plains. Narrow, low-lying isthmus permitted construction of Panama Canal and other interoceanic trade routes. Forests and woodlands cover 58% of the land.

Government
Under the Constitution of 1972, as amended, most recently in 2004, Panama is a democracy governed by three branches of government. The executive branch is headed by a president, elected for a five-year term; the legislative branch is composed of the unicameral National Assembly, which has 78 members elected for five-year terms; and the judicial includes the Supreme Court of Justice, its nine judges appointed for 10-year terms. Suffrage is universal and compulsory for adults 18 years and older.

Political Divisions

Capital	Panama City (Population in 2005 estimate: 1,436,025)
Other Cities:	Colón, David
Subdivisions	9 provinces and the territory of Kuna Yala

People

Population	3,191,319 (2006 estimate)
Growth Rate	1.6% (2006 estimate)
Ethnic Groups	Mestizo 70%, West Indian 14%, white 10%, Indian (including Kuna, Embera, and the Talamancan Teribe) 6%
Languages	Spanish, (official) English as native tongue 14%. (Many Panamanians are bilingual)
Religions	Roman Catholic 85%; Protestant 15%
Literacy	93%

Economy

GDP*	$22.8 billion (2005 estimate)
Natural Resources	Copper, mahogany and other forests, seafood, hydropower
Economic Sectors	
Agriculture	8% of GDP
Industry	18% of GDP
Services	74% of GDP
Agriculture	Bananas, rice, corn, coffee, sugarcane, vegetables, livestock, shrimp
Industries	Construction, petroleum refining, brewing, cement, sugar refining, paper, printing, mining, furniture, chemicals
Services	Finance, insurance, tourism, canal-related services.
Major Exports	Bananas, shrimp, sugar, clothing, coffee
Labor Force	
Agriculture	21%
Services	61%
Industry	18%

Sources: *The World Factbook 2006* (U.S. Central Intelligence Agency); *Background Notes* (U.S. State Department, 2005).

* Purchasing power parity

APPENDIX 7

BELIZE: BASIC FACTS

Official Name
Belize, formerly British Honduras

Geography
Area	8,867 sq. miles (22,923 sq. km). Slightly larger than Massachusetts
Borders	Mexico, Guatemala, and the Caribbean Sea
Elevations	Highest: Victoria Peak, 3,828 feet (1,160 m)
Terrain	Flat and swampy coastal plain with low mountains in the south. Forests and woodlands cover 73% of the land and some of the world's most extensive coral reefs lie offshore.

Government
Under the Constitution of 1981, Belize has a parliamentary government with three separate branches. The executive branch is composed of the British monarch as the chief of state (represented by the governor general of Belize) and the prime minister, elected for a five-year term as the leader of the majority party. The legislative branch consists of the bicameral National Assembly: the 29-member Assembly and the 12-member Senate; all serve five-year terms. Although assembly delegates are elected by popular vote, the senators are appointed: six recommended by the prime minister, three by the opposition party, and the remainder by different interest groups to the governor general. The judicial branch includes the Supreme Court; the chief justice is appointed by the governor general on the advice of the prime minister. Suffrage is universal for adults 18 years and older.

Political Divisions

Capital   Belmopan (population in 2004 estimate: 12,300)
Other Cities   Belize City (59,000), Orange Walk (15,000), San Ignacio (16,000)
Subdivisions   6 districts

People

Population   287,730 (2006 estimate)
Growth Rate   2.3% (2006 estimate)
Ethnic Groups   Mestizo 49%, Creole (African origin and African-European) 25%, Mayan 11%, Garífuna (Black Carib Indians) 6%, other (including whites, East Indian, Chinese) 9%
Languages   English (official), Spanish, Mopán and other Mayan, Garífuna, Creole
Religions   Roman Catholic 50%, Protestant 27%, including Pentecostal (7%), Anglican (5%), Seventh Day Adventist (5%), Mennonite (4%), other 14%, none 9%.
Literacy   94%

Economy

GDP* $1.8 billion (2004 estimate)
Natural Resources   Arable land, timber, fish
Economic Sectors
  Agriculture   22.5% of GDP
  Industry   23% of GDP
  Services   54.5% of GDP (2004 estimate)
Agriculture   Bananas, cacao, sugarcane, citrus fruits, lumber, fish, cultured shrimp
Industries   Clothing, food processing, construction.
Services   Tourism, government
Major Exports   Sugar, bananas, citrus concentrate, clothing, fish products, lumber
Labor Force
  Agriculture   27%
  Services   55%
  Industry   18%

Source: *The World Factbook 2006* (U.S. Central Intelligence Agency); *Background Notes* (U.S. Department of State, 2005).

* Purchasing power parity

298

APPENDIX 8

CHRONOLOGY

Pre-Columbian Central America

pre-10,000 B.C.E.   Peopling of the Americas from Asia
c. 2000 B.C.E.   Sedentary villagers
c. 1500 B.C.E.   Ocós culture and the rise of Olmec civilization
800–400 B.C.E.   Rise of early Mayan settlements and culture
250 B.C.E.   Mayan and other Mesoamerican urban centers
250–900 C.E.   Classic Period Mayan civilization
900–1200 C.E.   Terminal Classic and early Postclassic Mayan civilization; flourishing of lower isthmian chiefdoms
1200–1521 C.E.   Flourishing of highland Guatemalan Mayan city states; Aztecs gradually dominate much of Mesoamerica

The Spanish Conquest

1492   Christopher Columbus lands on Hispaniola
1501   Rodrigo de Bastidas explores Panamanian coast
1502   Christopher Columbus explores isthmian coast
1510   First successful Spanish settlement: Santa María la Antigua in Panama
1513   Vasco Núñez de Balboa reaches the Pacific Ocean
1519   Hernán Cortés anchors his ships off the Mexican coast
Pedrarias Dávila establishes Panama City
1521   Cortés conquers the Aztec capital in Mexico
1522   Gil Gonzáles Dávila explores Pacific coast Central America
1524   Pedro de Alvarado conquers the Quiché Mayans in Guatemala. Francisco Hernández de Córdoba founds Granada and León, Nicaragua; Pedrarias soon takes over

1524–26	Cortés and other conquistadores in Honduras. Founding of Trujillo and Puerto Cortés in Honduras, and San Salvador
1532	Francisco Pizarro battles for Peru
1536	First slaves shipped to Peru from Nicaragua
1537	First bishop appointed to Guatemala
1541	Conquest period ends
1542	New Laws, drafted by Bartolomé de Las Casas, promulgated
1543	Trans-isthmian overland route established in Panama

The Kingdom of Guatemala

1548	Royal *audiencia* installed in Santiago de Guatemala under the viceregal authority of New Spain (Mexico)
1560	The first successful Spanish colony established in Costa Rica
1567	Kingdom of Guatemala stretches from Chiapas through Costa Rica
1588	Defeat of Spanish Armada and British expansion in the Caribbean
1638	British logging and pirating based in Belize
1697	Canek, leader of the last Mayan stronghold, is defeated
1700	Charles II, last of the Spanish Hapsburgs, dies. Bourbons rule
1712–14	Tzeltal Mayan revolt in Chiapas
1746	Portobelo sacked; Spain abandons Panamanian trans-isthmian route
1763	Britain agrees to end pirate raids on Spanish territory in exchange for logging rights
1773	Earthquakes in Guatemala; Santiago de Guatemala (Antigua) abandoned for location of Guatemala City
1779	Wars begin between England and Spain. Captain General Matías de Gálvez curtails British activities in the kingdom
1798	Spain loses battle against British at St. George's Caye, Belize

Independence and the Central American Federation

1808	France invades Spain; the colony supports the government in exile in Cadiz
1810	Independence movements begin in Mexico and Colombia (including Panama); sporadic support breaks out in kingdom
1812	Liberal constitution enacted by Cadiz government in exile
1814	Ferdinand VII restored to Spanish throne
1821	Mexico wins independence; Kingdom of Guatemala declares its independence and joins the Mexican Empire of Agustín de Iturbide Slavery abolished in former Spanish territories
1823	Central America secedes from Mexico
1824	United Provinces of Central America established
1827–29	Civil war
1829–39	Under General Francisco Morazán, liberals lead federation
1831–38	Governor Mariano Gálvez implements liberal reforms in Guatemala
1837–40	Rafael Carrera leads uprising in Guatemala
1839	Federation crumbles
1840	Carrera defeats Morazán

Conservatives and Foreign Profiteers

1839–65	Carrera, the *caudillo* par excellence, controls Guatemala and dominates much of Central America
1840	Confederation pact by Nicaragua, Honduras, and El Salvador to counteract British occupation of Central American territories
1841	Britain blockades Caribbean coast
1847	Nicaragua grants United States trans-isthmian rights
1848	Central American nations declare their individual sovereignty
1850	Clayton-Bulwer Treaty between the United States and Britain
1852–68	Cornelius Vanderbilt's Atlantic & Pacific Ship Canal Company operates across Nicaragua

1855	Panama Railway completed
1855	William Walker and his filibusters arrive in Nicaragua
1856–57	The "National War" against Walker rids the isthmus of the filibusters
1859	Guatemala recognizes British claims in Belize in exchange for a road to the Caribbean coast

Making of the Coffee Republics

1870	Age of liberalism begins with emphasis on foreign investment and modernization and "land reform" for the new export crops: coffee and bananas
1870–82	General Tómas Guardia rules Costa Rica; institutes constitutional reforms and ends military dictatorships
1878	French granted rights to construct a canal through what is now Panama
1885	Guatemalan dictator Justo Rufino Barrios killed in El Salvador fighting for the unification of Central America
1893–1909	José Santos Zelaya installs a liberal government in Nicaragua and reclaims Mosquitía
1898–1920	Manuel Estrada Cabrera of Guatemala establishes the most long-lived Central American dictatorship
1899	United Fruit Company organized

Dollar "Diplomacy" and Dictators

1903	Panamanian independence from Colombia; the first U.S.-Panama Canal Treaty
1907	Central American Peace Conference, and the establishment of the Central American Court of Justice
1907–31	Meléndez family and the oligarchy dominate El Salvador
1910–17	Mexican Revolution ushers in unionism and reform movements
1912–33	U.S. Marines occupy Nicaragua
1914	Panama Canal opens
1916	Collapse of Central American Court of Justice
1917	Attempt at Central American unification fails

1920	Estrada Cabrera overthrown; other dictators soon forced out
1928–34	Augusto Sandino leads guerrillas aginst U.S. occupation of Nicaragua
1931–44	Dictatorships of General Jorge Ubico (Guatemala), and General Maximiliano Hernández Martinez (El Salvador) represses labor and communist and, indeed, any reform movements
1932	*La Matanza* slaughter of peasants in El Salvador after uprising organized by communist Agustín Farabundo Martí
1933–48	General Tiburcio Carías Andino controls Honduras
1934	Sandino murdered by order of Anastasio Somoza
1934–56	Nicaragua ruled by General Anastasio Somoza

Challenge to the Old Order

1944	Protests force Ubico and Martinez to resign
1944–54	Juan José Arévalo and Jacobo Arbenz usher in free elections and reforms in Guatemala
1948	Civil War in Costa Rica led by José Figueres Ferrar
1950	Costa Rica abolishes army
	Universal suffrage granted in El Salvador and Costa Rica
1948–56	El Salvador ruled by reform party of Major Oscar Osorio
1954	U.S. government assists in overthrow of Arbenz George Price's progressive party, advocating independence for British Honduras, wins elections in Belize
1956	Somoza assassinated; sons take over in Nicaragua
1957–63	Ramón Villeda Morales introduces civilian government and reforms in Honduras; a 1963 military coup ends reforms
1950s–60s	Riots in Panama
1958	Richard Nixon greeted with protests in Latin America
1959	Fidel Castro victorious in Cuba
1960	Central American Common Market established;

	Beginning of guerrilla movements in Guatemala and Nicaragua
1961	Alliance for Progress implemented
1964	Pan American Highway spans Central America to the Darién
1969	Soccer War between El Salvador and Honduras

Civil Wars

1968	Latin American bishops conference in Medellín
1969–81	Omar Torrijos rules Panama
1971	Guerrilla movements begin in El Salvador
1973	Colony of British Honduras becomes the nation of Belize
1975	Guerrilla warfare in Guatemala flares in Mayan highlands
1977	U.N. recognizes the independence of Belize
	Panama signs new Canal Treaty with U.S.
1978–82	General Romeo Lucas García implements scorched-earth policies in Guatemala
1979	Sandinista victory in Nicaragua
	Military coup institutes junta government in El Salvador
1980	Monsignor Oscar Arnulfo Romero assassinated in San Salvador
1981	U.S. and contra activity intensifies from bases in Honduras
1982	General Efraín Ríos Montt, with U.S. support, takes over Guatemala; La Violencia receives world condemnation
	Major Roberto D'Aubuisson president of El Salvador
1983	Contadora Peace Negotiations initiated
1987	Central American Peace Conference initiated by President Oscar Arias of Costa Rica
1990	Nicaragua holds an internationally monitored election; Sandinistas lose
1991–92	El Salvador Peace Treaty negotiated under U.N. auspices
1996	Guatemala Peace Treaty signed under U.N. auspices

The Challenge of Peace and Democracy

1996–99	Peaceful, democratic presidential elections take place in all Central America nations
1997	Unification initiative before the U.N. by Guatemala, Honduras, El Salvador, Nicaragua, and Costa Rica
1998	Hurricane Mitch devastates Honduras and Nicaragua
December 31, 1999	Panama Canal placed under Panamanian control
1999–2006	El Pacto implemented between former Sandinista president Daniel Ortega and conservative president, Arnoldo Alémán in Nicaragua
2003	General Ríos Montt defeated by Oscar Berger in Guatemalan presidential election
2004	Signing of CAFTA–DR (Central American–Dominican Republic Free Trade Agreement)
2005	Hurricane Stan ravages Guatemala and El Salvador
2006	Panama approves widening of the Panama Canal Nicaraguan presidential campaign symbolizes populist trend in Latin America with victory of Daniel Ortega

Appendix 9
BIBLIOGRAPHIC SOURCES

Alvarado, Pedro de. *An Account of the Conquest of Guatemala in 1524*. Edited by Sedley J. Mackie. Boston: Milford Houses, 1972.

Anderson, Charles L. G. *Life and Letters of Vasco Núñez de Balboa*. Reprint, Westport, Conn: Greenwood Press, 1970.

Angulo, Pedro de. Archivo General de Sevilla (Audiencia de Guatemala), Leg. 168.

Asturias, Miguel Ángel. *Men of Maize*. Translated by Gerald Martin. Pittsburgh: University of Pittsburgh Press, 1995.

———. *El Señor Presidente*. Translated by Frances Partridge. New York: Atheneum, 1964.

Barber, Willard F., and C. Neal Ronning. *Internal Security and Military Power: Counterinsurgency and Civic Action in Latin America*. Columbus: Ohio State University Press, 1966.

Barry, Tom. *Central America Inside Out*. New York: Grove Weidenfeld, 1991.

Baxter, Kevin. "Under the Volcano: Neoliberalism Finds Nicaragua." *The Nation*, April 6, 1998.

Belt, Thomas. *The Naturalist in Nicaragua*. 1874. Reprint, Chicago: University of Chicago Press, 1985.

Bierhorst, John. *The Mythology of Mexico and Central America*. New York: Oxford University Press, 2002.

Bumgartner, Louise. *José del Valle of Central America*. Durham, N.C.: Duke University Press, 1963.

Burgess, Paul. *Justo Rufino Barrios: A Biography*. Philadelphia: Dorrance & Company, 1926.

Burkhart, Louise E., and Janine Gasco. "Mesoamerica and Spain: The Conquest." In *The Legacy of Mesoamerica*, edited by Robert M. Carmack et al. Upper Saddle River, N.J.: Prentice Hall, 1996.

Calderón, Manuel Torres, Thelma Mejia, et al. *Deciphering Honduras: Four Views of Post-Mitch Political Reality*. Cambridge, Mass.: Hemisphere Initiatives, 2002.

Cambranes, Julio Castellanos. "Origins of the Crisis of the Established Order in Guatemala." In *Central America: Crisis and Adaptation,* edited by Steve C. Ropp and J. A. Morris. Albuquerque: University of New Mexico Press, 1984.

Cardenal, Ernesto. *From Nicaragua with Love: Poems 1979–1986.* Translated by Jonathan Cohen. San Francisco: City Lights Books, 1987.

Carlsen, Robert S. *The War for the Heart & Soul of a Highland Maya Town.* Austin: University of Texas Press, 1997.

Carmack, Robert M. *Quichean Civilization.* Berkeley: University of California Press, 1973.

Chavero, Alfredo. *Antiguedades Mexicanos.* 1892.

Chinchilla, Oswaldo Mazariegos. "Archaeology and Nationalism in Guatemala at the Time of Independence." *Antiquity* 72, no. 276 (1998): 376–86.

Chonay, Dionisio José, and Delia Goetz, trans. *Title of the Lords of Totonicapán.* Second printing. Norman: University of Oklahoma Press, 1967.

Cortés, Hernán. *Letters from Mexico.* Translated and edited by Anthony Pagden. New Haven, Conn.: Yale University Press, 2001.

Craddock, Bantz J. General. "Testimony before 109th Congress, House Armed Services Committee." Available online. URL: http://ciponline .org/colombia/050309crad/htm. Posted March 9, 2005.

Crowe, Frederick. *The Gospel in Central America.* London: Charles Gilpin, 1850.

Darío, Rubén. *Cantos de Vida y Esperanza.* Buenos Aires: Espasa-Calpa Argentina, SA, 1948.

Day, Jane Stevenson, and Alice Chiles Tillett. "The Nicoya Shaman." In *Paths to Central American Prehistory,* edited by Frederick W. Lange. Niwot: University Press of Colorado, 1996.

Democracy in Latin America: Toward a Citizen's Democracy. New York: United Nations Development Program, April 2004.

Denevan, William M., ed. *The Native Population of the Americas in 1492.* Madison: University of Wisconsin Press, 1976.

Dunlop, Robert G. *Travels in Central America: Being A Journal of Nearly Three Years Residence in the Country: Together with a Sketch of the History of the Republic, and an Account of Its Climate, Productions, Commerce, etc.* London: Longman, Brown, Green, & Longman, 1847.

Duran, Diego. *Book of the Gods and Rites and the Ancient Calendar.* Translated and edited by Fernando Hercasitos and Doris Heyden. Norman: University of Oklahoma Press, 1971.

Edmonson, Munro S., trans. *Heaven Born Mérida and Its Destiny: The Book of the Chilam Balam of Chumayel*. Austin: University of Texas Press, 1986.

Elhinny, Vincent. "U.S.-Central American Free Trade Agreement: Leaping Without Looking?" In *Americas Program*. Silver City, New Mexico: Interhemispheric Resource Center, 2003.

Equipo Maíz. *El Salvador, 10 años después*. San Salvador: Asociación Equipo Maíz, 2001.

Franck, Harry A. *Tramping Through Mexico, Guatemala and Honduras*. New York: The Century Company, 1916.

Fuentes, Patricia de, ed. and trans. *The Conquistadors*. Reprint, Norman: University of Oklahoma Press, 1993.

Gage, Thomas. *Travels in the New World, 1648*. Reprint, Norman: University of Oklahoma Press, 1985.

Gerla, Marisa P. "Toward a Deeper Union? A Comparative Assessment of Central American Integration." Unpublished paper, 2005.

Geyer, Georgia Ann. "The Amazing New 'Center' in Central America." In *Washington Quarterly* 22, no. 3 (summer 1999): 10–13.

Graham, Mark Miller. "Merchants and Metalwork in Middle America." In *Paths to Central American Prehistory*. Edited by Frederick W. Lange. Niwot: University Press of Colorado, 1996.

Graham, Mark Miller, ed. *Reinterpreting Prehistory of Central America*. Niwot: University Press of Colorado, 1993.

Handy, Jim. *Gift of the Devil*. Boston: South End Press, 1984.

Haugaard, Lisa, Adam Isacson, and Joy Olson. *Erasing the Lines: Trends in U.S. Military Programs with Latin America*. Center for International Policy. Available online. URL: www.ciponline.org. Posted December 2005.

Henderson, Captain George. *An Account of the British Settlements of Honduras*. London, 1809.

Heritage Foundation. Index of Economic Freedom 2006. Available online. URL: www.heritage.org/research/features/index/country. Downloaded June 15, 2006.

Inter-American Development Bank. "The Poverty Impact of Trade Integration." Available online. URL: www.iadb.org/news/articledetail.cfm?. Posted June 27, 2006.

Jones, Grant D., ed. *El Manuscrito de Canek*. Mexico: Instituto Nacional de Antropología e Historia, 1991.

———. "The Last Maya Frontiers of Colonial Yucatán." In *Spaniards and Indians in Southeastern Mesoamerica*, edited by Murdo J. MacLeod and Robert Wasserstrom. Lincoln: University of Nebraska Press, 1983.

Jones, Oakah L., Jr. *Guatemala in the Spanish Colonial Period.* Norman: University of Oklahoma Press, 1994.

Joyce, Thomas A. *Central American and West Indian Archaeology.* 1916. Reprint. New York: Hacker Art Books, 1974.

Kincaid, Douglas. "Demilitarization and Security in El Salvador and Guatemala: Convergences of Success and Crisis." In *Journal of Interamerican Studies & World Affairs,* 52, no. 4 (winter 2000).

Kinzer, Stephen. "Country Without Heroes." In *The New York Review of Books,* July 19, 2001, 31–33.

———. "The Trouble with Costa Rica." In *The New York Review of Books,* June 8, 2006, 56–59.

LaFeber, Walter. *Inevitable Revolutions: The United States in Central America.* Second edition. New York: W.W. Norton & Company, 1993.

Landívar, Rafael. *Rusticatio mexicano.* Facsimile edition, 1782. Guatemala: Editorial Universitaria, 1950.

Las Casas, Bartolomé de. *A Short Account of the Destruction of the Indies.* Edited and translated by Nigel Griffin. London: Penguin Books, 1999.

Latinobarómetro, Latin American Poll 2005. Available online. URL: www.latinobarometro.org. Posted October 2005.

Lehner, Ernst, and Johanna Ernst, compilers. *How They Saw the New World.* New York: Tudor Publishing Company, 1966.

León-Portilla, Miguel, ed. *Broken Spears: The Aztec Account of the Conquest of Mexico.* Translated by Lysander Kemp. Boston: Beacon Press, 1962.

———. *Pre-Columbian Literatures of Mexico.* Translated by Grace Lobanov and the author. Reprint, Norman: University of Oklahoma Press, 1986.

Lutz, Christopher H. *Santiago de Guatemala 1541–1773: City, Caste, and the Colonial Experience.* Norman: University of Oklahoma Press, 1997.

MacLeod, Murdo J. *Spanish Central America: A Socioeconomic History 1520–1720.* Berkeley: University of California Press, 1985.

Marure, Alejandro. *Bosquejo histórico de las revoluciones de Centro America desde 1811 hasta 1834.* Guatemala: 1837.

Maudslay, Alfred P. *Biologia Centrali-Americana. Archaeology.* 1889–1902. Facsimile edition. New York: Milpatron Publishing Company, 1974.

McCann, Thomas P. *An American Company: The Tragedy of United Fruit.* New York: Crown Publishers, 1976.

Ministry of Education, El Salvador. *Historia de El Salvador.* Tomos 1 y 2. El Salvador: Comisión Nacional de los Libros de Textos Gratuitos, 1994.

Mongabay. World Deforestation Rates 2000–2005. Available online. URL: http://news.mongabay.com Posted November 17, 2005.

Montejo, Victor. *Testimony: Death of a Guatemalan Village.* Translated by Victor Perera. Willimantic, Conn.: Curbstone Press, 1987.

Morison, Samuel Eliot, ed. and trans. *Journals and Other Documents on the Life of Christopher Columbus.* New York: Heritage, 1963.

Munro, Dana G. *The Five Republics of Central America.* 1918. Reprint, New York: Russell & Russell, 1967.

National Security Archive. U.S. Department of State memorandum, March 29, 1968.

Newson, Linda. *The Cost of Conquest: Indian Decline in Honduras under Spanish Rule.* Boulder, Colo.: Westview Press, 1986.

Nyrop, Richard F., ed. *Panama: A Country Study.* Washington, D.C.: U.S. Government Printing Office, 1981.

Paige, Jeffrey M. *Coffee and Power: Revolution and the Rise of Democracy in Central America.* Cambridge, Mass.: Harvard University Press, 1997.

Pendergast, David M., and Grant D. Jones. "Poor Beds of Sticks and Rings of Pure Gold." *Ancient Mesoamerica* 3 (1992): 281–90.

Ramírez, Sergio. *Adiós Muchachos: Una memoria de la revolución sandinista.* Mexico D.F.: Aguilar, 1999.

Recinos, Adrián, and Delia Goetz, trans. *The Annals of the Cackchiquels.* Third printing. Norman: University of Oklahoma Press, 1974.

Reents-Budet, Dorie. *Painting the Maya Universe.* Durham, N.C.: Duke University Press, 1994.

Restall, Matthew. *Maya Conquistador.* Boston: Beacon Press, 1998.

Rogers, Tim. "In Nicaragua, Old US Foe Rises Again." *Christian Science Monitor,* July 7, 2006.

Rohter, Larry. "Unending Graft Threatens the Democracies of Latin America as Frustrations Grow." *The New York Times,* July 30, 2005.

Roys, Ralph L., trans. *The Book of the Chilam Balam of Chumayel.* Norman: University of Oklahoma Press, 1967.

Rushdie, Salman. *The Jaguar Smile: A Nicaraguan Journey.* Reprint, New York: Picador, 2003.

Sahagun, Bernardino de. *General History of the Things of New Spain: Florentine Codex (c. 1583).* Translated by Arthur J. O. Anderson and Charles E. Dibble. 13 vols. Santa Fe, N. Mex.: School of American Research and University of Utah Press, 1951–82.

Sherman, William L. *Forced Native Labor in Sixteenth-Century Central America.* Lincoln: University of Nebraska Press, 1979.

———. "Some Aspects of Change in Guatemalan Society, 1470–1620." In *Spaniards and Indians in Southeastern Mesoamerica,* edited by Murdo J. MacLeod and Robert Wasserstrom. Lincoln: University of Nebraska Press, 1983.

Sieder, Rachel, Megan Thomas, et al. *Who Governs? Guatemala Five Years After the Peace Accords.* Cambridge, Mass.: Hemisphere Initiatives, 2002.

"Small, Vulnerable—and Disunited." *Economist,* 360, no. 8234, August 11, 2001, 28–29.

Spence, Jack. *War and Peace in Central America.* Brookline, Mass.: Hemisphere Initiatives, 2004.

Spence, Jack, Mike Lanchin, et al. *From Elections to Earthquakes: Reform and Participation in Post-War El Salvador.* Cambridge, Mass.: Hemisphere Initiatives, 2001.

Squier, E. G. *Notes on Central America, Particularly the States of Honduras and San Salvador.* New York: Harper & Brothers, 1855.

Stein, Stanley J., and Barbara H. Stein. *The Colonial Heritage of Latin America.* New York: Oxford University Press, 1970.

Stephens, John Lloyd. *Incidents of Travel in Central America, Chiapas, and Yucatán.* New York: Dover Publications, 1969.

Tedlock, Barbara. *Time and the Highland Maya.* Rev. ed. Albuquerque: University of New Mexico Press, 1992.

Tedlock, Dennis, ed. and trans. *Popol Vuh: The Mayan Book of the Dawn of Life.* New York: Simon & Schuster, 1985.

Tozzer, Alfred M., ed. and trans. *Landa's Realción de las Cosas de Yucatán.* Cambridge, Mass., Papers of the Peabody Museum, vol. xviii, 1941.

Turcios, Roberto. "El Salvador: Una Transición histórica y fundacional." In *Nueva Sociedad* 90 (July–August 1997): 112–118.

United Nations Development Program. "2006 Annual Report: Global partnership for development." Available online. URL: http://undp.org/publications/annualreport2006/index.shtml. Downloaded March 2, 2006.

———. "Human Development Reports: Latin America & the Caribbean 2005." Available online. URL: http://hdr.undp.org. Posted September 8, 2005.

United Nations Economic Commission on Latin America and the Caribbean. "Mexico and Central America. " In *Preliminary Overview of the Economies of Latin America and the Caribbean 2005.* Available online: www.eclac.org/publications. Posted December 2005.

U.S. Department of State. Background Notes. Available online. URL: http://www.state.gov/r/pa/ei/bgn/. Updated 2005–2006.

Vasconcelos, Pedro de. *Remittances 2005: Promoting Financial Democracy.* Washington D.C.: Inter-American Development Bank. March 2006.

Vásquez, Norma. "Revolution, War and Women in El Salvador." Monograph 5. Montevideo, Uruguay: LOLA Press, 1996.

Weiner, Tim. "Guatemalan Voters Reject a Former Dictator." *The New York Times,* November 10, 2003.

Wikipedia. "Latin America. "Available online. URL: http://en. wikipedia.org/ wiki/Latin_america. Updated July 12, 2006.

Woodward, Ralph Lee, Jr. *Central America: A Nation Divided.* 2nd ed. New York: Oxford University Press, 1985.

————. *Rafael Carrera and the Emergence of the Republic of Guatemala, 1821–71.* Athens: University of Georgia Press, 1993.

World Bank. "World Development Indicators 2006, Data & Statistics." Available online. URL: http://www.worldbank.org. Downloaded September 10, 2005.

World Factbook. U.S. Central Intelligence Agency Publications. Available online. URL: www.cia.gov/cia/publications/factbook/2006. Updated June 6, 2006.

World's Coffee, The. no. 9. International Institute of Agriculture, Rome: FAO Bureau, Villa Borghese, 1947.

Wortman, Miles L. *Government and Society in Central America, 1680– 1840.* New York: Columbia University Press, 1982.

Zorita, Alonso de. *Life and Labor in Ancient Mexico.* Edited and translated by Benjamin Keen. Norman: University of Oklahoma Press, 1994.

Appendix 10

SUGGESTED READING

Although this book's brief history is intended for the general reader, many in-depth works are also available. The following works in English include not only history and politics but also literature, art, anthropology, and ethnohistory.

Books Spanning Major Periods

Bolland, O. Nigel. *The Formation of Colonial Society: Belize from Conquest to Crown Colony*. Baltimore: Johns Hopkins University Press, 1977.

Bulmer-Thomas, Victor. *The Political Economy of Central America Since 1920*. Cambridge: Cambridge University Press, 1987.

Carmack, Robert M. *Rebels of Highland Guatemala: The Quiché-Mayas of Momostenango*. Norman: University of Oklahoma Press, 1995.

Edelman, Marc, and Joanne Kenen, eds. *The Costa Rica Reader*. New York: Grove Weidenfeld, 1989.

Grant, C. H. *The Making of Modern Belize: Politics, Society and British Colonialism in Central America*. Cambridge: Cambridge University Press, 1976.

Haggerty, Richard A., ed. *El Salvador: A Country Study*. Washington, D.C.: U.S. Department of the Army, 1990.

Hall, Carolyn, Hector Pérez Brignoli. *Historical Atlas of Central America*. Norman: University of Oklahoma Press, 2003.

Helms, Mary. *Middle America: A Culture History of Heartland and Frontiers*. Englewood Cliffs, N.J.: Prentice Hall, 1975.

Karnes, Thomas L. *The Failure of the Union: Central America, 1824–1975*. Revised edition. Tempe: Arizona State University Press, 1976.

LaFeber, Walter. *Inevitable Revolutions: The United States in Central America*. Second edition. New York: W.W. Norton & Company, 1993.

Langley, Lester D. *The United States and the Caribbean in the Twentieth Century.* Athens: University of Georgia Press, 1989.

Lindsay-Poland, John. *Emperors in the Jungle: The Hidden History of the U.S. in Panama.* Durham, N.C.: Duke University Press, 2003.

Morris, James A. *Honduras: Caudillo Politics and Military Rulers.* Boulder, Colo.: Westview Press, 1984.

Nelson, Harold D. *Costa Rica: A Country Study.* 2nd ed. Washington, D.C.: U.S. Government Printing Office, 1984

Nyrop, Richard F., ed. *Guatemala: A Country Study.* 2nd ed. Washington, D.C.: U.S. Government Printing Office, 1984.

Nyrop, Richard F., ed. *Panama: A Country Study.* Washington, D.C.: U.S. Government Printing Office, 1981.

Paige, Jeffrey M. *Coffee and Power: Revolution and the Rise of Democracy in Central America.* Cambridge, Mass.: Harvard University Press, 1998.

Pérez-Brignoli, Hector. *A Brief History of Central America.* Translated by Ricardo B. Sawrey and Susana Strettridi Sawrey. Berkeley: University of California Press, 1989.

Ropp, Steve C. *Panamanian Politics: From Guarded Nation to National Guard.* New York: Praeger, 1982.

Rudolph, James D., ed. *Honduras: A Country Study.* Washington, D.C.: U.S. Government Printing Office, 1984.

Rudolph, James D., ed. *Nicaragua: A Country Study.* 2nd ed. Washington, D.C.: U.S. Government Printing Office, 1982.

Smith, Carol A. *Guatemalan Indians and the State 1540–1988.* Austin: University of Texas Press, 1992.

Stone, Samuel Z. *The Heritage of the Conquistadors: Ruling Classes in Central America from Conquest to Sandinistas.* Lincoln: University of Nebraska Press, 1992.

Torres Rivas, Edelberto. *History and Society in Central America.* Translated by Douglass Sullivan-González. Austin: University of Texas Press, 1993.

Woodward, Ralph Lee, Jr. *Central America: A Nation Divided.* 3rd ed. Oxford: Oxford University Press, 1999.

Yashar, Deborah. *Demanding Democracy: Reform and Reaction in Costa Rica and Guatemala, 1870s–1950s.* Stanford, Calif.: Stanford University Press, 1997.

The Land and Its First Peoples

Bierhorst, John. *The Mythology of Mexico and Central America.* New York: Oxford University Press, 2002.

Boone, Elizabeth, H., ed. *Ritual Human Sacrifice in Mesoamerica.* Washington, D.C.: Dumbarton Oaks, 1984.

Christenson, Allen J., trans. and ed. *Popol Vuh: The Sacred Book of the Maya.* New York: O Books, 2003.

Coates, Anthony G., ed. *Central America: A Natural and Cultural History.* New Haven, Conn.: Yale University Press, 1997.

Coe, Michael D. *Mexico: The Maya.* 7th ed. London: Thames & Hudson, 2005.

Davies, Nigel. *Voyagers to the New World.* Reprint edition. Albuquerque: University of New Mexico Press, 1986.

Grove, David C., ed. *Regional Perspectives on the Olmec.* New York: Cambridge University Press, 1989.

Olmec World: Ritual and Rulership, The. Princeton, N.J.: The Art Museum, Princeton University, 1996.

Recinos, Adrián, and Delia Goetz, trans. *The Annals of the Cakchiquels.* Second printing. Norman: University of Oklahoma Press, 1967.

Sheets, Payson D. *The Ceren Site.* 2nd ed. Belmont Calif.: Wadsworth Publishing, 2005.

Sheets, Payson D., ed. *Archeology and Volcanism in Central America.* Austin: University of Texas Press, 1983.

Stone, Doris. *Pre-Columbian Man Finds Central America.* Cambridge, Mass.: Peabody Museum Press, 1972.

Tedlock, Dennis, ed. and trans. *The Popol Vuh: The Mayan Book of the Dawn of Life.* Rev. ed. New York: Simon & Schuster, 1996.

West, Robert C., and John P. Augelli. *Middle America: Its Land and People.* 3rd ed. Englewood Cliffs, N.J.: Prentice Hall, 1989.

The Mayans and Their Neighbors

Aveni, Anthony F. *Skywatchers of Ancient Mexico.* Rev. ed. Austin: University of Texas Press, 2001.

Carmack, Robert M. *The Quiché Mayas of Utatlán: The Evolution of a Highland Guatemala Kingdom.* Norman: University of Oklahoma Press, 1981.

Graham, Mark Miller, ed. *Reinterpreting Prehistory of Central America.* Niwot: University Press of Colorado, 1993.

Lange, Frederick W., ed. *Paths to Central American Prehistory.* Niwot: University Press of Colorado, 1996.

Lange, Frederick W., ed. *Wealth and Hierarchy in the Intermediate Area.* Washington, D.C.: Dumbarton Oaks, 1992.

León-Portilla, Miguel, ed. *Broken Spears: The Aztec Account of the Conquest of Mexico.* Translated by Lysander Kemp. Rev. ed. Boston: Beacon Press, 1992.

León-Portilla, Miguel. *Pre-Columbian Literatures of Mexico.* Norman: University of Oklahoma Press, 1969.

Miller, Mary Ellen. *The Art of Mesoamerica from Olmec to Aztec.* 4th ed. London: Thames & Hudson, 2006.

Quilter, Jeffrey, and John Hoopes, eds. *Gold and Power in Ancient Costa Rica, Panama, and Colombia.* Washington D.C.: Dumbarton Oaks, 2003.

Schele, Linda, and David Freidel. *A Forest of Kings: The Untold Story of the Ancient Maya.* Reprint edition. New York: HarperPerennial, 1992.

Schele, Linda, and Peter Mathews. *The Code of Kings: The Language of Seven Sacred Mayan Temples and Tombs.* New York: Scribners, 1998.

Sharer, Robert J. with Loa P. Traxler. *The Ancient Maya.* Sixth edition. Stanford, Calif.: Stanford University Press, 2005.

Stone, Doris. *Pre-Columbian Man Finds Central America.* Cambridge, Mass.: Peabody Museum Press, 1972.

Urban, Patricia A., and Edward M. Schortman. *The Southeast Maya Periphery.* Austin: University of Texas Press, 1986.

The Spanish Conquest

Alvarado, Pedro de. *An Account of the Conquest of Guatemala in 1524.* Edited by Sedley J. Mackie. Boston: Milford House, 1972.

Anderson, Charles L. G. *Life and Letters of Vasco Núñez de Balboa.* London: Fleming H. Revell & Company, 1941.

Carmack, Robert M. *The Quiché Mayas of Utatlán: The Evolution of a Highland Guatemala Kingdom.* Norman: University of Oklahoma Press, 1981.

Cortés, Hernán. *Letters from Mexico.* Translated and edited by Anthony Pagden. New Haven, Conn.: Yale University Press, 2001.

Elliot, J. H. *The Old World and the New 1492–1650.* 1970. Reprint, New York: Cambridge University Press. 1992.

———. *Imperial Spain 1469–1716.* New York: New American Library, 1963.

Fuentes, Patricia de, ed. and trans. *The Conquistadors.* Reprint, Norman: University of Oklahoma Press, 1993.

Kelly, John E. *Pedro de Alvarado, Conquistador.* 1932. Reprint, Port Washington, N.Y.: Kennikat Press, 1988.

Las Casas, Bartolomé de. *A Short Account of the Destruction of the Indies.* Ed. and trans. by Nigel Griffin. London: Penguin Books, 1999.

Recinos, Adrián, and Delia Goetz, trans. *The Annals of the Cakchiquels.* Second printing. Norman: University of Oklahoma Press, 1974.

Ricard, Robert. *The Spiritual Conquest of Mexico. An Essay on the Apostolate and Evangelizing Methods of the Mendicant Orders in New Spain, 1523–1572.* Translated by Lesley Byrd Simpson. Berkeley: University of California Press, 1982.

Sale, Kirkpatrick. *Christopher Columbus and the Conquest of Paradise.* 2nd ed. London: Tauris Parke, 2006.

Founding of the Kingdom of Guatemala

Friede, Juan, and Benjamin Keen, ed. *Bartolomé de Las Casas in History: Toward an Understanding of the Man and His Work.* De Kalb: Northern Illinois University Press, 1971.

Gibson, Charles, *Spain in America.* New York: Harper & Row, 1966.

Jones, Oakah L. Jr. *Guatemala in the Spanish Colonial Period.* Norman: University of Oklahoma Press, 1994.

Lutz, Christopher H. *Santiago de Guatemala, 1541–1773: City, Caste, and the Colonial Experience.* Norman: University of Oklahoma Press, 1997.

MacLeod, Murdo J., *Spanish Central America: A Socioeconomic History 1520–1720.* Berkeley: University of California Press, 1973. Reprint, 1985.

MacLeod, Murdo J., and Robert Wasserstrom, eds. *Spaniards and Indians in Southeastern Mesoamerica.* Lincoln: University of Nebraska Press, 1983.

Newson, Linda A. *The Cost of Conquest: Indian Decline in Honduras Under Spanish Rule.* Boulder, Colo.: Westview Press, 1986.

———. *Indian Survival in Colonial Nicaragua.* Norman: University of Oklahoma Press, 1987.

Sherman, William L. *Forced Native Labor in Sixteenth-Century Central America.* Lincoln: University of Nebraska Press, 1979.

Zorita, Alonso de. *Life and Labor in Ancient Mexico.* Translated and edited by Benjamin Keen. Norman: University of Oklahoma Press, 1994.

Life in the Colony

Crouch, Dora P., Daniel J. Garr, and Axel I. Mundigo. *Spanish City Planning in North America.* Cambridge, Mass.: MIT Press, 1982.

Floyd, Troy S. *The Anglo-Spanish Struggle for Mosquitia.* Albuquerque: University of New Mexico Press, 1967.

Gage, Thomas. *Travels in the New World, 1648.* Reprint, Norman: University of Oklahoma Press, 1985.

Haring, Clarence Henry. *Buccaneers in the West Indies in the XVII Century.* Hamden, Conn.: Archon Books, 1966.

Hoberman, Louisa Schell, and Susan Migden Socalow, eds. *The Countryside in Colonial Latin America.* Albuquerque: University of New Mexico Press, 1996.

Jones, Oakah L., Jr. *Guatemala in the Spanish Colonial Period.* Norman: University of Oklahoma Press, 1994.

Lovell, George, and Christopher H. Lutz. *Geography and Empire: A Guide to the Population History of Spanish Central America, 1500–1821.* Boulder, Conn.: Westview Press, 1995.

Lutz, Christopher H. *Santiago de Guatemala, 1541–1773: City, Caste, and the Colonial Experience.* Norman: University of Oklahoma Press, 1997.

MacLeod, Murdo, J. *Spanish Central America: A Socioeconomic History 1520–1720.* Berkeley: University of California Press, 1973. Reprint, 1985.

MacLeod, Murdo J., and Robert Wasserstrom, eds. *Spaniards and Indians in Southeastern Mesoamerica.* Lincoln: University of Nebraska Press, 1983.

Stein, Stanley J., and Barbara Stein. *The Colonial Heritage of Latin America.* New York: Oxford University Press, 1970.

Wortman, Miles L. *Government and Society in Central America, 1680–1840.* New York: Columbia University Press, 1982.

The Bourbons and Independence

Anna, Timothy B. *Spain and the Loss of the Americas.* Lincoln: University of Nebraska Press, 1983.

Bumgartner, Louise. *José del Valle of Central America.* Durham, N.C.: Duke University Press, 1963.

Floyd, Troy S., ed. and trans. *The Bourbon Reformers and Spanish Civilization: Builders or Destroyers?* Boston: D.C. Heath, 1966.

Fisher, Lillian Estelle. *The Background of Revolution for Mexican Independence.* Gainesville: University of Florida Press, 1966.

Gonzalez, Nancie L. *Sojourners of the Caribbean: Ethnogenesis and Ethnohistory of the Garifuna.* Urbana: University of Illinois Press, 1988.

Humboldt, Alexander von. *Political Essay on the Kingdom of New Spain.* Ed. by Mary Maples Dunn. New York: Alfred A. Knopf, 1972.

Lanning, John Tate. *The Eighteenth Century Enlightenment in the University of San Carlos de Guatemala.* Ithaca, N.Y.: Cornell University Press, 1956.

Möerner, Magnus, ed. *The Expulsion of the Jesuits from Latin America.* New York: Alfred A. Knopf, 1965.

Wortman, Miles L. *Government and Society in Central America, 1680–1840*. New York: Columbia University Press, 1982.

The Federation of Central America

Anna, Timothy E. *The Mexican Empire of Iturbide*. Lincoln: University of Nebraska Press, 1990.

Bumgartner, Louise. *José del Valle of Central America*. Durham, N.C.: Duke University Press, 1963.

Chamberlain, Robert S. *Francisco Morazán: Champion of Central American Federation*. Coral Gables, Fla.: University of Miami Press, 1950.

Karns, Thomas L. *The Failure of the Union: Central America, 1824–1975*. Revised edition. Tempe: Arizona State University Press, 1976.

Stephens, John Lloyd. *Incidents of Travel in Central America, Chiapas and Yucatán*. New York: Dover Publications, 1969.

Woodward, Ralph Lee, Jr. *Rafael Carrera and the Emergence of the Republic of Guatemala, 1821–1871*. Athens: University of Georgia Press, 1993.

Conservatives and Foreign Profiteers

Bard, Samuel A. [E. G. Squier] *Waikna; or, Adventures on the Mosquito Shore*. New York: Harper & Brothers, 1855. Reprint, Gainsville: University of Florida Press, 1965.

Dunlop, Robert G. *Travels in Central America, etc.* London: Longman, Brown, Green, & Longman, 1847.

Folkman, David. *The Nicaragua Route*. Salt Lake City: University of Utah Press, 1972.

Gudmundson, Lowell. *Costa Rica Before Coffee: Society and Economy on the Eve of the Export Boom*. Baton Rouge: Louisiana State University Press, 1986.

Langley, Lester D. *Struggle for the American Mediterranean: United States–European Rivalry in the Gulf-Caribbean, 1777–1904*. Athens: University of Georgia Press, 1976.

Scroggs, William O. *Filibusterers and Financiers: The Story of William Walker*. 1916. Reprint, New York: Russell & Russell, 1969.

Squier, E. G. *Notes on Central America, Particularly the States of Honduras and San Salvador*. New York: Harper & Brothers, 1855. Reprint. Ann Arbor: University of Michigan Library, 2005.

Woodward, Ralph Lee, Jr. *Rafael Carrera and the Emergence of the Republic of Guatemala, 1821–1871*. Athens: University of Georgia Press, 1993.

The Making of the Coffee Republics

Belt, Thomas. *The Naturalist in Nicaragua.* 1874. Reprint, New York: Cosimo, 2005.

Burgess, Paul. *Justo Rufino Barrios: A Biography.* Philadelphia: Dorrance & Company, 1926.

Karnes, Thomas L. *Tropical Enterprise: The Standard Fruit and Steamship Company.* Baton Rouge: Louisiana State University Press, 1978.

Langley, Lester D. *Struggle for the American Mediterranean: United States–European Rivalry in the Gulf-Caribbean, 1777–1904.* Athens: University of Georgia Press, 1976.

————, and Thomas Schoonover. *The Banana Men: American Mercenaries and Entrepreneurs in Central America 1880–1930.* Reprint. Lexington: University Press of Kentucky, 1996.

McCullough, David. *The Path Between the Seas: The Creation of the Panama Canal, 1870–1914.* New York: Simon & Schuster, 2004.

Schoonover, Thomas. *The United States in Central America, 1860–1911.* Durham, N.C.: Duke University Press, 1991.

Seligson, Mitchell A. *Peasants of Costa Rica and the Development of Agrarian Capitalism.* Madison: University of Wisconsin Press, 1980.

Stewart, Watt. *Keith and Costa Rica: A Biographical Study of Minor Cooper Keith.* Albuquerque: University of New Mexico Press, 1964.

Williams, Robert G. *States and Social Evolution; Coffee and the Rise of National Governments in Central America:* Chapel Hill: University of North Carolina Press, 1994.

Dollar "Diplomacy" and Dictators

Anderson, Thomas P. *Matanza: El Salvador's Communist Revolt of 1932.* Lincoln: University of Nebraska Press, 1971.

Conzemius, Eduard. *Ethnographical Survey of the Miskito and Sumu Indians of Honduras and Nicaragua.* Washington, D.C.: U.S. Government Printing Office, 1932.

Dozier, Craig, L. *Nicaragua's Mosquito Shore: The Years of British and American Presence.* Tuscaloosa: University of Alabama Press, 1985.

Grieb, Kenneth J. *Guatemalan Caudillo: The Regime of Jorge Ubico, Guatemala 1931–1944.* Athens: Ohio University Press, 1979.

LaFeber, Walter. *The Panama Canal: The Crisis in Historical Perspective.* Updated ed. New York: Oxford University Press, 1990.

Langley, Lester D. *The Banana Wars: United States Intervention in the Caribbean 1898–1934.* 2nd rev. ed. Lanham, Md.: SR Books, 2002.

McCann, Thomas P. *An American Company: The Tragedy of United Fruit.* New York: Crown Publishers, 1976.

McCullough, David. *The Path between the Seas: The Creation of the Panama Canal, 1870–1914.* New York: Simon & Schuster, 2004.

Macaulay, Neill. *The Sandino Affair.* 1967. Reprint, Micanopy, Fla.: Wachoota Press, 1998.

Morris, James A. *Honduras: Caudillo Politics and Military Rulers.* Boulder, Colo.: Westview Press, 1984.

Munro, Dana. *Intervention and Dollar Diplomacy, 1900–1921.* Princeton, N.J.: Princeton University Press, 1964. Reprint, Westport, Conn.: Greenwood Press, 1980.

Salisbury, Richard V. *Anti-Imperialism and International Competition in Central America.* 1920–1929. Lanham, Md.: SR Books, 1989.

Schmidt, Hans. *Maverick Marine: General Smedley D. Butler.* Lexington: University Press of Kentucky, 1998.

Schoonover, Thomas. *The United States in Central America, 1860–1911.* Durham, N.C.: Duke University Press, 1991.

Walker, J. W. G. *Ocean to Ocean: An Account, Personal and Historical, of Nicaragua and Its People.* Chicago: A. C. McClurg & Company, 1902.

Walter, Knut. *The Regime of Anastasio Somoza 1936–1956.* Chapel Hill, University of North Carolina Press, 1993.

Watland, C. D. *Poet-errant: A Biography of Rubén Darío.* New York: Philosophical Library, 1965.

Challenge to the Old Order

Ameringer, Charles D. *Democracy in Costa Rica.* New York: Praeger, 1982.

———. *Don Pepe: A Political Biography of José Figueres.* Albuquerque: University of New Mexico Press, 1978.

Arévalo, Juan José. *The Shark and the Sardines.* Translated by June Cobb and Paul Osegueda. New York: Lyle Stuart, 1961.

Asturias, Miguel Ángel. *Men of Maize.* Translated by Gerald Martin. Pittsburg, Pa.: University of Pittsburgh Press, 1993.

———. *El Señor Presidente.* Trans. by Frances Partridge. New York: Atheneum, 1978.

Barber, William F., and C. Neale Ronning. *Internal Security and Military Power in Latin America.* Columbus: Ohio State University Press, 1966.

Bell, John Patrick. *Crisis in Costa Rica: The 1948 Revolution.* Austin: University of Texas Press, 1971.

Cullather, Nick. *Secret History: The CIA's Classified Account of its Operation in Guatemala 1952–1954.* Stanford, Calif.: Stanford University Press, 1999.

Dunkerley, James. *Power in the Isthmus*. London: Verso, 1988.

Durham, William H. *Scarcity and Survival in Central America: Ecological Origins of the Soccer War*. Stanford, Calif.: Stanford University Press, 1979.

Etchison, Don L. *United States and Militarism in Central America*. New York: Praeger, 1975.

Fagen, Richard R. *Forging Peace: The Challenge of Central America*. New York: B. Blackwell, 1987.

Immerman, Richard. *The CIA in Guatemala*. Austin: University of Texas Press, 1983.

Leonard, Thomas M. *The United States and Central America, 1944–49*. Tuscaloosa: University of Alabama Press, 1984.

Rodríguez, Mario. *Central America*. Englewood Cliffs, N.J.: Prentice Hall, 1965.

Schlesinger, Stephen, and Stephen Kinzer. *Bitter Fruit: The Untold Story of the American Coup in Guatemala*. Rev. ed. Cambridge, Mass.: Harvard University Press, 2005.

Walter, Knut. *The Regime of Anastasio Somoza 1936–1956*. Chapel Hill: University of North Carolina Press, 1993.

Williams, Robert G. *Export Agriculture and the Crisis in Central America*. Chapel Hill: University of North Carolina Press, 1986.

Civil Wars

Aldaraca, Bridget, ed. *Nicaragua in Revolution: The Poets Speak*. 1981. Reprint, Minneapolis, Minn.: Marxist Education Press, 1991.

Alegría, Claribel, and Darwin J. Flakoll, eds. and trans. *On the Front Line: Guerrilla Poems of El Salvador*. Willimantic, Conn.: Curbstone, 1989.

Anderson, Thomas P. *Politics in Central America: Guatemala, El Salvador, Honduras, and Nicaragua 1982*. Rev. ed. New York: Praeger, 1988.

Barry, Tom. *Central America Inside Out*. New York: Grove Weidenfeld, 1991.

Bolland, O. Nigel. *Belize: A New Nation in Central America*. Boulder, Colo.: Westview, 1986.

Brockett, Charles D. *Political Movements and Violence in Central America*. New York: Cambridge University Press, 2005.

Carmack, Robert M. ed. *Harvest of Violence: The Maya Indians and the Guatemalan Crisis*. Reprint. Norman: University of Oklahoma Press, 1992.

Dunkerley, James. *The Long War: Dictatorship and Revolution in El Salvador*. London: Verso, 1983.

Eich, Dieter, and Carl Rincón. *The Contras: Interviews with Anti-Sandinistas.* Reprint, Westport, Conn.: Bergin & Garvey, 1987.

Flora, Jan L., and Edelberto Torres Rivas, eds. *Central America: Sociology of Developing Societies.* New York: Palgrave Macmillan, 1989.

Gettleman, Marvin E., et al. *El Salvador: Central America in the new Cold War.* Revised edition. New York: Grove Press, 1987.

Herrick, Bruce, and Barclay Hudson. *Urban Poverty and Economic Development: A Case Study of Costa Rica.* New York: St. Martin's Press, 1981.

LaFeber, Walter. *Inevitable Revolutions: The United States in Central America.* 2nd ed. New York: W.W. Norton & Company, 1993.

———. *The Panama Canal: The Crisis in Historical Perspective.* Revised edition. New York: Oxford University Press, 1990.

Lernoux, Penny. *Cry of the People: The Struggle for Human Rights in Latin America—The Catholic Church in Conflict with U.S. Policy.* Reprint. New York: Penguin, 1991.

Menchú, Rigoberta. *I, Rigoberta Menchú: An Indian Woman in Guatemala.* London: Verso, 1984.

Montgomery, Tommie Sue. *Revolution in El Salvador: From Civil Strife to Civil Peace.* Second edition, Boulder, Colo.: Westview Press, 1995.

Randall, Margaret, ed. *Risking a Somersault in the Air: Conversations with Nicaraguan Writers.* 1981. Reprint, Willimantic, Conn.: Curbstone Press, 1990.

Ropp, Steve. C., and J. Morris, eds. *Central America, Crisis and Adaptation.* Albuquerque: University of New Mexico Press, 1984.

Rosenberg, Mark B., and Philip L. Shepherd, eds. *Honduras Confronts its Future.* Boulder, Colo.: L. Rienner Publications, 1986.

Vilas, Carlos M. *The Sandinista Revolution: National Liberation and Social Transformation in Central America.* New York: Monthly Review, 1986.

Walker, Thomas W. *Nicaragua: The Land of Sandino.* 3rd ed. Boulder, Colo.: Westview Press, 1991.

———, ed. *Revolution and Counterrevolution in Nicaragua.* Boulder, Colo.: Westview Press, 1991.

Wickham-Crowley, Timothy. *Guerrillas and Revolution in Latin America: A Comparison Study of Insurgents and Regimes Since 1956.* Princeton, N.J.: Princeton University Press, 1992.

Williams, Robert G. *Export Agriculture and the Crisis in Central America.* Chapel Hill: University of North Carolina Press, 1986.

The Challenge of Peace and Democracy

Dunkerley, James. *The Pacification of Central America*. London: Verso, 1994.

Dye, David R. *Contesting Everything, Winning Nothing: The Search for Consensus in Nicaragua, 1990–1996*. Cambridge, Mass.: Hemisphere Initiatives, 1995.

Dye, David R., with Jack Spence and George Vickers. *Patchwork Democracy: Nicaraguan Politics Ten Years after the Fall*. Cambridge, Mass.: Hemisphere Initiatives, 2000.

Montejo, Victor D. *Maya Intellectual Renaissance: Identity, Representation, and Leadership*. Austin: University of Texas Press, 2005.

Paige, Jeffrey M. *Coffee and Power: Revolution and the Rise of Democracy in Central America*. Cambridge, Mass.: Harvard University Press, 1997.

Paus, Eva. *Foreign Investment, Development, and Globalization: Can Costa Rica Become Ireland?* New York: Palgrave Macmillan, 2005.

Robinson, William I. "Latin America in an Age of Inequality." In *Egalitarian Politics in an Age of Globalization*, edited by Craig N. Murphy. New York: Palgrave Macmillan, 2003.

Spence, Jack. *War and Peace in Central America*. Brookline, Mass.: Hemisphere Initiatives, 2004.

Spence, Jack, et al. *Promise and Reality: Implementation of the Guatemalan Peace Accords*. Cambridge, Mass.: Hemisphere Initiatives, 1998.

———. *Chapúltepec: Five Years Later; El Salvador's Political Reality and Uncertain Future*. Cambridge, Mass.: Hemisphere Initiatives, 1997.

Tice, Karin E. *Kuna Crafts, Gender and the Global Economy*. Austin: University of Texas Press, 1995.

Vickers, George and Jack Spence. *Endgame: A Progress Report on Implementation of the Salvadoran Peace Accords*. Cambridge, Mass.: Hemisphere Initiatives, 1992.

Walker, Thomas W., and Ariel C. Armony, eds. *Repression, Resistance, and Democratic Transition in Central America*. Wilmington, Del.: Scholarly Resources, 2002.

Warren, Kay B. *Indigenous Movements and their Critics: Pan-Maya Activism in Guatemala*. Princeton, N.J.: Princeton University Press, 1998.

INDEX

Boldface page numbers indicate major treatment of a subject. Page numbers in *italic* indicate illustrations. Page numbers followed by *m* indicate maps, by *t* indicate tables, and by *c* indicate the chronology.